The Love Affair as a Work of Art is itself a work of art of a high and rare order, simultaneously an exercise in belles-lettres and an essay in historical biography. Its gleaming theme is the role of memory in the essential relationships of people who give themselves up to profound experiences of feeling. We imagine we knew the people who embellish this theme—which shines like sunlight through the interstices of incident—but as we read we realize we're only now making their acquaintance. That even goes for Proust! This miracle of incorruptible empathy and literary sovereignty is a great, serious, and enchanting creation. —JAMES LORD

The stories told by Mr. Hofstadter are intrinsically interesting. Moreover, his own writing . . . is polished, refined and sophisticated without ever becoming mannered or self-conscious . . . A lush, delightful and extremely suggestive work of art in its own right. —RICHARD BERNSTEIN, *The New York Times*

The French elevated the love letter to rapturous heights from the 17th through the 19th centuries . . . In this enraptured study Hofstadter conveys the sheer glee he has taken in digging into dusty volumes of letters and diaries . . . his verve is irresistible. —AMY BOAZ, *Library Journal*

Read Dan Hofstadter's book. It is gemlike: finely cut, sparkling and most given to close examination . . . a delight to read. Seldom have I read a work in which the metaphors are as crisp as a French salad. —RAYMOND F. BETTS, *Lexington Herald-Leader*

There is no one else—*no one*—in the entire United States who can write like this. Hofstadter's verve, elegance, wit, and worldliness have no equal. —JOHN LUKAS

Hofstadter continues his intriguing and original inquiry into the enigmas of personality, the making of art, and the dynamics of deception [with] nimble analyses [and] piquant profiles . . . Literary history at its wittiest, most richly imagined, and creative. —DONNA SEAMAN, *Booklist*

THE

LOVE AFFAIR

AS A

WORK OF ART

THE

LOVE AFFAIR

AS A

WORK OF ART

DAN HOFSTADTER

The Noonday Press
Farrar, Straus and Giroux
New York

The Noonday Press
A division of Farrar, Straus and Giroux
19 Union Square West, New York 10003

Published in Canada by HarperCollins*CanadaLtd*
Printed in the United States of America
First published in 1996 by Farrar, Straus and Giroux
First Noonday paperback edition, 1997

The Library of Congress has catalogued the hardcover edition as follows:
Hofstadter, Dan.
    The love affair as a work of art / Dan Hofstadter.
        p.   cm.
    ISBN 0-374-19231-6
    1. Authors, French—19th century—Relations with women.
    2. Authors, French—19th century—Relations with men.
    3. Authors, French—19th century—Correspondence.   4. Love-
letters.   5. Love in literature.   I. Title.
PQ147.5.H64   1996
848'.70809354—dc20   95–45962

The author gratefully acknowledges the following publications, in which
some paragraphs of this book first appeared in very different form:
George Sand, *Story of My Life*, translated, edited, and with an intro-
duction by Dan Hofstadter, The Folio Society, London, 1984; *The
Despot and the Slave: An Autobiography in Fact and Fiction from the
Writings of Benjamin Constant*, translated and edited by Dan Hofstadter,
The Folio Society, London, 1986.

FOR NANCY

CONTENTS

ACKNOWLEDGMENTS

FOR AWAKENING MY INTEREST in the subject of this book I
wish to thank Sue Bradbury and John Letts. I also appreciated
the early encouragement of John Elderfield, Peter Gay, Robert
Gottlieb, and Victoria Wilson. For their advice and helpful
comments I am grateful to Robert W. Greene and John Lu-
kacs, who read intermediate drafts of several chapters. Joanna
Stalnaker proved an unusually efficient researcher.

I would not have been able to finish this project without the
office space and unstinting support offered by Judith M. Frangos and Dr. George D. Frangos.

I am indebted to the staffs of the Bibliothèque Nationale,
the British Library, and above all the Istituto Francese of Florence for their gracious assistance. This book was made possible
by a generous grant from the Solomon R. Guggenheim Foundation for the year 1992.

The loyal assistance of my literary agent, Irene Skolnick, has
been precious, as ever.

I shall never forget the delightful days I spent in Paris in the
company of Dr. Robert Naquet. Dr. Naquet, who is the husband of the late Michelle Maurois, not only placed the Caillavet family archives at my disposal but also took part in the

search for documents pertaining to Proust, unearthing some very enlightening letters.

To my editor, Elisabeth Sifton, I am especially beholden. My confidence in her superb grasp of prose structure and her deep interest in French literature has sustained me constantly during the writing of this book.

D.H.

And then it seemed to him that they might have joys which should make life worth living. Their existence might be a work of art, beautiful and hidden. They would think, comprehend, and feel together. It would be a marvelous world of emotions and ideas.

—*The Red Lily*

A NOTE ON USAGE

THE WORD "SALONNIÈRE" IS used here in its accepted English sense of "one who holds a salon" and not in its original sense, still valid in France, of "one who frequents a salon." French names have been standardized to suit the modern reader's expectations and do not necessarily represent the forms of address used in France during the last century; aristocratic titles have been left in their original languages, since they do not exactly correspond to the cognate English ones. All translations occurring in the text are by the author unless the notes credit another translator. Books are referred to by their English titles unless no translation is readily available, in which case they have been left in French.

INTRODUCTION

THE QUESTION "ANY MAIL for me today?" is one that a lot of us have stopped asking recently: in this age you don't want to be a person who writes or expects to receive letters. It dates you, folds you up in the past, suggests that you share a zip code with too many poodle walkers, too many old ladies in astrakhan hats. Point out that nobody answers your letters and your friends will give you a pitying look, as if to hint that you're the last person in the world to grasp what's going on.

I don't know if personal letters are really as passé as they sometimes seem to be, but I do know that writing and reading them used to be like getting your three squares, almost like breathing. The mail delivery was something you eagerly awaited each day. Though I've always loved Lewis Carroll's verses—

> He thought he saw an Elephant
> That practised on a fife;
> He looked again, and found it was
> A letter from his wife—

I've never been able to imagine, even in the Mad Gardener, such a degree of befuddlement. Generally it is easy, even for

the pottiest or most distracted among us, to recognize a letter—
I mean one just delivered and still unopened. Something in us
spots a letter straight off, as a duck spots bread on the water.

The decline of the letter has a lot to do with microcircuitry,
with the advent of the affordable long-distance telephone call
and the electronically conveyed message. Letters are simply un-
cool these days, as antiquated as fedoras or Mary Janes. So it
may surprise us to remember that letter writing was once considered a dangerous pastime, structurally analogous to seduction. For the first two or three centuries of the early modern
era, any letter sent to a member of the opposite sex, especially
to a young woman, was suspect unless worded with a studied
neutrality: everybody knew that a letter's integrally masculine
or feminine tone, the teasing secrecy afforded by its envelope,
and its naturally caressing mode of address made it a potential
prelude to intimacy. Early adulthood is still the one period of
our lives in which many of us exchange long letters, and when
we recall the excitement of rushing home to write them—how
fervently we looked forward to that blessed hour of privacy, its
freedom from interruptions, its delirious sharing of feelings and
impressions—we get a sense of the passion that filled the mails
before the triumph of the telephone. Even the formal aspects
of letter writing—the choice of an attractive paper, the subtle
coquetry of the handwriting, the bringing of the envelope to
the lips to be sealed—carry strong sensual suggestions.

In the times when literate people wrote to one another co-
piously all their lives, the letter was an important medium of
adultery, and adultery is what many of the great old correspondences, especially those written in French, are about.
There is to these illicit exchanges an aura of furtive celebration.
Withdrawing into his or her writing "cabinet," armed with
plume and inkwell and blotters, the adulterous correspondent
enjoys the pleasures of imaginary conversation and emotional
release; when these effusions have run their course, there is the
secret posting of the letter, the exquisite ache of awaiting a

reply, and, when it comes, the delight of carrying it about in one's pocket, of combing through it to see if one has missed anything, of reading it over and over, of being constantly assured that one is loved. These are simple, nourishing rituals, but out of them grow solemnities more elaborate and profane: the mutual return of letters, the sacrificial burning of letters, and the collection of letters for publication (with a check arriving by return mail, if one's in luck).

The sex appeal of the letter has not been sufficiently stressed of late. The intimate letter can be, among other things, a hand surrogate. The pen flourishes on an envelope call to mind its sender's touch, and the paper's small size and pleasant texture flatter the hand of the receiver. Once the letter is opened, its message can suggest the warm pressure of a palm. As an object the letter is almost weightless—special scales measure its imperceptible heft—but like a hand, it can end or maim lives: in eighteenth-century France, a great fuss was made over the King's prerogative of writing *lettres de cachet*, which contained secret orders of imprisonment. In the many notable paintings of women receiving or reading *billets doux*, the entire composition turns upon a hand holding a scrap of paper, and this sense of the little determining the large emerges, too, in real-life love affairs, in which a letter is often the vehicle of doom. A letter's size, which makes it easy to burn or tear up, also makes it easy to keep, and it may survive longer than its writer intended. Letters have a dismaying habit of resurfacing as exhibits in court.

The lightness of the letter—its role as, so to speak, a winged thought—suggests that it may really be a form of prayer, a cousin to both the paternoster and the prayer aria of grand opera, in which the voice is raised in heartfelt entreaty. By nature almost every letter prays for an answer (this is a theme in Proust), and the love letter yearns for a response that is nothing less than the surrender of the beloved. People who believe in the efficacy of prayer—the devout, or, if you will, the merely credulous—believe that prayer calms the winds of causality, breaks links in the food chain, stops the Furies dead in their tracks. Lovers often think so, too, and the love letter's prayerfulness, which can be reminiscent of a litany, probably accounts for one of its most commonly observed properties, its dullness. The more sincere the tender missive is, the more monotonous it is also likely to be for the general reader. Any series of love letters is usually both repetitive and predictable, and even if its author is wildly brilliant it will tend to resemble similar performances by any number of other people. Victor Hugo's mistress Juliette Drouet was not a person who aspired to literary distinction, and one forgives her the insipidity of her *Thousand and One Letters*; but the great bard himself was no better. His sweet-talk, though too genuine to be described as inflated, is full of stock phrases and false superlatives ("the most generous, the worthiest, the noblest of creatures"). Unalloyed love letters seldom make good reading unless you yourself are their object, so I suppose we can be thankful that most are alloyed. Devotion is admixed with resentment or spite, adoration with financial or legal worries. Often, like a drop of vinegar in an otherwise too sugary sauce, a good quarrel cuts the cloying taste of an amorous correspondence, giving it pungency and renewed verve.

Some of the finest correspondences between men and women turn into a kind of narration. To read one of these exchanges is like listening to two people make up a tale together, but the tale never grabs you till the pair disagree. In France, letter writing became an important form of literary expression in the seventeenth century, and by the latter part of the eighteenth, the period of Madame du Deffand and Madame de Charrière, the woman's story is already tugging away from the man's, or maybe pushing against it. In these duets, each writer may have an implicit ending up his or her sleeve, and often the two endings do not coincide. There are occasions, to be frank, when the woman seems to be trying to pin down the man. Even if the two are merely acquaintances, she may want a close friendship, or perhaps something more, whereas the man wants only to deter her familiarity without losing her attention. But that is only one species of written conversation, because they vary enormously. In some cases one correspondent may not really want to be a character in the story; in others neither correspondent wants a story to get rolling, but it does anyway. Sometimes a woman has trouble closing her letters because that seems to close the relationship, and sometimes her letters and her lover's replies "cross" each other in more senses than one.

In France, the cultivation of letter writing in the seventeenth and eighteenth centuries went hand in hand with two literary genres, the epistolary novel and the so-called novel of analysis. The former reached its apex with Montesquieu's *Persian Letters* and Laclos's *Dangerous Liaisons*, but scholars tell us that like most great works they are atypical. Letter writing is basically a domestic art, a distant relation of sewing and embroidery, and students of the epistolary novel still debate the question of women's role in its development. Nobody can deny that to write good personal letters you have to prize the affective life and have a tendency to look inside yourself, both conventionally feminine qualities. Exploring a marital problem that any woman might face, Madame de La Fayette wrote the first great novel of analysis, *The Princess of Clèves*, in the late 1670s, and maybe only a practiced correspondent could have invented a story like this one, which looks away from action and circumstance and toward the clashes inside people's minds. Many novels of this type, which see love as a source of weakness and pain, have been written in France since Madame de La Fayette's day; something about them—perhaps the extreme interiorization of the plot or the stress on a slowly mounting moral crisis—seems to derive from the habit of daily letter writing.

The people of the nineteenth century put the letter to new and arresting uses. George Sand and Alfred de Musset had totally opposed life scripts, but shared common rhetorical resources, and all the excitement of their letters lies in the tension between the tale and how it is told. An even odder scenario comes about when a pair of lovers partake in a spectral story, a story that happens mostly on paper: they may then pursue an ardent epistolary affair while hardly ever meeting in person. Such was the case with Louise Colet and Gustave Flaubert, in the 1850s. Another couple, separated for a long period, may quarrel more and more fiercely until they virtually lose faith in each other and their correspondence ends, leading the reader to assume that their involvement is finished. But the pair may have stopped writing because they are now reunited, have no need to correspond, and have forgotten what their quarrel was about. This happened several times with Anatole France and Madame de Caillavet in the late 1880s: their letters have powerful narrative energy, but it doesn't reveal where the two writers are heading.

People who study the history of the letter sometimes argue about whether or not it's an art form or whether or not it's a narrative form, but it's hard to see why that matters. Some letters use language imaginatively and entertainingly, and some don't. Certain features belong to the fixed terrain, the bedrock, of letter writing. Unlike most stories, which happen in the past, a tale told in a correspondence almost always happens in the present; the main pronouns are "I" and "you"; and not much real dialogue can occur, since there's always a time lapse between letters. The monologue is the rule, and the "moanologue" is not uncommon either. If the great divide of writing runs between fiction and fact, or between fiction and what is nowadays optimistically known as "nonfiction," then letter writing doesn't know where it stands, and never has. When a brilliant but confused letter writer convinces himself that he's in love with somebody, is he or isn't he? When a correspondent tells a shaggy-dog story that is perfectly formed but completely untrue, is it a lie or a short story? These issues are best left to theorists, but you can't help noticing how often the literary letter writer will make up a piece of enchanting pastoral and run with it as fast and as far as he can.

Truth has always been a great concern of the French—they're a nation of mathematicians and scientists and philosophers—and they have given a lot of thought to the problem of lying in letters, diaries, and memoirs. The personal letter originated as the very substance of sincerity, what sugar is to sweetness or salt to saltiness, but by the time of Laclos, who wrote his great novel a few years before the Revolution, it seemed an agency of deceit. Laclos has one of his male characters write a letter to a woman using the rump of another woman as an escritoire, and every phrase in the letter rings a pun on the place where it's being composed. For a while it has been modish among critics to deny that truth and lying are valid distinctions in the writing of personal history, but you wonder how they would feel in court, pursuing a divorce or a libel suit, if their antagonists invoked this doctrine to fib in their depositions: intellectual fashion has a way of running directly counter to the basic assumptions of civil society. A postwar French scholar named Henri Guillemin—one of those historians of an older generation who are "no longer read"—spent several decades adapting the detective's and the prosecutor's techniques to the analysis of literature, and what he thought he discovered was that most writers lied, and lied extravagantly. Guillemin wasn't always convincing, but it's hard to get his arguments out of your mind, especially when you're reading an intimate correspondence. Such romantic interchanges are often dreamy and delusive, so it's not surprising that a current of hot air blows through many of them.

The idea that a love affair may be a work of art is at least as old as Ovid, who wrote famously on the theme. But every art form needs a public, and love or courtship seldom attracts much of an audience unless it connects with some visible or audible activity, like poetry or ballroom dancing or—I've heard this said—bridge. Only in nineteenth-century France, it seems to me, is the situation different, because during this period the literary love affair comes briefly to look like an autonomous form of expression. A single grand passion might take shape in so many different kinds of writing—primarily in letters but also in diaries, memoirs, and *romans à clef*—that it acquired, and still retains, a semblance of aesthetic unity independent of any of these genres. Of course this is only an illusion, a mental construct created by the writers' mythologizing power, but it can induce us to read a quantity of hybrid material that does not otherwise cohere. Often of secondary or even quite inferior quality, the heterogeneous texts captivate us when examined in the light of the liaison they document.

The book that follows represents my attempt as an outsider, an American of the 1990s, to control my astonishment at some of the personal documents that I've been reading recently. It makes no claim to be a work of original scholarship and is not intended to add anything to the sum of human knowledge. To consider the love affair as a work of art is a game for a day, a sort of charade in which one tries to enter into the thoughts of some talented people of the past and so to vivify their experiences. It is not by nature a polemical enterprise, and I have resisted the temptation to view any of these attachments as a confirmation of some larger sociological verity, concentrating instead on their stylistic qualities.

In writing about love, Parisian literary people of the last century enjoyed two advantages that may never again be present at the same time. They felt free, within the bounds of decorum, to talk about the physical side of their relationships, and they were also trained to compose long, spontaneous, and beautifully organized letters. This happy conjunction has gone by the board, and the great era of the love letter is over—which perhaps explains why one is so impressed, looking back over the literary liaisons of nineteenth-century France, at the volume of correspondence left in their wake, at the number of couples capable of knocking out at least a book's worth of readable letters (not to mention all the memoirs and autobiographical novels). I felt that I had to make a selection, and I have consequently divided this book into two parts: the first deals with several couples who were active during the period stretching, roughly, from 1796 to 1834, and the second does the same for the period 1887 to 1915. My thought (derived from some of the popular fiction of the last century) was to explore a phenomenon within a certain time frame and then revisit it some decades later. I discovered that many of the issues, metaphors, myths, and even personalities of the first phase reappeared with uncanny persistence in the second.

The reader may be surprised, after what I have just written about letters, to discover that I have cited relatively few in my first two chapters. That is because many of the letters I wanted to read had been burned by their authors' descendants. Yet all the collateral texts that I have consulted, which include numerous letters written by interested third parties, are influenced by what you might call the epistolary tonality, and as time went by, I was able to quote more and more letters, to offer more and more of what Goethe called "the most immediate, the most beautiful breath of life." In our own, less romantic era we might say that letters are simply the horse's mouth, and though the equine exhalations in the following pages may not always be as sweet as Goethe might have wished, I believe that they do have a certain acrid fragrance.

PART ONE

NAKED IN THE
MARKETPLACE

*"The lovers are naked in the marketplace and
perform for the benefit of society. The matter
with them, to the perception of the stupefied
spectator, is that they entertained for each
other every feeling in life but the
feeling of respect."*

HENRY JAMES,
ON THE SAND–MUSSET CORRESPONDENCE

1

A HOSTILE SENSIBILITY

BENJAMIN CONSTANT IS ONE of those European writers who
have never really made it over here, never been asked to join
in the American jamboree. Seedy, anxious, and faintly disrep-
utable, his shade can sometimes be found among the invited
guests, wittily talking or being talked about, but basically he's
a friend we wish we didn't know. Few English-speaking people
are familiar with him, and most of those who are are not inclined to pursue the acquaintanceship. His political theory remains a subject for specialists, and his one great novel, *Adolphe,*
published in 1816, is affection-repellent—female readers especially find it very hard to take. It is true that Constant has
passed into the annals of gossip, since he was consort of a lady,
Madame de Staël, who continues to interest us; but even in
this role he is elusive. We Americans have a wide range of
colloquial qualifiers for the word "lover"—we speak of Latin
lovers, demon lovers, and just plain great lovers—but this dry
fellow doesn't rate any of them. Though his accent was French,
his forebears came from the humid and quite un-Latin province
of Artois; his only demon was the imp of self-analysis; and he
seldom seemed capable of much fondness for anyone, least of
all himself.

When his friend Julie Talma died, of tuberculosis, at the age of forty-nine, Constant wrote a eulogy that came to serve as a milestone in the history of French letters. The year was 1805 —almost two hundred years ago—but reading his grief-stricken lines we still feel that they summon us to mourn not only the death of one person but romantic love itself. Julie was the widow of the great classical actor François-Joseph Talma; she had suffered much and was widely admired for her elegant fortitude. She was also able to think like a man, and one of her talents, Constant tells us, was for helping lovers out of hopeless situations, consoling the lady for being discarded while explaining to the gentleman the manner of disentangling himself with the least possible brutality. (It didn't seem to occur to Constant that sometimes a woman might want to be free of a man, and here he betrayed not only the prejudices of his era but also a secret of his intimate life. He was thinking, as it happened, about himself and a certain Anna Lindsay, and about Julie's role as a mediator between them; that she had strenuously objected to his treatment of Anna he conveniently banished from his mind.) Constant thought that Julie had grasped the abhorrent, blinding truth about love: that the "natural state" of one sex is only the "passing fever" of the other. She had had the courage to admit that

> a woman who has given away her heart and the man who has obtained it stand in precisely inverse positions. . . . The woman begins to have a purpose, that of keeping her lover, for whom she has made what feels like a great sacrifice; whereas the man ceases to have a purpose, since what has been his purpose is now a bond. Small wonder that two people placed in such an unequal relation will soon be unable to get along, and that is why the institution of marriage is so admirable: to supplant a goal that no longer exists, it proposes common and enduring interests.

Here, in a few sentences, was the theme of *Adolphe*, which Constant began writing about a year later: that a man and a woman want such different things from love that they naturally tend toward dissension. It's a restatement of the ancient idea that love is an antinomy, and it forms the cracked pedestal of the art of fiction in nineteenth-century France.

With this notion Constant turned his back on Jean-Jacques Rousseau and looked ahead toward the decades of positivism. There are stirrings of proto-social Darwinism here, intimations of the sociobiological theories of human mating that have gained credence in our own day. But if he had some of the prophet's wild foresight, he also had much of the superficiality, the smug reductionism, of the modern social scientist; and with the surmise that some simple explanation could be found for the infinitely varied, colorful folkways of the war between the sexes, he drifted into a sort of schematic thinking that would impoverish his powers as an artist. Genuinely oracular, Constant's message also has the oracle's deeper obscurity and crossed purposes.

His own posthumous fortunes as a novelist were mixed. Despite all that continues to be said and written about him, despite the discovery of more and more of his private papers in attics and archives, few people now read him for pleasure, as George Eliot and Middleton Murry and Harold Nicolson once did, and we may suspect that this holds true even among the French. Constant is studied, but he isn't enjoyed. In the mid-1920s, Guy de Pourtalès described Adolphe as a creature who had lived on into our own century, a type who might still be spied haunting the streets of Paris; one might add that since then he has made his way to London and New York, where he is daily sighted all over the place. We see him in cafés, in theater foyers, haggard, nervous, biting his lip; he slouches through the features pages of the women's magazines. Perhaps a student or an intellectual or a mediacrat, this fair-haired boy seems devoted to an adoring soulmate, but on a deeper level his emotions are stunted; he's unable, as the magazines say, to "make a commitment." He's the counterpart and archenemy of that equally ubiquitous figure the girl who desperately wants to get married. A peculiarly modern type? It may be: Pourtalès said that in creating Adolphe, Constant had "enriched the world with a new form of suffering." Yet we may also suspect that he's as old as our species.

Adolphe is devoid of self-irony, of humor, and this humorlessness is one of Constant's problems as a writer. Yet for anyone interested in how to get from the dirty laundry of life to something fit to hang out on the literary line, his imaginative use of certain tones of voice repays close scrutiny. One of these tones, which perhaps engenders all the others, is that of disenchanted filial affection. Defying convention, Constant dispensed with the reverential note in discussing his father, whom he talked about as a lovable but exasperating equal. In our own era of filial impiety, such a tone is not uncommon; what's unusual is that old Colonel Juste de Constant—a man of archaic formality, a father almost of stone—is portrayed in luminous language which reaches across the years. Constant's tone of recollection, as virtually all his expositors have noted, mingles the elegiac with the guilt-ridden: he felt that the past could never be candidly or honestly treated without some tincture of remorse. In another manipulation of tone, which today we might call "narcissistic," he flaunted his unhappiness, his timidity, his doubts, qualms, and scruples, but it is his misfortune that this tone does not appeal in writing as it does in speech. In a friend, as in a stand-up comic, such foibles may be charming, which Constant the man apparently was; but on the printed page they seem self-induced, as though the writer is malingering or maybe just pleading for sympathy.

One of the strangest things about Constant's private writing is that he apparently pursued it—not always, but often—as a sort of makeshift expedient or poor substitute for some other, more active pursuit. It was a reflection on what he would have done if he'd had the presence of mind, or a rehearsal of what he ought to do if he could summon up the nerve. Stung into writing by his obsessions, by the bees in his bonnet, he seems unable to pace himself, to allow his mind any leisure or margin of maneuver. This poorly measured pace gives his diaries, which are largely devoted to his tie with Madame de Staël, a weirdly claustrophobic and, to be frank, largely subliterary quality, like that of a neurotic's logbook or errand list. Constant had no gift for capturing conversations, no gift for describing people or places. It is unfair, of course, to compare this poor-substitute writing to the glossy finish of a novel like *Adolphe*, but the truth is that all the plot lines in Constant's life, the real and the fictional alike, play out against the same biographical scenery: you can't get interested in the novel without poking into the personal papers, and in the end their dimensions coincide. Reluctant though you may be to indulge in this sort of mildly prurient reading of Constant, it is actually more rewarding than the purer sort of study— a fact acknowledged in the standard French edition of *Adolphe*, which prints Constant's diaries and autobiographical works together with the novel in implicit deference to the way people actually want to read it. The liaison between Constant and Madame de Staël may have been a wretched business, but as Henry James once regretfully pointed out, "When we wish to know at all we wish to know everything."

ALL THE MISERY BEGAN one afternoon early in the autumn of 1794, when Madame de Staël, who was traveling on the lakeside road from Geneva to Lausanne, grew aware that she was being furiously pursued by a lone horseman; as she halted her carriage, she recognized a young Swiss aristocrat of Huguenot extraction whom she'd met at a party about two weeks before. Historical sources tell us that Benjamin, then in his late twenties, was a lanky fellow who wore his carroty hair in a pigtail and had a way of smiling with half his face; he was not handsome, but Madame de Staël recalled that he talked with unusual verve. On dismounting, he told her that he had just come from her doorstep, where he had learned of her departure and rushed after her in hot pursuit. Flattered and amused, she invited him to resume the journey in her carriage, and soon the pair were engaged in a conversation that would continue for fifteen years.

At twenty-eight, Germaine de Staël was Europe's leading woman of letters and a formidable champion of liberal ideas. She was also enormously rich. Her father, Jacques Necker, the self-made Swiss millionaire who as Louis XVI's finance minister had tried to avert revolution in France, doted upon her and treated her to immense sums of money. Unabashedly vain of his wealth and power, Germaine held court in his château, Coppet, overlooking Lake Geneva. There she had surrounded herself with brilliant and often eccentric men, in part because she liked them and in part because they helped satisfy her need for self-dramatization.

Germaine of course would have numerous lovers, but not on account of her appearance. Her figure was bovine and her features overlarge, as though seen through a magnifying glass. She dressed like an odalisque, in décolleté gowns and a turban, but had a chambermaid's brisk gait, and in the amateur theatricals that she often arranged, she strode mannishly about, striking attitudes suited more to a satyr than a nymph. Even so, she exuded a certain animal magnetism, and if no portraitist managed to capture a trace of her sex appeal, that is probably because it resided primarily in her voice. Talk, with Germaine, was a performance art, and when she sketched a thought in the air with her arms, which were perfectly formed and always left naked, that thought seemed to find an embodiment. Benjamin took note of that voice and those arms.

The story of the liaison of Germaine and Benjamin is told by Benjamin alone. Germaine's version, which we would so much like to hear, went up in the flames that later consumed almost all her intimate letters to him. Fortunately, Benjamin's private papers, his *Adolphe,* and his unpublished fragment *Cé-cile* are among the most revealing documents ever penned, for the conversation initiated that day on the Lausanne-Geneva road was to become one of the most interesting ever pursued by a woman and a man. Their liaison was not so much a love affair—not, anyway, after the first two years—as a searching dialogue, by turns amiable and disputatious, about the nature of love and freedom and what the age called "sensibility." Germaine and Benjamin conversed in Germany and in France, they conversed joyfully and angrily, and even, on occasion, cleverly extending their discourse by other means, they conversed by making love. Yet talk, not sex, was the true vehicle and conductor of their affection. Talk secured their bond against the attrition of infidelities and intrigues, secured it indeed against every human failing but one: sheer beastliness.

There is a folktale common to many cultures in which a pair of lovers, disengaging from an embrace, find to their horror that their kiss has magically disfigured their faces. This ghoulish conceit aptly characterizes the attachment of Benjamin and Germaine. Both were brilliant, adventurous, and rich, and together they embodied the close connection between artistic freedom and political liberalism. Yet in private they argued to the point of exhaustion, to the point of mutual hatred. Tending to view their life as a melodrama, which was standard fare in the theater of their day, they pursued in deadly earnest quarrels that may seem ridiculous to us. Both were northerners and brooders (the notion that all northerners *are* brooders was an inescapable false truth of their era), and in their frequent storms of rage and grief they fogged each other's sense of reality. Germaine, and perhaps also Benjamin, seemed to believe that love would be easier in Italy than it was in the north, as though all their problems would evaporate in the sun. This was not to be—they never made it to Italy together—but one doubts that they would have been happier there. For theirs was an intrinsically painful bond, and their both being writers didn't help matters any. Quite the contrary: both spoke too candidly, too forcefully, and too often out of turn. The gifts that drew them together also thrust them apart.

Benjamin Constant was congenitally unhappy. His mother had died a month after his birth, and he had the orphan's tendency to melancholia, to cramped self-reliance and compulsive nomadism. As a student he had rioted away his youth in six countries. He spoke nearly perfect English, good German, was well versed in Greek and Latin, and had a keen ear for both music and poetry. On his favorite social topics, politics and religion, he discoursed with graceful fluency, and by the time he met Germaine he was already talking about "the passions" in surprising, novel ways. What, he would ask, did it mean to be "sincere," and weren't the thoughts of all civilized people so artificial as to render this word meaningless? Benjamin was ruthless, self-probing, attractively vulnerable. With his great interest in the psychology of love, he had already proved irresistible to many women.

It is curious that Constant never wrote about his mother's death, since it unsteadied him for life and filled him with a wary ambivalence toward those he loved. Benjamin's favorite cousin, Rosalie, with whom he was to carry on a lively correspondence, wrote that his mother, Henriette Constant, née Chandieu, had been "beautiful, and of an angelic disposition," and that his father, Colonel Juste Constant de Rebecque, had been devastated by her loss. Benjamin resembled her—he had her red hair—but he was not, as they used to say, "reared in her memory," with the result that there was no one, not even the venerated image of a deceased parent, to counterbalance his father's influence. And that influence, scholars agree, was mostly baneful. The Pays de Vaud was then a virtual colony of Berne, and Juste, like many in the local gentry, had been obliged to take up mercenary soldiering in the service of another Protestant power, namely, the United Provinces. The Colonel dragged his son all over Europe, consigning him to tutor after tutor in a way that could only exacerbate the boy's feelings of rootlessness. After numerous unsuccessful educational experiments, he sent Benjamin off at fifteen to the University of Edinburgh, where he effortlessly learned to speak English (Scottish-accented) and also became a confirmed gambler. The gaming obsession was then common among young aristocrats, but for Benjamin it may also have afforded a means of confronting the force of blind fate that had carried away his mother.

On his return to the Continent, the adolescent boy began to woo older women obsessively. One of the most sympathetic of these was an English lady named Harriet Trevor, who lived near Lausanne; impelled by a need to test his attractiveness, Benjamin wrote her a sham declaration of love. "The agitation caused by the uncertainty of this overture," he would later avow, "threw me into a sort of fever that closely resembled the passion I was feigning." This phrase is pure Constant: over and over he would return to the notion that utterance generates feeling rather than the other way around. With Harriet his efforts apparently succeeded, but when they miscarried he was thrown into despair. A rebuff sustained at the hands of an unmarried Parisienne whom his father strongly favored, the well-dowried Jenny Pourrat, left him so humiliated that he took a suicidal dose of opium in her and her mother's presence. His embarrassment, as he later wrote, "left me indifferent to the outcome of my act, and I accepted . . . antidotes to the opium with such pliancy that my audience must have been convinced that they were watching not tragedy but comedy. Often after some extravagant deed I suddenly grow tired of the solemnity necessary to sustain it." This tantrum, with its farcical denouement, is usually (and convincingly) read as the archetypal Constantian act, but it also has a tacit and touching subplot. The spoiled youth playing the clown is also the lonely son trying to attract his father's attention. Father and son were never on the same plane: their lives spiral around each other like the twin tiers of those old newel staircases on which people going up never meet those coming down.

Behind most prodigal sons there are difficult fathers, and such, undeniably, was Juste de Constant. Born in 1726 to a family of the Huguenot military nobility that had emigrated to Geneva from Artois, Colonel Constant had served valiantly in the forces of the United Provinces and been seriously wounded several times. He usually found himself fighting the French crown, the hereditary enemy of his forebears, but he bore the Bourbons no grudge: a devoted citizen of the canton of Vaud, he reserved most of his considerable bile for the patrician oligarchy of Berne, against whom he would rail for hours at a time. Ill-formulated and self-contradictory, his harangues may have been largely intended to perplex or shock his entourage. Juste's sarcasm wounded everyone he met, and whenever more than three people gathered in a room he simply refused to speak. Though his bearing was impressive—his lieutenants aped his mannerisms—his family found him distressingly chilly, and only as an adult did Benjamin begin to understand that Juste was simply too inhibited to express paternal affection. The Colonel had been about forty years old at the time of his wife's death, and he stood aloof from the little boy whose red hair may have stirred painful memories. In time, like many of the ill loved, Juste grew almost pathologically litigious (he even sued a provincial postal service), and eventually he lost much of his fortune in a nine-year court case, a sort of Dutch *Jarndyce and Jarndyce*, pursued against a crowd of mutinous subordinates.

By far the most baroque deed of Juste's life was his public abduction, when Benjamin was about two, of the nine-year-old daughter of a local Vaudois peasant family. She was an exceptionally bright child, and Juste had advanced ideas about how to bring up bright children; when somebody questioned his wisdom, he simply kidnapped the girl (subsequently conciliating her horrified parents) and embarked on a series of pedagogical experiments. This was a very eighteenth-century thing to do, and no molestation of the child was involved, though the Constant clan feared that the good people of Vaud would see the event "under every imaginable color." The girl was familiarly known as Marianne; surprisingly, she adjusted gracefully to her new condition, and when she reached the age of twenty Juste asked her to take charge of Benjamin, who was then four. "I am really too moody and impatient to rear a child properly," he told her, using the brilliant little boy as a bait for her affection and loyalty. When, for legal reasons, Juste moved from Switzerland to France, she became the steward of his domain and, at an unknown date, his second wife. She would serve the cross-grained Colonel till the end of his days, supervising his kitchen, playing his clavichord, and bearing him two children; later, Juste told Marianne that in looking after Benjamin for several years she had performed "a greater service than saving my life."

Benjamin was long denied knowledge of Marianne's true role in the family, and his feelings toward her were mixed. Only when he was about twenty-three did he learn that Marianne, whom he called "Friend," was actually Juste's mistress (or possibly, by then, his secret wife) and that her children were thus his half siblings. The revelation shocked him and further complicated his relations with his father, who by this time was nursing a deep disappointment over his son's preference for literature over soldiering. So Marianne was enormously important to Benjamin, indeed the second most important person of his youth, yet scholars have devoted scant attention to her. This may be because so little is known of her character, and because Benjamin's feelings toward her varied so greatly that they are difficult to interpret. At times he regarded her as the "source of all my father's woes" and the snake-like usurper of a part of his fortune; at others he showed more understanding of her uneasy position. What is certain is that her presence as stepmother—often a wicked stepmother

13

out of a Perrault fairy tale—strongly colored his relations with the opposite sex.

THERE IS AN OLD tradition which holds that Benjamin's intellectual character was molded by the last older woman he befriended before he met Germaine de Staël. This was the celebrated Madame de Charrière—the "Zélide" of James Boswell's correspondence and of Geoffrey Scott's stylish biography of 1925, *The Portrait of Zélide*. Isabelle de Charrière, née van Tuyll van Serooskerken, was a woman of frosty beauty and wide-ranging talents. Born in 1740 to one of Holland's most aristocratic Protestant families and reared in a stiflingly proper home, she had married a dull Swiss gentleman in 1771 and moved to the manor of Le Pontet, at Colombier, near Neuchâtel, where she dwelt in a state of anguished disappointment. Letter writing, the harpsichord, the composition of novellas, and tincture of opium were Isabelle's avocations; her life at Le Pontet, her biographer tells us, was like an "old, unfinished, ill-written play, and the chief interest of her mind was that it could find no harmony within itself, nor acquiesce in the discord." At fault, Scott supposes, were her philosophical ideals, which embodied "a certain harsh clear cult of . . . reason which at every crisis falsified her life." For those of us who cannot accept the idea that a woman's emotions are driven by her rhetorical style, this charmingly stated argument is not quite convincing; but Isabelle must indeed be viewed as an Enlightenment type holding out against the march of Romanticism. "Belle," as she was familiarly known, had shown a precocious gift for science and mathematics conjoined with a willfulness which often disconcerted her family. The spirited girl was what we would now call a manic-depressive, and she would suffer from lifelong insomnia—one of her early letters has her sleeping three hours out of forty. A bust by Houdon shows how comely she was, with that doll-like, capacious forehead so favored by the eighteenth century; sensual, high-strung, and flirtatious, she speaks in one of her earlier letters of her "wretched vitality."

The gifts of Belle de Zuylen were almost too abundant, yet the great affair of her overlong youth was nothing other than the sordid old business of finding a husband. And here Belle's very originality became an obstacle. She was so fastidious and, in a way, so self-exasperated that the marriage auction, with its nudges and winks and hints of tempting bids, turned into a labor of some thirteen years. All her energy, her vast capacity for moral casuistry and social analysis, turned around this question, which she framed in carefully balanced antitheses: one had to please but also to be pleased, to avoid duplicity while satisfying nature, to suit oneself without offending one's family, to maintain or increase one's fortune without crassly selling oneself; and to these issues Belle devoted an endless, elegant, and quite sophistic suite of letters. Belle was brilliant, she was considerate, she was lovely as a Dresden shepherdess; yet she was also morbidly indecisive. About the age of thirty, she seemed suddenly to realize that her long intellections bore on a topic that would soon be out of date. Having rejected a number of hands, among them Boswell's, and already approaching frank unmarriageability, she grew fretful and morose, at one point writing a friend that she thought herself "incapable of loving." And then at last she bit the bullet, married M. de Charrière, and went off with him to the sad prim country of Neuchâtel, where she settled in like a person who was mortally wounded but had gone on living anyway. Later, when her spirits had improved, she began to write tales, several of them still worth reading, and she was much appreciated in Paris, where, ironically, one of her admirers was Madame Necker, the mother of the woman who would one day take Benjamin away from her.

More or less forgotten at her death, Madame de Charrière was rediscovered in 1833, when Gustave Planche, a literary critic and an intimate of George Sand, wrote an essay about her for *La Revue des Deux Mondes*; it was followed eleven years later by one of Sainte-Beuve's long treatments for the same journal. Charles Augustin de Sainte-Beuve was the predominant French literary critic of the last century, and his appreciation of Belle is valuable if only because it presents her attachment to Benjamin as the richest chapter of her mature life and the decisive phase of his education.

Belle and Benjamin's friendship was most intense from 1787 to about 1789, and the letters he wrote to her during this period are its finest literary product. Sainte-Beuve saw that some of them explored a vein of writing, tender and lively, that Constant would never rediscover; here everything was painted, nothing needed explaining. Reading them today you feel you're peeking through a stereopticon: before you unfolds a succession of views of the aristocratic home life of the late eighteenth century. You see the pretty lady bent over the harpsichord, trying out alternative fingerings, while Mademoiselle Rose dresses her hair; you see the gangly young gentleman writing notes for a book on the backs of playing cards. Or perhaps the pair are sitting in the kitchen; the clock shows ten past ten; now and again Rose breaks a bundle of twigs and lays it on the fire while Belle and Benjamin speak of the affinity of wit and madness. Benjamin's renderings of Belle's interior have a strangely elegiac touch, as when we feel that the death of a beloved person has turned everything in that person's room into a sacred still life. The enchantment of her chambers is precious; the hours chase each other round and round; and if we cannot help detecting an element of reprisal in this adolescent's attachment to a middle-aged woman, which forms a mirror image of Juste de Constant's liaison with Marianne, Belle and Benjamin also achieved a rare intimacy. When they were not together, and sometimes even when they were, long letters flew regularly between them. Sent away by his father in 1788 to the Court of Brunswick, Benjamin regaled Belle with a private feuilleton that recorded the sensations of each fleeting hour: perhaps nowhere else in literature is the connection between the love of writing and the apprehension of death so troublingly apparent. By a curious irony, at roughly the same period the young Germaine Necker was questioning the moral soundness of such self-attention in her own *Journal de jeunesse*, and though she did not yet know Benjamin, her remarks seem prophetic. "There are impulses," she observed one day, "which lose their naturalness the instant one becomes aware of them, or aware that one may later remember them. . . . Woe to the man who can express everything; woe to the man who can bear to read the record of his withered emotions."

Most of Belle and Benjamin's heart-to-hearters took place in the watches of the night. While others slept they maintained their vigil, upholding Reason against prejudice and convention; to the ease of life in a castle was added the thrill of staying up all night. This exchange has often been complacently celebrated, but one is hard-pressed today to see what in their wool-gatherings was so profound. The two seem overcerebral, a pair of cephalopods warily swimming through an ocean of false ideas. Repelling other creatures, they formed what we would nowadays call a mutual admiration society, and we have to remind ourselves that the nightmares they resisted were really of their own making.

The question whether Belle and Benjamin were lovers in the physical sense has exercised many minds, giving rise to an amusing speculative literature. Yet it has never been satisfactorily answered. The two were obviously in love somehow, and Sainte-Beuve, who enjoyed nosing into people's indiscretions, could see no reason why they shouldn't have "made that little experiment." The evidence works against this easy assumption. Nothing in their letters points to a carnal passion, and both had good reason to resist it. Belle was no romantic—she took a scrupulous view of matrimony—and her years probably made her feel too vulnerable to indulge her tenderness for her young protégé. Benjamin, though emotionally drawn to her, was more physically attracted to girls of his own age, and he respected Belle so deeply that he may have wished to spare her unnecessary pain. In a much discussed letter dated November 8, 1794, Belle asked Benjamin, "Since ours are neither marital nor lovers' quarrels, why are they so harsh?" which hints at a regret that they didn't have something more substantial to bicker about. Perhaps they had made a chastity vow that was beginning to get on Belle's nerves—we'll never know, nor, most probably, are we meant to. Gustave Rudler, in his great biography of 1909, *La Jeunesse de Benjamin Constant*, suggested that it wouldn't be displeasing if the puzzle of Belle and Benjamin's love should remain forever unsolved. "I'd see it," he wrote, "as an aesthetic propriety, an interesting artistic effect." The rhythm of the couple's letters allows us to suppose that this effect was consciously cultivated, that the quelling of any irritable need for a physical resolution gave shape, perhaps even strength, to their bond.

Sainte-Beuve read their correspondence differently. He viewed the amorous friendship of Isabelle and Benjamin as an act of deliberate moral corruption, as a jaded woman of the world setting out to foster a young libertine's cynicism. The critic was appalled at Benjamin's more jaundiced remarks— that the world, for instance, was "a magic lantern"; or that God had "died, with the world half-finished"; or that he, Benjamin, had already entered on a "premature old age." The element of posturing here set Sainte-Beuve's teeth on edge: couldn't the boy stop whining for a minute and kick up his heels for the joy of being alive? Sainte-Beuve's essay damaged Constant's reputation, and as late as the mid-1920s Scott was at pains to show how misguided Sainte-Beuve had been. Scott claimed that Sainte-Beuve missed the element of mutual consolation in this friendship; yet Scott may have missed something equally important—the component of bluster, the aura of two people putting a brave face on disappointment. What neither analyst considered was the possibility that both Belle and Benjamin were chiefly disappointed not in other people—not in "society" or "convention"—but in themselves.

So many insightful pages have been devoted to this famous liaison that its basic contradiction may have been lost in the shuffle. The first term of this contradiction, simply put, is that the baton of sensibility is generally believed to be best relayed by an older female to a younger male. Though affairs between older men and younger women have doubtless always been more common, they involve the conferral of a different favor —call it status or protectedness, a feeling of being prized. What an older woman is supposed to teach a younger man is a soft attentiveness to feeling. And in this sense Belle's choice of a young friend was happy, because the large feminine component in Benjamin was accented by such a need for mothering that he proved ideally receptive to what Rudler called her "intellectual maternity." Here, however, an irony intrudes, and with it the other term of the contradiction: it is that Belle was transmitting a quality she didn't really have. It's one thing to value sensibility and quite another to possess it, and little in Belle's correspondence suggests any profound concern about other people's feelings. What she seems to have transmitted to Benjamin, then, or at least nurtured within him, was a sort of counterfeit or intellectualized sensibility that consisted mostly in the analysis of motive. And like most mentor-pupil relationships, theirs was not free of prickliness: she forced him to scrutinize the inherent tensions of the writing life, forced him to admit that he wasn't going to be able to wave the flag of literary ambition as the Constant males had formerly waved the banner of military glory. Fighting well had won his elders praise, but writing well might entail his forfeiting praise; it might even entail his going his own disgruntled way, as Belle herself had done.

In 1787, the year in which she met Benjamin, Belle had published a novella, *Caliste*, that would serve as a kind of template for his novel *Adolphe*. The story of *Caliste* is as simple as a fairy tale, which in some ways it is. We find ourselves at Bath, where the narrator, a young lord named William, meets a lovely but mysterious woman who lives in semiseclusion in a charming house where she spends most of her time playing the clavichord. Mistress Caliste encourages William to call on her—he, too, adores music—and soon the pair fall violently in love. Will they marry and find happiness together, or will some obstacle arise to force them apart? Well, Caliste, we discover, has been a professional actress and, worse still, the mistress of a wealthy gentleman, now deceased, from whom she inherited her fortune. As it happens, William's father opposes his union with a woman of such dubious background. After much waffling, William decides not to marry her and is betrothed to somebody else; the embittered Caliste accepts the proposal of another suitor, a man from Norfolk who "has no father" and shows a blithe disregard for the social forms that have William tied up in knots. The marriages are concluded, but neither one is happy, and Caliste falls mortally ill; before she dies she seeks out her true love, and he more or less admits that he has been "the dupe of a phantom called virtue."

Caliste is to all appearances a sentimental novella that renews an old French idea, that of constructing a morally edifying tale around an unconsummated affection (the classic example being Madame de La Fayette's *The Princess of Clèves*, of 1678). It's an attack on the social prejudices that destroy the lives of decent and loyal women like Caliste (who at one point describes herself as "two people, one of whom [is] continually occupied in gagging the other"). But *Caliste* is more than a period piece, which partly accounts for the revival the novel is now enjoying in France. Among other qualities, Madame de Charrière had a great sensitivity to one of the most ravenous of all human drives, namely the desire for respectability. There is a particularly delicious moment when William consults Caliste's servants as to the advisability of making her his mistress, and they, shocked by the very idea, tell him that they would have to give notice.

Madame de Charrière, who had lived in Britain, had such a gift for mimicry that she was able to make William the narrator of *Caliste.* It has long been known that *Caliste* served as the prototype for Constant's *Adolphe*, but only quite recently has anyone made the rather crucial observation that Madame de Charrière's adoption of the male viewpoint enables the writing to breathe. The critic Béatrice Didier has suggested that the usual habits of eighteenth-century feminine storytelling—the sighing sentences, loose punctuation, and "floods" of sensibility—would have ruined this tale; if Caliste herself had been the narrator, employing a characteristically female voice, the result might well have been a self-pitying monologue. There's a suave audacity to Madame de Charrière's strategy of talking through a male mask: it puts her intonation to a test, but then, when she comes to creating the character of Caliste, she's home free.

Scholars have viewed Benjamin's attachment to Belle as "formative," but the word may be misleading. It's not certain that Benjamin ever *was* formed—he was always dissolving and reshaping himself—and his letters to Belle reveal not so much a mind conventionally hardening up or finding its governing idea as a spirit that has been given license to indulge a vast sense of superiority to other people. Predictably, it was just this superiority that began to backfire toward the end of their liaison. Benjamin found himself bridling at Belle's distaste for his worldly ambitions, and also at her refusal to agree with him that his father, who had been embroiled in his great lawsuit for about seven years, was always and unquestionably in the right.

Benjamin was now in his late twenties. Though he had been nominally married since 1789 to a certain Minna von Cramm, whom he would soon divorce, he was much the same melancholy rake that he had been at eighteen. ("There are two persons in me," he later confessed, echoing Caliste, "one of whom is always studying the other.") Unable either to enjoy life or to forgive himself for not doing so, he kept on shuttling between Paris, Germany, and the Pays de Vaud in search of a proper sphere for his talents. He had published nothing; he had run for no office. He was just beginning to despair of ever achieving anything when he met Madame de Staël. Belle sensed what was coming, and being Belle, she coiled up defensively. The Necker girl, she snobbishly reminded Benjamin, was not really of the best society—she was spoiled, bombastic, and pretentious. What Madame de Staël took to be artistic temperament, Belle said, was really only intellect; but perhaps the young man should get to know her, he should try to give her her due. Unhappily, Benjamin did more than that. "I don't find it at all difficult to give her, as you put it, her due," he told Belle. "On the contrary, the more I see of her, the more difficult it becomes for me not to praise her extravagantly. . . . She's the second woman I've met for whom I'd have given everything in the world. . . . You know who the first was." That *was* must have hurt. Twelve days later he wrote to Belle:

> I think you judge her rather severely. I think she's very energetic, rash, talkative, but also very kind, very trusting. She's no mere chatterbox—the proof is the real concern she shows for anyone she knows who's in trouble. . . . It's true, as you say, that she has a silly side: she's as much of a name-dropper as any parvenu, and like a girl from the country she can't resist talking about Paris society. But I don't think she's vain, she simply knows that she's very intelligent, she must talk and let herself go. . . . She does overpraise people, but that's because she wants to make friends.

From this Belle must have deduced that Germaine had taken to flattering Benjamin, and she may have regretted that she herself had not: one of the most wounding letters she received from him after he joined Germaine's circle accused her of having turned his literary ambition into a corpse that Germaine was raising from the dead. Considering all that Belle had toiled to give him, this seems almost wantonly cruel; and that, clearly, was how Belle felt it.

There is in the public library of Neuchâtel a slip of paper with a fragmentary poem in Madame de Charrière's hand: "Alas! If I were still young, they would see me run / The risk . . . But when one feels oneself growing older, / Such an attempt is no longer likely to be favored. . . . /Dear Benjamin, it is, then, all over . . ."

IN THE AUTUMN OF 1794, Germaine invited Benjamin to stay with her for a while at a country estate she had rented near Lausanne. While she felt no voltaic charge between herself and this compulsive talker with his bandy legs, green-tinted glasses, and occasional outbreaks of acne, he was enthralled by her: she had "replaced the entire universe" and was "a world in herself." In his unfinished autobiographical novel, *Cécile*, Benjamin describes his first meeting with a woman he names Madame de Malbée, who is modeled on Madame de Staël:

> When I first met her, she was twenty-eight. Rather on the short side, and a little too stout to be graceful, she had irregular, overly pronounced features, a poor color, the finest eyes on earth, beautiful arms, dazzlingly white if too large hands, and a superb neck. Moving abruptly, and coming to rest in mannish postures, she seemed unpleasing at first, yet irresistibly seductive as soon as she spoke and gestured.
>
> Her mind, the most far-ranging that any woman (and perhaps any man) has ever had, showed more strength than grace in intellectual matters, while in her personal relations a tinge of solemnity and affectation prevailed. But there was in her gaiety an odd charm, an unguarded childlike warmth, which in moments of brief but expansive intimacy won over the hearts of her listeners. . . . Within an hour

she had secured over me the greatest sway that a woman can gain over a man. I decided to settle near her, and soon I was living in her house. I spent the whole winter telling her of my love.

Benjamin soon discovered that Germaine's house was a sort of menagerie for her many admirers, any one of whom might suddenly be discovered with her in some declamatory or amatory pose. Feeling spurned, he decided to take an overdose of opium. It was a reprise of the buffoonish suicide attempt at Jenny Pourrat's, though with one crucial difference: he had divined that deep down, unknown even to herself, Germaine was attracted to him. "Live, my dear Monsieur Constant!" she commanded, as he lay on his impromptu *lit de parade*; obediently, he prolonged his existence. He pursued her for a year and a half, until April 1796, when she yielded to his entreaties and became his mistress.

There are several reasons why Germaine proved irresistible to Benjamin. With her full figure and musical voice, she was attractive in an approximate sort of way. Her intelligence fascinated him, she had well-developed maternal instincts, and she was rich enough to indulge a lover with settled vices—an important point, because Benjamin's gambling habit now went hand in hand with a speculative interest in securities and real estate. Yet another reason was Benjamin's ambition: Germaine's connections reached tendril-like through a broad section of the French ruling class, and for Benjamin connections were indispensable. The poet Béranger later wrote that Benjamin never heard of anyone else's success without displaying the most transparent envy; though he may have believed that he loved Germaine, in reality he "loved nothing but the emotions she aroused in him." Even those emotions were feigned, Béranger thought, for if Benjamin had been cut out of her circle he would have been thrown back on the society of provincial courts, on dowager duchesses and botanizing abbés—people of gifts too paltry to interest him. Germaine's social set served much the same function in his life as a gambling den; the social intrigue was like a good game of cards, it shook him and woke him up. Béranger respected Constant's mind, but he did not like him, and what he perhaps missed was the tonic effect of Germaine's bloated ego on Benjamin's moody disposition. Like many people who have grown up motherless, he was prone to black humors; in a diary entry for May 1, 1805, he would write: "I have in my character an element of chronic discouragement that [Germaine] alone can dispel, and if my intellect can do without the whole world, this part of my character cannot." Only she could help him take heart, and that, more than any other reason, may explain why he would stick by her for so many years.

Another important tie binding Benjamin to Germaine was a child. Albertine de Staël was born in June 1797, and she was almost certainly his daughter. She had his red hair and his facial features, though miraculously softened and refined. "My Albertine is a charming child," Benjamin wrote in his diary in September 1804. "I've never seen more wits or more of *my* wits, which for me is a great merit." And though he could not, for social reasons, acknowledge her as his daughter, he felt deeply grateful to Germaine for bringing her into the world. At the time of Albertine's birth, he wrote to his aunt Anne de Nassau that he had received "such great proof of the devotion of a [certain] person . . . that I could never without the rankest ingratitude and . . . most bitter regret consider doing anything painful to her." But if for many people parental love tends to simplify life, it did not do so for Benjamin. He would soon grow distant from Albertine—distracted, unaccountable—and as inwardly estranged from his love for her as his own father had been from his affection for himself.

Germaine's daunting ebullience can perhaps be attributed to the unconditional love she had always received from her powerful father. Reared in Paris according to the doctrines of *Emile*,

Rousseau's treatise on education, she was granted a little wooden stool in her mother's salon, where she listened raptly to the luminaries of the day. Since the Neckers were Protestants, they could hold their at-homes on Friday without forgoing meat, and the combination of meat and philosophy attracted the likes of Diderot, d'Alembert, Grimm, and Gibbon. Germaine was one of those children who are dazed, or cursed, by the spectacle of an adored parent's rapid rise to fame and fortune, and in 1777, when she was eleven, Jacques Necker was appointed Comptroller General, the highest position in French public finance. She hated her mother, an austere, strong-willed Swiss beauty, and sometime not long after puberty she made the welcome discovery that her father also detested Madame Necker. The father and the daughter worshiped each other unabashedly, and once, at a ball, when Monsieur Necker caught sight of Germaine dancing with her fiancé, he cut in and rebuked the young man with the words "I shall show you how one dances with a girl one is in love with."

The man Germaine married was Eric Magnus de Staël, a Swedish diplomat and intermittent ambassador of his country to France. The marriage, concluded in 1786, was one of convenience (though Staël would not altogether retire from the scene until his death, in 1802). For Germaine, the two chief amenities were a grand apartment in the Swedish Embassy, in the rue du Bac, and diplomatic immunity, which would prove useful in her future struggles with Napoleon. It was Napoleon, not Staël, who in the mythic order of things—the publicist's, journalist's, and caricaturist's order—was Germaine's true counterpart. On the continent of Europe, only she, for a while, counterbalanced him; only her huge eyes, buck teeth, and striped turban merited a place beside his stern countenance. Deeply humane, almost unfailingly (if starchily) eloquent, she saw through his pretensions as surely Madame de Charrière had seen through her own: never was man scolded so relentlessly by woman. Madame de Staël's vanity was piqued by the idea of playing unicorn to Bonaparte's lion, but he was not placed on earth to debate, and in 1800 he started actively to harass her. (In 1803 he banished her from Paris, and she was followed by her young friend Madame Récamier, the great beauty, whose devotion soon became legend.)

Benjamin had always shown a partiality to the female point of view, and he must often have discussed Germaine's work in progress with her. His *Adolphe* would differ hugely from her novels, but she probably contributed to his conviction that circumstantial suspense is less compelling than the sort generated by a search for answers. This was to some degree a feminine insight. Germaine believed, like many women of her day, that it had fallen to her sex to detect the nuances of character and the shades of the affections. With their "dreamy" sensibility and pity for sufferers, women had observed that a ruminative inquiry into the feelings of one's family and friends could become a self-sufficient artistic entertainment. Of all the civilized nations, the most advanced in what Madame de Staël called "sentimental morality" was clearly Germany. Since so many of the people across the Rhine were Protestants, and thus able to dissolve marriages with relative freedom, the exercise of sensibility within marriage became a positive duty for them, and the failure to be romantic was condemned as immoral. Such conceits struck Germaine as slightly absurd—German couples, she wrote, had a way of ogling each other that itself wished to be ogled, and even the moon, that bauble from the prop room of sensibility, was now the "subject of their obligatory enthusiasm"—but if the Germans' oafish benignity brought a smile to her lips, she certainly preferred it to the old French *esprit de bravoure*, the aristocratic code of callous seduction. This code she put down to a puerile claim—"the pretension," as she put it in one of her many interesting phrases—to "what is evil."

Germaine shared the common view that women had achieved a certain paramountcy in France, thanks to the institution of the salon. The personalities in a salon revealed themselves not through decisions or deeds but through wit, and this, being a derivative of psychological acumen, was a natural part of the Frenchwoman's mental equipment. In a salon the men cultivated what pleased the women, and if the hostess was highly placed, a male guest's good manners or fine conversation could lead to his rapid social advancement. Still, some vestige of the old code also made it difficult for a woman to be a novelist in France. Though it was proper for her to give voice to her thoughts about her husband or lover, to exhibit "a personality that is always *à deux*," it was another matter for her to write them down. The obtuse old squires looked askance at lady scribblers: if a woman, a protected being, took up writing, she exposed herself to the barbs of public opinion, implicitly refusing the protection of her family and so dishonoring it. It was almost impossible, Madame de Staël argued, to "bear *nobly* the reputation of authoress, to reconcile it with the independence of an elevated rank, and withal to lose nothing of dignity and . . . naturalness." Though the novel of sensibility was the cutting edge of fiction, it took a lot of courage to write one, which Constant saw and appreciated some time before it occurred to him to try his hand at this largely, if not exclusively, feminine genre.

Madame de Staël's first full-scale novel, *Delphine*, was published in 1802. It was written in epistolary form, like many eighteenth-century tales, and true to its type, it contained more meditation, a female prerogative, than decision, a male one. Years later, when Sainte-Beuve felt inspired by his friendship with George Sand to write a long essay on Madame de Staël, it was precisely the immobility of the prose in *Delphine*, the sensation of beholding a succession of "figure groups in starched draperies," that he took issue with. The characterization was crude and overinsistent; each correspondent earnestly proclaimed what he or she believed in; the plot was not propelled by action. In a way, the whole thing was like the sort of amateur theater in which the players stop, pose, and declaim set speeches—there was no room for fluid gestures, stage business, running and jumping. Sainte-Beuve's characterization may or may not have been valid, but it suggests how Madame de Staël's liaison with Benjamin Constant may have appeared to outsiders after their first few years together. If that liaison were a work of the imagination rather than a historical fact, we, too, would probably regard it as overrhetorical, excessively static, and devoid of clear climaxes.

Because so few personal letters from Germaine to Benjamin have survived, it is hard to weigh what she felt for him, or to know when she felt it. She writes about giving him durable happiness and about her conviction that no one can replace her in his heart, but these sentiments appear in desperate late billets, dated April and May 1808. Her description of the character Henri de Lebensei, in *Delphine*, may give an indication of her feelings about Benjamin in the period 1798–1802:

A savage, proud timidity often makes [Lebensei] silent in company. But since his mind is lively and his character serious, the smaller our conversational circle becomes, the more charm and resourcefulness he displays in speech. When the two of us are alone, he is even more engaging. . . . I trust in my happiness because I understand him objectively, independently of the feelings I arouse in him: I am the one person with whom he can give play to all his virtues and also his faults. When intimacy has reached the point where two lovers find happiness in childlike games, private jokes, countless little things the meaning of which is known only to the pair, then the heart is held captive by a thousand ties. . . . Beneath a cold and sometimes harsh exterior, he is more compassionate than anyone else I know. He conceals this secret out of fear that someone might take advantage of it, but I know it, and I trust in it. If it were nothing but the fear of hurting me that kept him from leaving me, I'd probably still be happy with him; but while I glory in the love I call forth in him, I'm secure in the thought that two virtues guarantee my possession of his heart—his honesty and his kindness.

A hysterical current runs beneath these sentiments. Germaine seemed to be searching for a means to satisfy her craving for male fealty, and since the weakest and most dependable of her vassals was Benjamin, she made use of the oldest trick in the feudal book: she enslaved him through hospitality. She lifted him out of his frequent depressions, lent him money, furthered his ambitions, and, most famously, persuaded him to sign a document declaring his obligation to love her:

> We promise to consecrate our lives to each other; we declare that we regard ourselves as indissolubly bound to each other, that we will share for ever and in every respect a common destiny, that we will never enter into any other bond, and that we shall strengthen the bonds now uniting us as soon as lies within our power.

> [Codicil]
> I declare that I am entering into this engagement with a sincere heart, that I know nothing on earth as worthy of love as Madame de Staël; that I have been the happiest of men during the four months I have spent with her, and that I regard it as the greatest happiness of my life to be able to make her happy in her youth, to grow old peacefully by her side, and to reach my term together with the one soul who understands me and without whose presence life on this earth would hold no more interest for me.
> Benjamin Constant

The ersatz betrothal, which was probably drawn up late in 1796, sealed Benjamin's servitude for the next thirteen years. Like any motherless child, he had grown up unprotected, a deluge lapping at his feet; now he was up to his ears.

Between 1795, when the pair became active in Paris, and 1803, when Madame de Staël was exiled by Napoleon and took up residence in Weimar, the two writers plied their pens with exceptional speed and assurance. In *On the Influence of the Passions* (1796) and *On Literature* (1800) Germaine developed an influential theory of the romantic imagination, and she also produced a steady stream of political tracts. Benjamin found her ideas congenial, and under her aegis he wrote two important essays, *The Strength of the Present French Government* (1796) and *On Political Reaction* (1797), both of which were heavily influenced by the main trends of contemporary English social thought; he served with distinction in the short-lived Tribunate, a government assembly which, though powerless, afforded him a place in the public view. Benjamin was fundamentally a liberal, and as such he represented the one ideology that was (and remains) paradoxically anti-ideological; though critical of Bonaparte, both he and Germaine always felt that principles must be brought into rough congruence with the world as it is, and their political conduct—for they were actors, too, in the march of public events—revealed that they were at times prepared to compromise or even jettison their principles when it suited their ambitions.

They were no less self-indulgent in their personal lives. The doctrine of laissez-faire found its bedroom counterpart in a complaisant tolerance of infidelity, the principle of free speech in a weakness for self-absorbed monologues. Matrimony was high diplomacy—the *entente*, more or less *cordiale*—of a ceremonial spouse and a half-dozen paramours. The idea of sexual fidelity as something regulating their own lives would have struck these creatures of the eighteenth century as preposterous. Yes, one might choose to be faithful, but only out of inclination, not out of principle or fidelity to a vow. The love affair as an expression of personal style is as subject as any other to the whims of fashion, and Germaine, when engrossed in her Circe role, would keep several of her admirers at Coppet and invite them simultaneously to dinner; jealousy was not supposed to figure in this carousel. Count Adolf Ribbing, Prosper de Barante, Mathieu de Narbonne, Mathieu de Montmorency, the Schlegel brothers, and John Rocca were among the chatelaine's suitors whom Benjamin was to encounter at Coppet or in one of the great houses she rented; on balance, he seems to have enjoyed their conversation. And of course he arranged amorous interludes of his own, though most often he resorted to prostitutes. Yet Germaine, falling episodically in and out of love with Benjamin, was prone to fits of jealousy on his account; nothing else explains her rages at him.

Benjamin wholeheartedly supported Germaine's political position and helped her to compose some theoretical tracts; his maiden speech before the Tribunate, in June 1800, was an outright challenge to Napoleon. But the two titans also dwarfed him; he sensed that he was fast becoming a miniature, with the miniature's oddness and pointless complication. Within a few years the imagery of his diaries and letters begins to make him look slightly absurd, placing him not beside but behind Germaine, running or panting, "breathless with trying to follow [her] chariot." Sometimes it seems that every one of her pronouncements or pamphlets closes off for him some useful back avenue, precludes some fragile demarche.

Benjamin's liaison with Germaine was so complicated, so cyclical, so full of fencing and fancy footwork, that within six months of Albertine's birth it had lost the attributes of romance. The hours became oppressive and sterile; they lengthened slowly into days and months and years. The couple's physical tenderness for each other dwindled, and as the seasons came and went at Coppet and in the rue du Bac and in scores of great estates in France, Germany, and Switzerland, Germaine and Benjamin struggled to find a new footing for their friendship. Two terms occurring often in Benjamin's writings are "scene" and "explanation," a scene being a violent argument in the presence of uninvolved parties, including (if not, indeed, for the benefit of) servants, and an explanation also being an argument, though a little more debate-like in nature and usually conducted in private: couples abandoned the company of others for an explanation, tearing out of drawing rooms, rushing into bedchambers, marching outside to whatever manorial park happened to lie at their feet. These scenes and explanations are full of speechifying, ultimatums, declarations of principle as wooden as the platform of some antiquated political party, and they rarely cause any change in the equipoise of the lovers; the impression the reader gets is of one form of expression being caged inside another, of people who wish to act being constrained only to speak, and being constrained, moreover, by something in the script itself, some stilted language or dull, hypnotic beat.

During the first six or so years of the liaison, many in Constant's family came to regard him as a scapegrace; one who did not was his spinster cousin Rosalie de Constant, a tart, witty hunchback—she had dislocated her shoulder as a little girl—who loved flowers and painted attractive floral illustrations, and would correspond late in life with some famous people, including Chateaubriand and his wife, Céleste. Rosalie was nine years older than Benjamin—he called her his "sister of the heart"—and as a devoted friend she took it on herself to tell him firmly and frankly what she thought of his conduct. Rosalie cordially despised Madame de Staël. She felt that Germaine unremittingly crammed poor Benjamin (and, by extension, all the Constants) with humble pie, and she resented Germaine's habit of dragging him about Europe to a succession of castles, most of them far from the Pays de Vaud, where she lived and where she wished that her dear cousin would also settle. Though not devout, Rosalie respected the principles of her Protestant faith, and she found it disgraceful that a married woman should carry on as Germaine did. She could not bring herself to refer to Germaine by name, calling her, instead, "the Lady of Coppet," and in 1804 she sent a note to that Lady declaring that Benjamin had "always held in our family the position of a precious object ever surrounded by some peril. . . . My prayers and my unquietness shall follow him."

In writing regularly to Rosalie, Benjamin had chosen a correspondent who candidly opposed his attachment to Germaine, and their letters took on a conspiratorial tinge. By May 1803, we find Benjamin begging Rosalie to help "illuminate" him: if she will share with him her feelings about Germaine, he promises, he will burn her letters after reading them. What he wishes, he tells her, is a woman who is comforted by his love, yet he has made Germaine so wretched that he himself is "unhappy on account of the unhappiness that she tells me I cause her" (a typically Constantian verbal construction). He tells Rosalie of his sleeplessness, his terrible debts, his long rides on horseback to cast off his despondency. Wishing to be free, he is chained to Germaine by the "supernatural influence" of her beautiful voice. Yet when Rosalie tells him that he must save himself, he bridles at the advice. He cannot leave Germaine now, he says, invoking his overstrained eyes or an illness of Albertine's—any concern that may provide him with a pretext for inaction. Rosalie tells him again that he must save himself; he replies that she judges the matter without knowing Germaine, that he could not bear to cause pain to his companion. He admits that his situation as the proclaimed lover of an enormously rich woman who has no intention of marrying him is degrading (her husband, the Baron de Staël, has recently died), and actually he is bent on leaving her if he can find a sweet somebody to share his existence. But he hastens to warn Rosalie not to tell Germaine, for his determination must await the right moment to be announced, when he is certain he will not make her suffer.

By February 1806, Benjamin has spent "not one hour that is not miserable" in the past few months of his "dark, heavy life"; yet in June 1807 he still "weeps like a child over the pain" that he would cause Germaine if he should abandon her.

And even when he finally writes Germaine a farewell letter, a letter that will surely shatter their bond, he feels an affection so profound that he wants only to enfold her in his arms and console her, and he throws the letter away. A month later, she threatens to kill herself, and the worst of it is that she has taken her servants into her confidence, created a "scene," so that now even these menials regard him as a monster. In Paris many influential people see him as hard and ungrateful, a man preparing to break off without ceremony an intimacy of more than ten years—truly this enslaving attachment to Germaine seems to have "issued from the bowels of the earth." We do not have a record of Rosalie's response to his lamentations—he seems to have burned most of her letters, as he promised—but her correspondence with her brother Charles suggests that the Lady of Coppet continued to be discussed in the harshest terms by the elders of the Constant tribe.

In 1804, Constant began to keep his famous *Journaux intimes*, which in France are regarded, somewhat perplexingly, as a masterpiece of the diary genre. Like most diary writers, Benjamin wants to discover his true feelings, to resolve certain personal dilemmas, and to arrest the stream of time, but unlike most others, he also wants to diagnose a painful ailment and to forge the will to heal himself, a will that he feels he lacks. Repeatedly he conveys the impression that as a moral being he is missing one or more organs. *What has gone wrong with my nervous system?* he seems to ask himself. *Why am I unable to move?* The reader pictures a defective version of one of those anatomical models so popular in the eighteenth century. As anxious as a chronic invalid, he nonetheless fails to summon up any genuine care for his wounded self, and the fear of death, the undertone of mourning, so unsteadies his voice that the reader may feel that orphanhood is the occult subject of his diary, that the tensions in the writing reflect some struggle with the call of the grave, some resistance to emotional petrifaction. Here all reflection is gridlocked by doubt, any course of action calls up a rebuttal, and the author's oceanic largeness of mind is attested to by his ability to entertain minute but disabling scruples. A diarist is one who by nature must turn emotions into words, but Benjamin's words rigidify unduly, and the diary begins to resemble something that has been hung up and desiccated, like a headhunter's wizened trophy. In the grief-laden months after Julie Talma's death there is even a general reduction of sentences to clauses, of words to symbolic abbreviations—metaphorically speaking, of fully fleshed body to shattered bone. Often regarded as an example of unusual clarity simply because their language is clear, the *Journaux intimes* are in the long run absolutely opaque, as though spring water were holding a dense silt in suspension. The contrast between the limpid style and the murky emotions suggests the diary of a muddled fictional character, a diary that has to be interestingly written because it is part of a work of art, yet also as confused as the person who keeps it. In the evolution of the diary genre, Constant's daybook is perhaps the first that feels like a fragment of an artfully composed tale, and it is this feeling that drives us, if our curiosity is excited, to want to read all the other fragments.

BENJAMIN'S PRIVATE WRITING IS honeycombed with references to various females who he hoped might help him to escape from his dependency on Germaine. The most forceful challenge to this addiction was posed, late in the autumn of 1800, by a winsome young woman named Anna Lindsay. Born Anna O'Dwyer to an Irish innkeeper at Calais, she had attracted men's attention since her teens but was perennially in need of a protector. She had served as the plaything of a succession of aristocrats, principally the Scotsman James Lewis Drummond, who on acceding to the earlship of Perth abandoned her along with the child of their union. Her situation improved in 1789, when she became the proclaimed mistress of the Marquis de Lamoignon, with whom she lived in luxury and by whom she would have two more children; Chateaubriand, who frequented the Lamoignon establishment, would recall Anna as "pleasing of countenance, noble, elevated," and "dryly witty, with a tendency to curtness."

Anna was thirty-six years old when Benjamin met her at Julie Talma's; they were to conduct a clandestine affair for rather less than a year, inviting turbulence and tribulation. Anna wrote gracefully—she had worked as a literary translator—and were it not for the loss of a portion of her letters, their correspondence would make for a balanced equation: on both sides there is much descanting on the subject of angels, of destiny, of the purity of the flesh. The pair's rhetorical fluency puts one in mind of an epistolary novel (a thought that fleetingly occurred to Benjamin), but the exchange was not, to say the least, intended for publication. What Anna with her insecure background desires is simply to achieve a "dignified" attachment, for the promise of security is the key to her heart, just as it was to Madame de Charrière's heroine Caliste. She has spent her life, she tells Benjamin, trying to win the favor of people she despises: "Having by misfortune lost caste, having been pushed into a saddening career, I have fought desperately to reconquer the trifling position that I was entitled to expect." Benjamin, though much taken with Anna, does not have the strength to break with Germaine, and his polished prose is governed by the dual purpose of retaining her interest while putting off her pent-up craving for marriage.

A poetics of engulfment, of self-loss, shapes Benjamin's letters to Anna. Everything but Anna becomes foreign to him: she is his oxygen, his lifeblood, "without which I smother and cannot survive." He visualizes her as clinging ivy covering the dead masonry of his soul: "You have seized, entwined about, and devoured my existence; you are the only thought, the only feeling, the only breath that still animates me." The outside world, he tells her, does not exist. One might think that this is amorous blather, but it isn't: what distresses Benjamin about Anna is precisely his craving for her—he wants her as much as she wants him but feels that he can't have her. When, snatching up her favorite word, he tells her that she has given him back the "feeling of my dignity," and that if only he had met her earlier he would by now be "strong with your strength," an unsuspected symmetry is revealed; he understands her because he is *like* her. "I understand you because I resemble you, because I too have made the voyage of life alone." It is not exactly that he, too, is socially déclassé, but that he has squandered most of his advantages and lost face in the eyes of Paris society, a loss that amplifies his orphan's fear of being found wanting. He is a fallen man who, like Anna, craves a mystical reinstatement, and it is his very similarity to her, with its attendant sensation of passivity, that he secretly fears and resents. "I hate suffering," he blurts out to her. "More than anything else, I'm afraid of suffering." And then—it has to happen—he finally explains why he cannot leave Germaine:

Any scandal would hurt you, and its effect upon your circle would sadden you deeply, perhaps for always; as for me, a rupture with *her* could incur the reproach of ingratitude and churlishness, and draw the attention of my many enemies, fanning their hatred. Inaction and silence, for a man who has entered public life by no design of his own and so contracted more than his fair share of duties, offer only false security: if a man forfeits the protection of anonymity, he has no choice but to win that of courage and recognized talent. I must defend my political ideas, and treat with elementary tact a bond that has nothing in common with the sort of feelings I have for you. I must work for the Tribunate and for my reputation, and put some order into my life; I cannot allow myself to be swept away.

That last phrase was enough to undeceive Anna, and in the spring of 1801 she decamped to Amiens, where she remained for some months in seclusion. "Though his protestations sometimes calmed me," she wrote on a scrap of paper later discovered in her copy of the correspondence, "and even restored my earlier ecstasy, his strategy, ever skillfully pursued and plain even to one blindly in love, soon caused me to be plagued with doubts, then with the knowledge that all my hopes had been dashed. The coldest heart in the world was trifling with my own, and presently the lover, as a crowning gesture, made it my duty to renounce him."

Only one person of consequence knew the details of Anna and Benjamin's affair, and that was Julie Talma, who tried to mediate between them, and in this way the correspondence became a triangular debate. By now Anna had a perfect grasp of Benjamin's character: she told Julie that he would never escape from his self-contrived treadmill, but that she, Anna, was "going to put an end to his indecent pursuit of me—I'm not going to offer his heart the delicious spectacle of a soul subjugated by him and reduced to despair." This Madame Talma duly considered, and then she, in turn, wrote to Benjamin.

What, my friend, do you want? . . . I have a bone to pick with you. With me you talk about Anna as if you were a detached observer, a person chatting conversationally about love. Alone with her—that is to say, in English—you speak like an ardent lover: you want to run away with her, you say a thousand wild things, and you don't really believe a single one of them. Is this is how you respect her peace of mind? A fine logic! Did you think she wouldn't tell me what you had told her? Well, listen, I'm going to tell her that you don't love her. I'm as sure of it as the day is long. To give her a place equal to the five or six others whom you've loved—that is not loving her.

You think to deceive us as one deceives a child.

Julie was twelve years older than Benjamin, and in effect, she was calling him on the carpet. Yet none of this figures in the famous eulogy he wrote for her a year later: her reprimand seemed to pass out of his memory.

A love affair decanted into a bundle of letters, with its aroma of spoilage clinging to it: such, even today, is the correspondence of Anna Lindsay and Benjamin Constant. The involvement seems so painful for both that the embarrassed reader prays that it will simply disappear, but it does not do so. Benjamin never ceased being fond of Anna, nor she of him, and his diaries reveal that the half-life of their mutual affection would last as long as she did.

AND SO BENJAMIN REMAINED Germaine's consort, growing more and more bitter and limp-willed. The story of how he got out of this pickle is fantastically, perversely complicated, involving one turned-down marriage proposal to Germaine, two wedding ceremonies with another woman, two phases of getting right with God, and more double crosses, zigzags, defeated altruism, and junked self-respect than anyone outside Hollywood can imagine. This mess has never been effectively chronicled because it cannot be mentally encompassed, but one or two moments in the life of our wayfarer may be enlightening to observe.

"The fear of boredom," he wrote in a notebook, about two years after the breakup with Anna,

> is my guiding emotion, and the greatest danger I would run in changing my situation is precisely that of being bored. My present position is obviously false, but it has its brilliant compensations. Though I have to put up with the inconvenience of a stormy liaison in which I play the secondary role, I find more apparent connections there than I

might elsewhere. The movement sweeps me along without my having to do anything. I can sit in the stern of the boat while still going forward, and at least I don't have to row. If I severed this bond everything would change. I'd be free of the pain of trying to resist the whirlwind that is carrying me along and the tedium of being caught up in an unsuitable celebrity, of the taint of Germaine's many imprudences, of the animosity which a famous woman excites and which also discredits her lover. But I would have far fewer connections in France, where I prefer to live, and I would lose the enjoyment of Germaine's quick, far-reaching mind and excellent heart—I'd lose her matchless devotion. Let us look into the future, however. For a long time I have had no love for Germaine, though my great flexibility helps me make up for my want of love without acting in bad faith. A striking intellectual similarity draws us together, but can this last? My heart, my imagination, and especially my senses need love. . . .

For eight years Germaine caused me to live in a continual tempest or overlapping of tempests. It is a mixture of [political ambition], a craving for love like an eighteen-year-old's, the need for companionship, the wish for glory, despondencies like barren wastes, the need for financial credit, the desire to shine, everything in my spirit that gainsays and confounds itself.

. . . Scene after scene, torment after torment. For three days running Germaine has been beside herself, and she showers me with so much invective and so many tears and reproaches that I waver between fury and indifference. How terrible it is when a man no longer loves a woman who cannot give up the wish to be loved! Their conversations are so brutal or superficial that he grows ashamed of his insensitivity to suffering, his feigned incomprehension. Since I am still deeply fond of Germaine, her suffering from not getting what she needs from me pains me enormously. Yet her unfairness repels me: when she accuses me of being about to leave her only because she is unhappy, I feel indignant.

Benjamin's disharmony with Germaine was thrown into relief by the death of Jacques Necker, in the spring of 1804. In the diary entries for this period, which, unlike most others, reflect deep thought and careful composition, Benjamin depicts the emotional strains arising from the passing of a beloved patriarch. There was much for him to ruminate about, for Germaine was still violently attached to her father. "Of all the men in the world," she had once written, "he's the one I would have preferred for a lover." She had lived much of her life through him, sharing in his fortune, protected by his power, basking in his importance as a larger-than-life historical failure. Never mind that his schemes to save monarchy in France had been blown away like so many promissory notes in the wind; in her view, his intellectual credit had survived the Revolution unimpaired. He had loved her, and while he lived he had repaired her follies and made her feel eternally young. He had also been fond of Benjamin, and it was the latter, of all her friends, who took it on himself to ride from Lausanne to Weimar to break the dreadful news to her.

April 9. Necker is dead! What will become of Germaine? What despair for the present, what loneliness in the years to come! I will go to see her in Germany, console or at least support her.

April 10. . . . I do not know anyone aside from myself who can feel for others; indeed, I feel more for others than I do for myself, because pity continually overwhelms me and because my grief, which would grow numb if it issued from some sorrow of my own, is ceaselessly renewed by the thought that it is not I who stand in need of consolation. . . . [Germaine] is far from suspecting the woe that has befallen her.

April 16. . . . [Germaine's] mental superiority and boldness have so cowed her entourage that no one freely tells her anything that might cause her pain: those who love her deceive themselves in order to delude her. They have loudly flattered her hopes about her father's health, and the result of this condescension will be horrible suffering.

April 22. Germaine's first feelings were convulsive. What absurd and revolting condolences people offer her! What a lack of sensibility in almost everyone! I am hardly surprised that people accuse me of having none. They use this word as if it meant everything that it does not. They think it refers to the conventional formulas with which the so-called friends of the so-called bereaved bestow on the latter as an excuse to rid themselves of their false sorrow as soon as possible. No, my sensibility is certainly not of that order: that is not the way I feel compassion for suffering people.

June 6. Quarrel with Germaine over my "scant" sensibility. No, my sensibility is not scant, only irritable. The sensibility of others never quite accords with it: theirs always seems solemn or flippant: it grates on me. Most often I think that they merely want—ignobly, to my mind—to rid themselves of their grief. My sensibility is always offended by *any* demonstration of the sensibility of other people: it is, as Germaine justly says, essentially hostile.

Germaine's emotional needs, enormous at the best of times, had been exacerbated by her father's death. Perhaps she felt that Benjamin's grief was paltry or shallow, for she had adored Jacques Necker so deeply that nobody's misery could keep hers adequate company. Benjamin, bitterly proud of his devotion, rejected the idea that his sensibility could be found wanting, but he did characterize it as "hostile." Sensibility of course has two faces: on the one hand, the word connotes an empathetic awareness of the feelings of others—our contemporary "sensitivity"; and on the other, it suggests an almost epidermal irritability in the one who possesses it—what the French usually call "susceptibility." And both sides of Benjamin's sensibility were being radically fused. As he became more and more critical of others, he settled into a passive, wounded state. His sense of what one might call true emotional pitch was increasingly offended by Germaine's friends, but most of all it was offended by Germaine. Never before had the clash between her sensibility and his own been so brutal. Hers, though coarse, was expansive, life-embracing, whereas his was touchy and fastidious. She needed him to absorb the flood of her effusions, but for him that meant washing out the fine discriminations that made him who he was. He wanted to channel feeling, to chasten and refine it, not to watch it swamp his mental landscape.

Germaine now hounded Benjamin like a creditor (which, materially speaking, she was, since he owed her a huge sum of money). Adrift without outside female assistance, he began to cast about for someone to marry, and the person he increasingly looked to was an old flame named Charlotte von Hardenberg, who in fact became the second Mme Constant. One would need an intricate flowchart to detail his oscillation between Germaine and Charlotte, but several of his diary entries for the years 1806–7 reveal his dominant moods. By this time Benjamin's mind had become such a matrix of indirection that he felt obliged to devise a numerical code for his many recurrent muddles and funks.

> 1 indicates physical pleasure; 2 the desire to break my eternal bond, of which there is so often question; 3 the bond renewed on account of memories or some fleeting charm; 4 work; 5 discussions with my father; 6 feelings of tenderness toward my father; 7 travel plans; 8 marriage projects; 9 weary of Mme Lindsay; 10 sweet memories and upsurge of love for Mme Lindsay; 11 hesitation about my marriage plans with Charlotte; 12 love for Charlotte; 13 uncertainty about everything; 14 plans to settle at Dôle in order to break with Germaine; 15 plans to settle at Lausanne with the same goal; 16 plans for overseas travel; 17 desire to patch up relations with several enemies.

By the early autumn of 1806, Benjamin has done little to free himself, but he has stealthily reclaimed much of the emotional territory ceded to Germaine over a decade. He is frankly "tired of the man-woman whose iron hand has ruled me for ten years"; she is "the most selfish, frantic, ungrateful, vain, vindictive woman in the world." He hesitates before a "necessary" step; yet the longer he wavers, the worse he feels: "She's hateful to me, unbearable. I must break off with her or die."

By early 1807, his inner pendulum is swinging even more briskly back and forth between revulsion and remorse:

February 28. Madame de Staël told me a true thing: I shall lose my talent through dryness of character. But what causes my dryness? My hatred of my predicament.

March 10. Gentle conversation [with her]. The truth is a singular thing—one might say that it breaks down doors. It crossed my mind to leave Madame de Staël without telling her, and then she told me that she had grown terrified of this very possibility without knowing why.

April 4. Madame de Staël shows a sweetness that both touches and distresses me. Let's allow her a few more good moments.

September 20. Yesterday was the fourteenth anniversary of this fatal attachment. For twelve of those years I've been trying to escape it. I'm not sure of anything yet, but I must remember that extreme actions produce contrary results. One must bend one's will to one's aim. And since I'm forced to scheme, scheme I shall. 12, 7, 8—any one of them is well and good so long as I get 2, and the first time she's a hundred leagues away, I'll choose one of these three courses of action.

The obsessive self-encryption reveals Constant's conspiratorial, noirish side. This character trait had come to the fore during his championing of his father's lawsuit, which at times edged toward real gutter danger, and sometimes it resembled a persecution mania. Constant seems to have been terrified lest Madame de Staël read his diary, terrified of the steps she would take if she were able, so to speak, to peer inside his brain. That terror, built into his perceptions, was a consequence of his lifelong tendency to see women as a hostile force.

CONSTANT BEGAN TO COMPOSE *Adolphe* in 1806 and rewrote it several times before its near-simultaneous publication in Paris and London, in 1816. Loosely based on his skirmish with Anna Lindsay, it also contains passages that sound like distant echoes of his long war with Germaine; yet, by and large, the fiction is so imaginatively conceived that it frustrates an autobiographical reading. It may be viewed as sort of a parable of what characteristically befell Benjamin with women—or, rather, of what he imagined befell him.

In a literary feint typical of the period, the story purports, by means of several fictional "publisher's notices" tacked onto the text, to be a memoir discovered by chance in a southern Italian town; the publisher rather priggishly announces that he's issuing it in hopes that it will "shed some light on human misery." Superficially, the tale is simple enough. Adolphe is the son of a government minister in a small German state; having reached his early twenties, and feeling that the time has come for him to acquire a mistress, he lays siege to the female companion of Comte P., a man of substance and an old friend of his father's. Ellénore, as she is called, is a Polish refugee, well-born and beautiful, but also impoverished and beset by colossal insecurities. Her many prejudices are opposed to her personal interests, and none more so, considering her improper past, than her attachment to the proprieties: uncertain of Comte P.'s esteem, she can't bring herself to explain to her two young children that they are illegitimate. She is nervous, mercurial, and sharp-tongued, and people observe her "as they might a beautiful storm." Adolphe thinks her a worthy conquest, and he writes her an insincere love letter. When she firmly but kindly rebuffs him, he suddenly feels that his love is authentic and presses his suit, hinting at a possible suicide. Soon she yields, and the pair become lovers.

At first Adolphe is happy with her, but before long he grows restless. Ellénore is "no longer a goal—she has become a bond." They cannot stay together forever, he feels, and he begins to betray the truth that he doesn't really love her. But he's so squeamishly afraid of wounding her that he's defenseless against her reproaches, which grow ever more vehement; and he complaisantly allows her to abandon Comte P. and her two children for a new life with himself. By now Ellénore has become a butt of contempt in the little German state, and Adolphe's father, alarmed at his son's behavior, arranges secretly to have her deported. But Adolphe manages to frustrate this scheme, which only breeds a new feeling in his heart, an all-consuming pity for his mistress.

Much has been said about Adolphe's layered emotions, about the way his ruefulness hobbles his will, but maybe the biggest attraction here is simply to watch Constant get so many different *types* of affect running—or at least staggering —at the same time. He takes over from women writers like Madame de Charrière the idea that inner conflicts are the key to people's lives, then heats those conflicts up to a pitch of psychological suspense.

In the midst of Adolphe's soul-searching, Ellénore's father recovers the occupancy of his former estate through an improvement in the fortunes of the Polish gentry. The couple travel to Poland and move into his country house. But Adolphe's father now manages to enlist a diplomatic associate, a baron who is stationed in Warsaw, to try to convince Adolphe of the folly of his love affair. Adolphe vacillates—some of the language here echoes Constant's diaries—and Ellénore makes the mistake of asking a female friend to plead her case with her lover. But this minx actually encourages him to abandon Ellénore, and after much thought he makes up his mind. He writes the baron, promising that he will break with Ellénore, and the baron perfidiously forwards his letter to her; on reading it she develops a high fever. Apparently stricken with a respiratory ailment, she begins to waste away before Adolphe's eyes, and to his horror dies in his arms. Only after her death does he discover, among her papers, a letter to him in which she confesses that she has been secretly wishing all along that he would leave her.

> Adolphe, . . . what is this strange pity that prevents you from ending a bond that you can't abide and that forces you to stay with someone you regard as a pathetic wretch? Why do you refuse me the one sad pleasure of . . . appreciating me as a person of dignity? . . . What do you want? That *I* should leave *you*? Can't you see that I'm not strong enough? It is for you—you who don't love—to find the strength in your heart.

Such, then, is the story of *Adolphe*. It must be said that this slender romance, which infuriated Germaine de Staël, now sticks firmly in the craw of almost every woman who studies French literature (and most students of French literature, outside France, are women). If some males profess to see Adolphe in themselves, very few females can identify with Ellénore, and the bittersweet tale, wholly misunderstood by British reviewers in 1816, has in the long run failed to win over the Anglo-American public. This suggests a larger, and perhaps insurmountable, problem. Just as individual French words often lack exact equivalents in English (*pain* is not "bread," nor is *vin* the beverage of Ernesto and Julio), so French literary genres do not quite translate into Anglo-American counterparts, and we have nothing that resembles the "novel of analysis." Like many such novels, *Adolphe* seems overrhetorical and didactic to us: it is less an artistic entertainment than a sort of moral workbook. It also feels overly stripped down, pared of the details of social background and tricks of speech that we nowadays expect of a novel: though we are told that Ellénore speaks a charmingly incorrect French, we are never offered an example, and on those rare occasions when she actually talks, she sounds like anyone else. She is flattened out, undercharacterized, as are all the people in the book except the narrator himself—if ever there was a novel coming perilously close to being all tell and no show, it is this one. Many years before the writing of *Adolphe*, the young Constant wrote Belle de Charrière a letter in which he confessed to having recently abandoned work on a novel "because I'm just too much of a talker. All those fictional characters who wanted to use my words were really trying my patience. *I* want to do the talking—especially when you are the listener." This would be a pertinent reflection on *Adolphe*; that the story works as well as it does suggests that the novel of analysis is one of those genres honored only in the breach, acquiring a semblance of life exclusively through the delicate colorings of its central moral theme.

Constant's tale enjoyed a limited vogue at the time of its appearance, then gradually lost favor with the public. It was dreary; it was downbeat; it was derelict in certain novelistic duties, such as the portrayal—always a measure of a writer's talent—of two people falling in love. It takes Ellénore and Adolphe only one perfunctory paragraph to grow fond of each other; convinced of the primacy of words, Constant apparently felt that the sudden transition from a woman's refusal to allow a man to speak to her of love to her encouraging such words was enough to describe her emotions—which it isn't, and wasn't, especially to the romantic sensibilities of early-nineteenth-century readers. *Adolphe* went into eclipse.

It has since been rediscovered three times—first by Gustave Planche, Sainte-Beuve, and Balzac in the 1830s and '40s, then by Paul Bourget, Anatole France, and Emile Faguet in 1889–91, and finally in our own time by a host of academic writers. The earlier, intellectual revivals were flashy and exciting, but they weren't always very judicious; the current university revival, which coincides with the study and publication of many of Constant's and his friends' private papers, has led to a much clearer understanding of *Adolphe* and its author. *Adolphe* has its place in the canon now, and yet it remains unloved. One problem with a university revival is that it may be carried out for professional purposes by scholars who avert their eyes from the artistic defects of what they are studying, and the consequence is a sapping of critical vitality.

Adolphe's main flaw as a fictional being—what sometimes makes him seem unmodern, unreal—is his lack of any comic or ironic sense. What *is* real-seeming about him is his relentless self-scrutiny. His thoughts are like arrows taking flight, then turning around in midair to torment the archer. But it's a patterned effect—rehearsed, almost dance-like—and Constant was by no means unaware of this. Skeptical of confessions and disdainful of Rousseau's belief that civilized people can dig their way back to a substratum of innocence, Constant refused to concede that sincerity is anything but a hypothetical alternative to the necessary deceits of social life. He allows us to suppose that Adolphe inflates his remorse to win his readers' sympathy, that he's putting one over on us in the same self-deluding way that he put one over on Ellénore. Several modern writers have even gone so far as to suggest that Adolphe's tone has more to do with the uses of the confessional voice—that is, with verbal atmospherics—than with an ethical intention. Historically, this argument is untenable—Constant was as deeply concerned with the edifying content of his novel as, let us say, Jacques-Louis David was with that of his paintings— but it raises a serious issue. Once a "novel of analysis" has been drained of its moral impact, once we decline to accept its applicability to our lives, why should we actually bother to read it—what real meaning does it have?

When people like Planche or Balzac read *Adolphe*, they felt they were taking their moral temperature. One didn't want to find oneself turning into Adolphe; one nervously checked one's mistress for symptoms of Ellénore. Of the vast body of writing devoted to *Adolphe* in the past few decades, however, almost none pays heed to its moral import, and maybe our continuing interest in the tale can be explained only by our "postmodern" tendency to empty out content, to turn everything into pure style.

Some twenty-five years ago, Tzvetan Todorov wrote an influential essay on *Adolphe*, in which he tried to rescue it as a story of genuine moral urgency. Todorov saw that Constant's idea of the inherent opacity of sexual relations is paralleled by a sense of verbal deficit. Just as the waywardness of the male sexual impulse eventually renders the loved one unloved, so speech negates or reverses all feelings. The paragraph in *Adolphe* that begins: "Charm of love, whoever has felt you could never describe you!" is not only the conclusion of one of the celebrated rhetorical set pieces in French literature, it is also the expression of an unpleasant truth. Women want to hear the language of love, but as soon as the lover speaks of love, describes or exalts it effectively, he also begins to denature it. "We cannot verbalize with impunity," says Todorov, reaching for a darker element of moral complication in *Adolphe* than any previously imagined: "To name things is always to change them."

Though feelings are usually anterior to words, putting them into sentences often scrambles them beyond recognition: emotions that felt true in the heart suddenly sound false when floated on the air. At one point in Constant's tale, Adolphe, having tried to reassure Ellénore that he loves her, inwardly laments, "Who can explain this fickle effect: that the very emotion that had prompted these words expired before I'd finished pronouncing them?" Here feelings thought to be true turn false on formulation, but the opposite can also take place: the sham can begin to seem real. Earlier in the story, when Adolphe is pretending to love Ellénore merely in order to seduce her, he observes that "the love that one hour before I had congratulated myself upon feigning, I now believed that I felt, and with fury." It is not the feeble or deceitful use of language that erects a barrier between the lovers, it is something in the very nature of speech when used as a vehicle for feeling.

In *Adolphe* Todorov finds a loose morphology of the use of words and silences in a failing marriage or love affair. The hero's affection for his mistress declines through a series of archetypal verbal situations which anyone can recognize and which Constant had studied closely in his own intimacy with Germaine de Staël. First comes a quarrel in which "irreparable words" are spoken, causing incurable wounds; though the pair may never repeat those words, they also cannot forget them. Next a habit of dissimulation appears: one frightful thought haunts both the man and the woman, but they are so afraid to give voice to it that instead they talk of their love, thereby cheapening it. It is inevitable that the woman will eventually air this secret that the man is trying to ignore, which is that he, though wishing to love her, really only pities her; and this thought, precisely for being expressed, for making her appear sexually diminished and pathetic to them both, becomes a reality. If, finally, the woman should persuade a friend to intercede with the man on her behalf, this conversation merely desanctifies the privacy of the two lovers, and their affection goes up in smoke. (In *Adolphe* the woman gets the blunt end of this process, but there is no clear sexual dimorphism here, no reason why the man can't be the loser.)

About five years after the appearance of Todorov's essay, a scholar named Han Verhoeff wrote a short book about *Adolphe*—he called it a "psychocritical study"—that has also proved extremely influential. His was a rebarbative, Freudian analysis, to which Constant's novel doesn't lend itself, but he did stress one very important matter that everyone before him had apparently overlooked. This was the question not of Ellénore's suffering as a lover but of her fitness as a mother. *Adolphe*, as it happens, does contain a number of passages in which Ellénore is portrayed as being curiously ill at ease with her two children. The most important is when she announces to Adolphe that she is going to leave her protector, Comte P., for his sake, and Adolphe, suddenly alarmed, warns her about the effect of such a decision on her reputation. What about her little ones, he asks her; she replies, "My children are also Monsieur P.'s. He has recognized them as his own. He will take care of them. They will be only too happy to forget a mother with whom they have nothing but shame in common." This answer is an astonishing piece of what we call (not in French novels, but in everyday life) humbug, and it requires some serious consideration.

Let's concede, as we diverge from Verhoeff's analysis, that many of the novelists of Constant's period enlist quite casual devices to eliminate characters who have become a liability to the plot. Inconvenient persons are destroyed by smallpox or suddenly dispatched to the Indies. But Ellénore's two children are in no way essential to the intrigue of *Adolphe*, so we wonder why they're there in the first place. And it is hard to avoid the impression that they are present not for a literary reason but on account of a psychic compulsion—which is to say that they partially vitiate the design of the book. If *Adolphe* is to work as a parable, it must show what goes wrong not only between this woman and this man but between woman and man as such. If we are to care about Ellénore's misfortune, we have to regard her as being on a par with women in general; and yet, as we've just seen, she is not. Most women, even the most irresponsible, would not abandon their children, and even if they were forced to do so by, let us say, a family court, they would be very unlikely to give them up with one humbugging phrase. So Adolphe misses something obvious here—he misses a point that no character in the most routine farce or bedroom comedy would normally overlook. It may also be observed (as Balzac would later do) that if Ellénore so easily agrees to leave her protector of many years, she could one day just as readily leave *him*. As a suitable object of his affections, she has disqualified herself; she's unworthy to become the woman in his life. Yet Constant doesn't figure any of this into his moral equation: he creates a stage set with doors the players never use.

There are other dimensions to *Adolphe* that lie beyond the sightlines of its author's moral understanding. There is, for example, the matter of Adolphe's faint desire for the beautiful woman who has given herself to him. One of the many ways in which Adolphe resembles the William of Isabelle de Charrière's *Caliste* is in the strange dullness of his passion. There is a scene in Belle's tale in which Caliste, despite her fierce adherence to the proprieties and her insistence on marriage, is so tormented by her physical desire for William that she encourages him to kiss her. She's sitting at her clavichord, all bare throat and glossy ringlets, gazing into his eyes, when he, in his confusion, backs off. She's dismayed to find that his inability to defy convention and marry her is equaled by his unwillingness to follow his instincts and seduce her. The reader is prepared to put William's backwardness down to gentlemanly restraint or misplaced tenderness, but the author herself will have none of this. Precisely to show that his will is self-maimed, she presently introduces a rival suitor, the "man of Norfolk," who comes from the same social class as William but has no father; this Norfolk chap is undismayed by Caliste's sensual history and regards the young lord as an "imbecile." There can be little doubt what this word meant for Belle: a man who allows his parents or the social chorus or his own inner fears to stand in the way of his normal affections and desires. And one suspects that any woman of today who picks up this novel will still read it exactly as Belle intended: in a provocative essay on Madame de Charrière's narrative style, Béatrice Didier has wondered whether William's masculinity isn't somehow defective, whether he isn't afflicted by a weak sexual drive. For if this possibility remains tastefully unstated in *Caliste*, it certainly fell within the compass of Belle's psychological perceptions. The same cannot be said for Constant, who seems to regard Adolphe's instant loss of appetite for Ellénore, his lack of any uxorious faculty, as perfectly normal. Adolphe is all consciousness: there's no animal playfulness in the man.

For a work so intent on dragging everything out into the light of self-awareness, *Adolphe* has an awful lot of unexplained shadows. So many of the hero's actions are prompted by quarrels with his father that filial revolt becomes a universal subtext and perhaps the real explanation of what's wrong with Adolphe; but somehow Constant never comes to this point. And why, one wonders, must Ellénore be so unattractively portrayed? Could anyone so greedy for status, so stridently déclassé, really compel the loyalty of an intelligent young aristocrat? Surely one of the undeveloped themes of this love affair is class aesthetics. Another is the disparity in age, the mature-woman-and-younger-man relationship: here again the reader, or at least the modern reader, is left unsatisfied. Isn't it odd, we wonder, that Ellénore's thirty-six years of social experience never amount to anything but a liability for her? Isn't it odder still that she has no wisdom to impart to Adolphe or, rather, that he never learns anything from her? Biographically, this pedagogic sterility has a cruel implication. It suggests that Constant may have learned not too much from Madame de Charrière, as Sainte-Beuve thought, but too little; and that even if he proved the more powerful artist, she had the greater insight into humanity. By featuring a male narrator in *Caliste* she put her psychological acumen to the test, forced herself to grasp the man's viewpoint before going on to express the woman's. Constant, in declining to reverse this arrangement—in retaining the male as protagonist—fell into the trap she'd so deftly avoided. He expended his sensibility on his author-surrogate and had none to spare for Ellénore.

Still, the main problem with *Adolphe*—the problem the reader can't shake out of his head—is that the female personage set beside the hero doesn't correspond to any observable type.

The artistry that created an archetypal male couldn't invent a plausible feminine counterpart. Ellénore is so feckless, so passive, so whiny that most women, starting with a certain Mme de Coigny, to whom Constant read a version of his tale in February 1807, and who found it offensive, can't see themselves in her. On finishing the novel, his contemporary Mme de Rémusat exclaimed, "Oh, what dry reading, and what a disagreeable book!" And when Constant sent a copy to Albertine in 1816, she wrote back caustically to her father: "Having never yet had the experience of being too *loved*, I cannot altogether comprehend the hero's unhappiness."

But is there another way to read *Adolphe*? I think there probably is, and it may have something to do with the relation between art and life. Though nothing about the Staël–Constant liaison was very pretty, its written records add up to an astonishing dossier. Poring over this voluminous scrapbook, which contains *Adolphe* and many other texts, you completely forfeit the distance of fiction, completely confuse the lark and the tree, but you also get immersed in an imaginative act that resembles a myth or lived paradigm. There's an almost musical quality to this myth, to its foreshadowings, echoes, and latencies, and though Constant wasn't consciously banking on any of this, he was scarcely unaware of it either. We have to hand it to him that his record of his plight left a fascinating writerly trail. Of course it's a trail that goes around in circles, but here, as elsewhere, he anticipated our own period, when the moral imagination is less often employed in making positive decisions than in trying to kick some vicious habit, or in admitting that it can't be kicked.

And Benjamin himself—would he ever get free of *his* addiction? The answer is yes, but sloppily, languidly, and over a period of about four years, with the help of Charlotte von Hardenberg. It was a slow struggle, because Charlotte was irresistible and Germaine immovable. The long war between them culminated in a scene in a hotel, with Germaine bursting

into Charlotte's rooms while the latter was soaking her feet—
an exquisite detail, under the circumstances—and precipitat-
ing a verbal duel that lasted almost all night long. Finally, on
May 9, 1811, Germaine and Benjamin said goodbye forever
on the grand stairway of the Auberge de la Couronne, in
Lausanne.

Unlike Ellénore, Germaine did not die of a broken heart
but went on pursuing her frantic love life. She never got over
Benjamin, though, and years later she was still writing him
agitated letters: "Is it really possible that you have ruined everything? Is it really possible that my despair could not restrain
you? No, you are guilty!—though your admirable mind still
casts its deceptive spell on me. Farewell, farewell! Ah, if you
only knew what I suffer!"

2

THE TOUCH AND ACCENT
OF THE ENCHANTER

IF YOU TAKE THE Paris métro to the Sèvres-Babylone stop, then walk around the corner into the rue de la Chaise, you come to a large portal, faced in stone and adorned by a single carved garland, that is clearly somewhat older than the surrounding masonry. This portal is all, or very nearly all, that remains of the façade of the Abbaye-aux-Bois, an Augustinian nunnery that stood on this site between 1718 and 1906 and has its place in history. From old photographs we know that the central cloister of the abbey was spacious and attractive. It enclosed a formal parterre shaded by tall acacias, and from its steeply pitched mansard roof two rows of austere dormer windows looked down. In the abbey's best days the superiors, the sisters, and the young boarders came from the first families of France; and attached to the main building was a wing, a sort of annex, which served as a house of repose for distressed gentlewomen seeking refuge from the cruel world.

It was in this wing that Madame Récamier lived and maintained her celebrated salon, from 1819 until some months before her death, in 1849. She was, by all accounts, the most beautiful Frenchwoman who has ever lived—or, if that seems too sweeping a claim, the most beautiful of whom we have record. The presiding genius of her salon was François-René de Chateaubriand, her platonic friend and former lover, who would sit stiffly in his own special chair and accept the homage of her many friends. Among these, at one time or another, were Benjamin Constant, Eugène Delacroix, Alexis de Tocqueville, Alphonse de Lamartine, Prosper Mérimée, and Sainte-Beuve; you might say that almost no one of note failed to climb, at one time or another, the stairway to her cramped interior.

Madame Récamier's accommodations were never luxurious, and during the first period of her residence they were almost primitive—two cells connected by a shadowy corridor. In a famous passage in his memoirs Chateaubriand describes how, arriving at the approach of dusk, he would labor up the three flights of stairs and pause to glance into the cloister below, where groups of nuns slowly revolved around the central garden and young girls skipped along the pathways, calling to one another. The cat's-paw leaves of an acacia trembled outside Madame Récamier's windows; as the abbey bells finished ringing the Angelus, she would seat herself at the piano, her loveliness scarcely dimmed by the years, and play for him awhile. Her tiny parlor also contained a harp, a portrait of Germaine de Staël in the character of Corinne, and a view of Coppet by moonlight. About seven years later, Madame Récamier moved upstairs to a more commodious apartment, and there, on either side of the mantelpiece, she hung portraits of Germaine and Chateaubriand; on an adjacent wall she placed a large painting representing the *Triumph of Corinne*. The new parlor was furnished with good sofas and chairs—Louis XVI juxtaposed with Empire—and a little table to hold the ever-growing manuscript of Chateaubriand's sweeping pageant, *Memoirs from Beyond the Tomb*.

The prime event at Madame Récamier's evenings was always the reading of the latest installment of these memoirs; naturally enterprising, she had arranged for the memorialist to receive a handsome advance for the vast work, which was to be published at his death. He did not read aloud—others did it for him—but his noble, careworn head, rendered ever more monumental by a progressive loss of hair and doubling of chin, expressed many nuances of emotion as he listened to the solemn voices re-creating his past. Of course, not everyone adored Chateaubriand's prose—Sainte-Beuve, for one, did not—but reverence for the aging writer was the keynote of Madame Récamier's salon; indeed, it was the price of admission, since she frowned on open discord. The setting, after all, was a convent, so an ecclesiastical hush seemed appropriate, and anyway, people felt privileged to be ushered into this celebrated sanctum. The atmosphere was one of general goodwill, of spirits doing their best to be kindred, and if, as Sainte-Beuve later put it, "all the charity rather detracted from the element of truthfulness," that was only because the hostess stubbornly averted her mind from malice and egoism and wickedness. She cultivated a kind of politic innocence, and though not herself a wit, she had a shrewdly benign sense of how to bring others' wits into complementarity.

About five years after committing himself to write his great book, Chateaubriand came to the heart of it all—those chapters devoted to the lady herself and to what she had meant for his lifework. The year was 1839—he was then seventy-one, she sixty-two—and it is a pity that no report has come down to us of the reading of this portion of his masterpiece and of the listeners' response, for it was a high point in the story of the Romantic movement. Though his account of their liaison (which he would take up again, at a later stage) was expressed in somewhat antiquated language—in prose striving not for naturalism but for ideal beauty—it managed to convey a lofty sense of how a man and a woman might live in harmony. The gallantry of the style was no empty artifice but a candid reflection of Chateaubriand's personal manner with Madame Récamier, and when he told his public that his life had been a dark storm illuminated only by the glow of her beauty, they had no reason, given what they witnessed every day, to question the simile.

The pair were known to their friends as Juliette and Chateaubriand, and their long intimacy, as portrayed by him—no other firsthand portrayal exists—has a high rosy sheen to it. They seem a loving couple enlaced atop a Sèvres tureen. He was a creator in word and deed, she the very type of mature female beauty, so it is satisfying to picture them conjoined; yet their embrace is more than aesthetically pleasing—it is morally edifying. Their story, we are told, is one of successful love, of affection ripening through middle life to old age, and also of a shared sense of the duty to resist tyranny: Chateaubriand's liberal heart had been deeply moved by Juliette's decision to throw in her lot with Madame de Staël when Germaine was being hounded by Napoleon. Yet if the liaison was in some ways exemplary, it was also problematic from the start. When they met, neither was young, and in each a world of reminiscence stirred like a sunken treasure ship beneath the placid surface of everyday speech. Both prized the past, both valued vintage friendships, but they had very few memories in common. Though Madame de Staël, for instance, had been Juliette's dearest friend, she remained for Chateaubriand a somewhat distant figure. She had died in 1817, just before the beginning of his attachment to Juliette, and though he had met her several times he had never paid court to her at Coppet. Once, it is true, Germaine had invited him there, but he had not found time to make the journey; she had repaired his error by sending him a long account of what *would* have happened if he *had* come—a dramatic dialogue between the two of them, in which she triumphed. At the time this had probably struck him as amusing, but years later, after he had fallen in love with Madame Récamier, the incident saddened him, since by not making the pilgrimage he had passed up an occasion to meet Juliette and so unwittingly left their intimacy in its chrysalis stage. Their paths might have crossed many times but had not; and when in middle age they found each other, they tried to resurrect large segments of the past, with the consequence that much of their conversation consisted of an exchange, a crossbreeding, of memories. It is for this reason that one must, if one wishes to understand their affection, sort through all the cluttered baggage of reminiscence—the stained letters, faded calling cards, and battered carnival masks—that the pair brought with them to their final destination.

SOMETIME AROUND 1800, AN ugly caricature of Juliette Récamier was published in Paris; she discovered the affront by accident, when she entered a printseller's shop and he casually showed her the picture. It gave her a jolt, but she also noticed that the shopkeeper had not been able to recognize her from the likeness, which suggests that she was one of those rare people whose features are immune to graphic parody. Her face was, simply, too perfect: it set the standard for an age. Today, wondering what was so lovely about her, we must look to the painting and sculpture of the period, for many supremely gifted artists wished to portray this woman who was also an idea. David, Gérard, and Canova were among those who tried, but strangely, their portraits do not seem to depict the same woman. They also do not depict the real woman. In none of them does Juliette seem as transcendently beautiful or charming as she certainly was; in none can we sense the enigmatic contradiction between her kindness and her oft-noted coquetry.

Canova, it must be granted, had an acceptable excuse for this failure, since his aim was to render her in a style halfway between realism and the *beau idéal*. In posing her, the great Venetian covered her ringlets with a shawl and made her glance heavenward, beatifically; but by encouraging her to let a faint smile play about her lips, he also lapsed into the somewhat kitschy taste that sometimes bedevils his work. With David things went rather better, for a woman's beauty has a lot to do with color. He tried to render her delicate complexion and the warmth of her auburn hair, and his portrait is more vivid than Canova's and also more celebrated—it was, after all, through this work that she acquired the honor of bequeathing her name to a sofa. But Juliette and David did not hit it off, and their discord shows in the picture. He found her spoiled—she was often late for sittings—and she felt that he was unable to catch her likeness or to discover what made her beautiful. She was hurt, and he apologized, regretting that he had placed her under a top light that veiled her eyes with shadows. His composition is bare of all furnishings except for a Pompeiian lamp and the severe couch on which she reclines, barefooted, wearing only a headband and a Roman-style peplos. The setting seems to imply something about her character, and a modern authority on David has detected in its taut blank surfaces a "hint of sexual fear"—presumably some anxiety that the painter detected in his model. Yet Juliette's only documented fear was that she would look bad in the picture—she was very anxious about that—and the spare arrangement, borrowed from Roman mural decoration, was intended as a symbol not of anxiety but of republican simplicity: this was Year X of the revolutionary era. David's portrait is really a history painting in which Juliette figures as a sort of keeper of the flame, though how she feels about this onerous role is not apparent from her gaze.

Gérard's more conventional image of Juliette, seated and, once again, barefooted, most closely matched her vision of herself. Here, in a filmy, off-the-shoulder gown, she is more frankly seductive but scarcely more knowable. Psychologically she comes into a better focus in a letter to the painter, penned some years later, which hints at the contrasts, the chiaroscuro, of her nature. "I admit that I don't know much about painting," she writes, "and that I judge of your talent simply by your success. I own that I shouldn't admire your pictures so much if you weren't perfectly kind and didn't feel a certain friendship for me. What are you going to do with my portrait?

You saw into the future when you gave me that sad and dreamy expression, which pleases me more than it resembles me." Her tone here is slightly put on, at once plaintive and disarming. By this period she has learned that beauty is a burden, and that life in its service will always entail some element of ritual sacrifice.

Baptized Jeanne-Françoise-Julie-Adélaïde Bernard, Madame Récamier was the daughter of a Lyonnais lawyer who had been summoned to Paris to serve as a revenue officer in the Ministry of Finance. She was educated in a convent, where she studied the piano, and was married in 1793, at the age of sixteen, to the banker Jacques-Rose Récamier, then about forty. Récamier was tall, blond, hearty, and indulgent—so much so that a squadron of his nephews lodged in his house. He was also very rich, and showed little discrimination in the company he kept and no particular regard for his marriage vows. Much later, Juliette confessed to one of her intimates that he had never treated her as anything but a "child, whose beauty charmed his eyes and flattered his vanity." All the evidence suggests that the marriage was never consummated, and so was not legally sound; certainly Juliette was thought by all who knew her to be a virgin. No one has ever explained why Récamier took so little interest in his young wife, but one plausible, if purely conjectural, explanation is that he either had syphilis or knew he ran a strong risk of contracting it. He did not presume to interfere in the affections of Juliette, who, for her part, tried loyally to observe the proprieties of married life. Their union was a typical eighteenth-century contrivance—a triumph of delicate stagecraft.

About five years after the marriage, in 1798, Récamier acquired the townhouse that Germaine de Staël's father, Jacques Necker, had built in the rue du Mont-Blanc (now the Chaussée d'Antin). The interior had to be wholly redone, and all the new decorative elements—the furniture, *boiseries*, and bookcases, the bronze sconces and fittings—were ordered from the cabinetmaker Jacob, who produced an extensive ensemble in the Directoire style. At Juliette's first receptions the guests gaped at the vast pier glasses, frescoed ceilings, and glittering chandeliers, and she herself proved a gifted hostess, welcoming princes and parvenus with equal attentiveness, playing the piano with tears in her eyes, and now and again vouchsafing her visitors a glimpse of her huge bed, which had four gilded swans at the corners.

It was during the purchase of the Necker townhouse that Juliette met Germaine, who would exercise an enormous sway over her for almost twenty years. Spiritually the two fit together with almost machined precision, like pieces of the boulle cabinetwork of the period. Benjamin Constant, recalling the two women's first meetings, spoke in terms of male and female: Germaine had a "virile intelligence, which penetrated everywhere," while Juliette had a "delicate and sensitive intelligence, which understood all." Juliette, one is told, raised listening to a fine art: with her eyes fixed unwaveringly on the speaker's, she would instantly grasp the trend of his thought, and whenever the gossip grew unusually wicked she would bring her handkerchief to her mouth and let her eyes twinkle over the crumpled lace. In time, Germaine would write some astonishingly steamy letters to Juliette, which have given rise to much speculation; yet hers was a deeply heterosexual nature, and far from wooing the young beauty, she seemed, instead, to want to annex her. Juliette had the physical grace Germaine longed for: the character of Corinne, in Germaine's eponymous novel, is to some degree a conflation of the two women.

There was always an aura of luminous blankness about Juliette Récamier. Born into a society that fancied powdered wigs and white facial creams, she was quintessentially lunar. Her skin was white, her dresses were almost unvaryingly white, and her only adornment was pearls; though she spoke and wrote well, her sole foray into literature was a translation of some stanzas by Petrarch—an exercise in reflectancy. Her surviving letters are scant, a testimony to her moonlike powers of self-occultation, and she caused most of her private papers to be burned. Her biography was not written until the late 1980s, and even Sainte-Beuve, in the important obituary that he devoted to her memory, announced that he would refrain from relating the details of her history. "Is a woman's life recounted? It is observed, perceived, *felt*. I shouldn't even care to furnish dates, which would savor of ill breeding." The chivalry was disingenuous—he had already written several long biographical notices of women—but it would have pleased the evasive Juliette. Though she did acquiesce in the composition of a brief celebrity memoir, an as-told-to account transcribed (and embroidered) by Benjamin Constant, it is both coy and cloudy —a peepshow seen through a frosted lens: she seems the center of a good deal of passion, but it leaves her essentially unexplained. If she does not emerge as a realized character in this little work, that, the reader feels, is because of an unspoken complicity between Juliette and Benjamin: neither one really wants to find the contours of her personality. She cannot bear the scrutiny, while he wants to borrow her voice to air some ideas of his own.

These "Memoirs of Juliette," set down in 1815, when she was thirty-eight, deal mostly with her relations with men—or, rather, with men's amorous pratfalls in her vicinity. Her first admirer of note was Jean-François de La Harpe, a small, gargoylish, combative man, no longer young, who had been a protégé of Voltaire's. La Harpe had failed as a playwright before making a name for himself as a social and literary critic and also as an inveterate diner-out who denounced social conventions while dragging his sleeves in his plate. Juliette, though attracted by his fame and intelligence, knew nothing of his checkered past, and apparently her ignorance released him from a certain cramped sense of constraint. In her presence La Harpe made a spectacular fool of himself, and she laughed at him, though merrily rather than mockingly. This, too, was among her gifts: to poke fun at people without wounding them, to make them feel honored to bring a smile to her lips. The next man to become infatuated with her was the young Lucien Bonaparte, Napoleon's embarrassing little brother, who for a year wrote her love letters in an attitudinizing style. To this courtship she responded with the classic squelch—she showed the letters to her husband—yet she would later tell Benjamin that Lucien's language planted in her mind "an unsatisfied need for emotion, which often gave rise to daydreams and sadness." All this prompted her to begin reading novels, especially those of Madame de La Fayette; and there she found the source of Lucien's vocabulary, though the novels were free of his mannerisms, which rang false to her, and also of his manic intensity. "I liked those stories in which duty opposes and finally tames feeling," she told Benjamin, "yet this sort of reading is actually rather dangerous, because it makes the reader accept the struggle between passion and virtue as something natural. . . . Though I did not miss the pleasures of love, I missed the pain. I thought I was made to love and suffer, but I loved nobody and nothing, and suffered only from my own indifference."

Then, at Germaine's, Juliette met Adrien de Montmorency, who was tall, blond, and affable—a flower of an ancient noble family of the Ile-de-France. Whereas Lucien had behaved like a character in a melodrama, Adrien seemed subtle, fully rounded: he was reticent, but gracefully so; eloquent, yet with that well-trained salon manner which proclaims a readiness to drop any subject that may "fatigue" the assembled company. He soon felt attracted to Juliette, and his conversation began to presuppose intimacy, gaining charm from its very uncertainty. The pair were suspended in what she felt to be "an agreeable half-light," and according to Benjamin's transcription of her narrative, she expected to fall in love with him. She never did. "I would have liked more passion," she admitted to Benjamin. "A few minor squalls would have been worth their price." She noticed with distress that she and Adrien were always meeting in public, and that their little secrets were so innocent that she could have divulged them to the multitudes: "I reproved my heart for its abandon, yet what really troubled me was its indifference." The dalliance dwindled, but the two would always remain close friends.

Only once did Juliette come close to giving herself to a man: that was at Coppet, in 1807, when Germaine introduced her to Prince August of Prussia, a dashing nephew of Frederick the Great, who rowed her about Lake Geneva and courted her with all the tempestuousness she had read about in fiction. She grew desperately fond of August, and she wrote her husband a letter requesting a divorce; from Paris Récamier sent her a pained reply expressing his compliance if she should absolutely insist, but also his regret—this after fifteen years of unconsummated marriage!—that he had too greatly respected her "virginal susceptibilities and repugnances." Those repugnances did not vanish in the presence of Prince August; "Though our relations were very intimate," she would later confess to a friend, "there was one thing he failed to obtain"—and during one of his long absences in Germany her interest in him evaporated.

By this period Juliette had acquired a reputation as a frigid coquette, a woman incapable of giving herself. Writing of her "sweet genius—that ambition of the heart, which, beneath all her delicacy, showed so much strength and perseverance," Sainte-Beuve later suggested that the great question of her life was whether she had ever loved. He felt that she had not— not passionately or ardently—and that her need to love had reshaped itself into a need to *be* loved and to repay her admirers' affection with kindness. Was this Sainte-Beuve's polite way of saying that she was a compulsive, if undeniably amiable, flirt? Coquetry, as George Sand would later observe, is a "system of provocation," and in Juliette's day women who practiced it stood accused not so much of being provocative as of being systematic: they were seen as breaking faith with the Romantic engagement to act spontaneously. Even Sainte-Beuve conceded that Juliette was a manipulator, but hers, he said—singling out the enduring paradox of her nature—was an "angelic" manipulation. She seemed to want to wound men in order piously to heal them. Most of her male friends fell headlong for her, and yet—this was the startling thing—she *kept* those friends. "She was a sorceress," he wrote, "in her manner of coaxing love into friendship while leaving intact its vernal bloom. It was as though she wished to arrest all life in its April. . . . To new friends she often spoke of bygone years and the people she had known. 'This,' she would say, 'is my way of adding a little past to *our* friendship.'"

If Juliette blew hot and cold to the world, it must also be said that the world blew hot and cold to her. Women in particular were reserved in her presence. During a trip to Rome in 1806, she grew close to the elderly Elisabeth Forster, Duchess of Devonshire, a well-known essayist and salonnière. Though Juliette was greatly impressed by this handsome lady —her magnificent eyes glowed out of a gaunt, almost spectral face—the latter, who could be a little acerb at times, sent a letter to Germaine in which she expressed the hope that an acquaintance of theirs had not fallen for "*that siren.*" Laure Junot, the Duchesse d'Abrantès, wrote in her *Memoirs* of the "uneasy timidity" that Juliette experienced in the midst of her splendor: "It was evident that she was pained by the envious glances of the females, who could not wholly suppress the ill will with which they witnessed her monopoly of homage." And when the distinguished German dramatist August von Kotzebue visited Paris in 1803–4, he was forewarned against Juliette by a wave of gossip that led him to expect a "vixen, hardened by wealth." Kotzebue changed his opinion when he met her, at the Opéra, where she sat withdrawn from the public gaze "like a violet in the grass"; he felt that there could be "no way of dressing the hair more unassuming[ly] yet more graceful[ly], than in the numerous chestnut brown locks which often, even without looking in the glass, she artfully unites under her comb. For many weeks, I saw her almost every day, but never decked with brilliants." To his surprise, he found her warm-hearted, self-sacrificing, and—an interesting point, this—unimpressed by the trappings of success. A rigidly dutiful wife, she welcomed him into her house, whose grand staircase "resembled a terraced flower garden"; and though her residence was altogether wonderful, it was wonderful in taste rather than in expense. Kotzebue remarked that when Juliette rode through Paris she used a plain carriage, changing to a phaeton only when she wanted to leave the city. Having adored the nuns at her convent, Juliette retained some vestige of schoolgirl piety: charitable works occupied much of her time (one might add that she would later found and endow a school for indigent girls, in the parish of Saint-Sulpice). Once, arriving at her house, Kotzebue found her sitting in the drawing room with a deaf peasant girl whose education she was providing for, and feeding her with her own hands. She was also devoted to her niece and adopted daughter, Amélie Cyvoct, a rather straitlaced child who had lost her mother to an epidemic.

Kotzebue's report deepens our sense of the enigma of Juliette. If her coquetry cannot possibly have been "angelic"—this is one of Sainte-Beuve's purely literary conceits—neither did her real impulses correspond to those of the stereotypical flirt. Amélie, who knew her as well as anyone and left two dithyrambic tomes about her aunt (*Souvenirs de Madame Récamier, tirés de ses papiers*), remembered her as anxious, unsoothed by the luxury about her; Amélie felt that Juliette craved those affections which compose the "veritable felicity and true dignity of woman." Neither wife nor mother in a biological sense, Juliette was eager for tenderness, and found only a pale substitute in the passing attentions of worldly men. Clearly she wished her life to be otherwise, but was powerless to improve it, and we may suppose that if she remained dauntingly opaque to her many admirers, she was even more of a riddle to herself.

UNLIKE MANY OF HER friends, Juliette Récamier was not an adventuress; she wasn't even an adventurous person. But she *was* mysterious, and she refused to let people clarify anything about her that she didn't want to have understood. One man who tried to elucidate her, by breaking her long carnal fast, was Benjamin Constant. The attempt won him nothing but ignominy, and the scores of billets he fired at her, which later became the subject of a scandalous trial, cast light only on himself. The form in which we receive information is often the most revealing thing about it, and this is certainly true of Benjamin's passion for Juliette. All of our knowledge about it comes from him, none from her, and though she wrote occasional replies to his letters, not a single one has survived. "He never had the ghost of a chance," wrote Amélie, and the one-sidedness of the record seems to confirm her judgment It's a case of what you might call unrequited writing. But just for this reason, Constant ended up having the last word: he found posthumous revenge in the fact that Juliette's side of the story would remain forever untold.

His erotic obsession was born during a private meeting that she arranged, on August 31, 1814, in order to further a strictly political aim. Juliette, as it happened, had long been a friend of Caroline Murat, whose husband, Joachim, had been installed by Bonaparte on the throne of Naples. Wishing to help the royal couple, Juliette set forth the merits of Murat's position to Benjamin and asked him to write a memorandum on the Kingdom of Naples, which she would then dispatch to the forthcoming peace congress in Vienna. Though friendship and flirtation were almost indistinguishable in Juliette's mind, there is no evidence that she consciously wished to excite Benjamin's interest in her; having watched him for years in his former role as Germaine's consort, she knew that his romantic adventures had "inflamed his head more than they had touched his heart," as her niece later put it, and that he craved "constant turmoil, which he sought everywhere, not excluding the gaming table." It was inconceivable that Germaine had not discussed Benjamin with Juliette during their intimate chats: Juliette had even helped to patch up quarrels between Germaine and Benjamin. And even if Juliette had been fond enough of Benjamin to offer him her virginity, which she emphatically was not, she would have had other good reasons for stalling him off. During the previous summer he had given her a manuscript copy of *Adolphe*, which was hardly good publicity for him as a lover, and when he began writing her phrases like "I am in the same situation with you that a certain person once was with me"— a clear reference to Anna Lindsay—she could hardly have felt reassured. He was an open book to her, and she knew far too much of the plot to want to be part of the denouement. But she did admire his talent, and she may have secretly hoped that he would write not only a report about Naples but also a line or two about something vastly more interesting—her own life. As things turned out, Benjamin would oblige her in both wishes, composing not only the diplomatic memorandum but also, a little later, the "Memoirs of Juliette."

Benjamin's famous diary entry *"Mme Récamier. Ah, ça! Deviens-je fou?"* abruptly introduces his violent and, for the reader, stupefying infatuation. The next day he sends her a declaration of love, and for many months his journal and letters register with barometric exactitude the ups and downs, the elations and despondencies, of a gravely wounded soul. Again and again he fawns shamelessly on her, bites and claws her with his words, decides that he is "cured," and almost at once relapses into what he calls "the paroxysm." His writing flows with a tremulous cadence, brimming over with "feminine" punctuation, and by using phrases like "it is all the same to you" and "this caprice of yours," he implicitly stakes out the passive, one might almost say the feminine, role in the contest. He weighs every shade of meaning in his madonna's greetings and farewells, employing all his sense of the tragic in a hopeless attempt to understand her.

Some historians have wondered whether Juliette cast an inadvertent spell on Benjamin in her keenness to enlist his writerly skills. This may be; it is also possible that Benjamin, who attempted in the sequel to wrest some political leverage out of Juliette's position as a supplicant, slighted her feminine pride. Nobody, least of all a coquette, enjoys being used as a fulcrum for somebody else's ambitions, and Juliette feared the fading of her charms. Now nearly forty, she may have addressed Benjamin with especial vivacity merely as a way of gauging her attractiveness to men.

On September 19, Benjamin made an entry in his diary in which he mentions a "big album":

> Night of delirious suffering, morning no better. I weep unceasingly. Wrote her. She told me to come at two. But what is the point of it all? I am recopying this diary in a big album. When I have finished the recopying, what will my situation be? I wonder.

Benjamin's review of the stages of his passion proceeded apace with its forward evolution, and some weeks later, as he continued to transcribe his diary—or the relevant material from it—into his album, he came to the entry in which he had wondered how he would feel later on, when recopying it. It's a moment of unnatural, freakish density, which prompts us to think up burlesque parallels. We picture, for instance, a man who, on folding up his umbrella, reminds himself that he mustn't forget this moment of folding up his umbrella the next time he opens it, and who, on reopening it, remembers that he wasn't to forget the moment when he last folded it up. It would be one thing if such memory jogs helped to elucidate Benjamin's emotions, but in fact they only neutralize or cauterize them, at least for a while. Time becomes a mirror; nothing seems real; and though Benjamin's notion of recopying the record of his passion into an album betrays a romantic hope that it can assume, of its own will, an aesthetic form, he is by now too defeated to apply himself to this project.

For us the interest of this strange mnemonic exercise lies in its similarity to musical composition, to the task of stating and recovering themes. But for Constant himself its utility probably lay in its power to transcribe suffering, to get misery down on paper; there's always a touching optimism to such transcription. But Benjamin is always the gambler: what he does not see, and what his language reveals, is that Juliette herself is a wager, perhaps the greatest of his life. Since she is a virgin, much of his attraction to her lies in the wager's fantastically low odds, and the course of his turmoil begins to resemble that of a cardsharp at a "faro" table who, in one anxious and seemingly endless night, tries to recoup some initial loss and so squanders his fortune. Over and over, like a player shunned by "Lady Luck," he speaks of his desperate inability to see into Juliette, to grasp her aims, motivations, desires. She is inexplicable. He fancies that his beloved is sadistically cruel, or that only his disappearance will touch her, though this suicidal scenario has the inconvenient side effect of removing him from the scene.

Benjamin's obsession with Juliette went on for the better part of a year. It had the shapelessness of his long involvement with Germaine, and one day, as suddenly as it had come, it was gone. Sometime toward the middle of it all, in late January 1815, he sat down—it was his sole endeavor of this sort—and tried briefly to work out with pen and paper what he'd learned from her view of himself. He decided, basically, that he talked too much—an insight that was long overdue. Endless talk, he felt, had made him caustic and dry; it had made him unable to tell right from wrong. All he talked about was emotions, but he didn't have any, or he had too many, which amounted to the same thing. Talk was the great corrupter!

Juliette was scared by Benjamin and she was fascinated by Benjamin. She seems to have been plagued by the psychic equivalent of what neurologists call *anaesthesia dolorosa*, or painful numbness. She felt her lack of feeling—"suffered from my own indifference," as she put it—and perhaps in her loneliness she hoped to grow fonder of him; but she can't have hoped so for very long. You know this if you read his letters to her, because you suddenly sense, from something in the texture of the prose, that she no longer answers him regularly: he's repeating himself, reasking the same questions. She does not find it exalting to be desired by a person whom she doesn't love, and she writes him only when begged to.

THE MAN WHO WOULD one day solve the riddle of Juliette was nine years her senior, a short, swarthy Breton with brooding eyes and telegraphic eyebrows. In the famous portrait by Girodet his head lurks between his shoulders while his eyes peer suspiciously sideways; Napoleon, who thought him an interesting troublemaker, remarked on seeing this picture that he looked like a "conspirator who has come down through the chimney." The Vicomte François-Auguste-René de Chateaubriand was an adventurer, politician, writer, lover; while he has never been much read by English-speaking people, because he wrote primarily about France and Catholicism, he is still regarded by his countrymen as one of the great essayists and memorialists of the last century. It is probably safe to say, however, that of his many books there is only one the French still read with any real interest (some read it with considerable affection) and that, paradoxically, is the *Memoirs from Beyond the Tomb*. This opus was published serially in 1848–50—its author was no longer alive by the time the final installment appeared—and though its sepulchral title suggests that it was scribbled by a man at death's door, or perhaps even dictated by a ghost, its creation had actually occupied vast stretches of its author's middle and later life.

Chateaubriand was proud of his prodigious memory. As a student he learned his logarithmic tables by heart, and once he recited a sermon back verbatim to the curate who had delivered it; in old age he could recall many intricate details of his early life, and so never lost touch with his youth. In the singular calisthenics of memory that are his *Memoirs*, his writing becomes a sort of contortionist's exercise, pushing to an extreme the hyper-awareness that Constant cultivated in his "big album" about Juliette. If you wish, for instance, to discover what Chateaubriand did in London in 1793, you must turn to the chapter written in London between April and September 1832, and so dated; in order to read in his recollections of the Paris of 1803, you must find the chapter dated "Paris, 1838." Some chapters bear an additional date, representing a subsequent revision, but Chateaubriand never tries to rid his text of the effect of superimposed angles of vision or the optics of affective memory. Instead, he seems to take positive pleasure in suspending one period of time within another, so that the past wells up to permeate the present and the present fills all impressions of the past.

One of the charms of the *Memoirs from Beyond the Tomb* is that one cannot plainly state what they are about. Though the work is recognizably a celebrity's life story and is governed by a metaphor of the *vanitas* type—in these pages, the reader soon senses, the mighty are going to do a lot of falling—otherwise it is very hard to place. Nowadays scholars try to distinguish between "autobiographies," which recount the author's own life and rise to fame, and "memoirs," which relate what he has seen of important political, diplomatic, or artistic events, but Chateaubriand's book does nothing to oblige twentieth-century academics. Here personal history, eyewitness reportage, social chronicle, and travel journal are all bundled up inside one plush vehicle; raw materials sit beside passages of highly groomed artifice, carnival humor rubs elbows with moral casuistry, and so many other forms of utterance butt in and jostle for attention that the reader scarcely knows what to make of so much incontinent chatter. One theme, however, recurs: that of Chateaubriand's resistance to Bonaparte—the pen's opposition to the sword. The story of this contest becomes a sort of armature on which many dissimilar anecdotes and meditations are elegantly arrayed.

Chateaubriand tells us that two accidents of birth greatly affected his destiny. The first was his noble lineage and upbringing, which attached him to such aristocratic traits as chivalry and the love of liberty (in the archaic, feudal sense of freedom from tyranny). He felt, however, that if the aristocracy had initially imposed itself as a superior class, at least in the martial sense, it had gradually declined into a picturesque and essentially useless appurtenance of society. His own father was the very embodiment of quixotic nobility: tall, thin, cadaverous, with fleshless lips and deep-set, glaucous eyes, whose pupils, in moments of anger, "seem to speed toward you like bullets," he was inordinately preoccupied by his ancestry. He had bought at great expense the dumpy, drafty château of Combourg, and there in his declining years he ruled with tight-lipped despotism over his family, vassals, and tenant farmers, arousing fear in everyone he encountered. This haughtiness ran in the veins of the ancient Breton clan: "Odious in my father," wrote Chateaubriand, "it was pushed to ridiculous extremes by my brother, and a little of it was passed on to his eldest son. Despite my republican bent, I am not sure that I have quite cast it off, though I have carefully tried to hide it." Often, though uneasily, Chateaubriand touches on his bloodline, and his *Memoirs* come in time to seem haunted by the spirit of noblesse oblige, with its burden of ironies and guillotine humor.

The other thing Chateaubriand's Breton heritage gave him was his closeness to the sea. His mother had told him how the roar of the surf on the Breton coast, whipped up by a late September storm, had drowned out his cries at birth, and no day went by when he did not meditate on "the rock where I was born, the bedchamber where my mother thrust life upon me, the howling tempest that rocked my first slumbers." In the *Memoirs* the sea reaches everywhere, now raging, now becalmed, but always in flux, imperiously bearing the mind away on its unseen currents, a mirror for the traveler's solitude.

Chateaubriand's father seldom broke his self-imposed silence. His mother, a naturally vivacious woman enjoined to a matching silence by her husband, managed to vent her feelings by noisily sighing in his presence. As a writer Chateaubriand does not probe for the underlying causes of his father's pathetic pride of blood—he mistakes the symptoms for the ailment—but he does offer an unforgettable picture of his parents, himself, and his sister Lucile suffering through wretched winters in the family castle: his father had acquired Combourg in 1771, when Chateaubriand was not quite three, and the son lived there off and on from his tenth till his twenty-second year. The Comte's bedchamber, filled with antique weapons and genealogical parchments, was in the east turret; he rose at four every morning and pored for hours over estate business and ancient legal grievances. At eleven-thirty dinner was served in the great hall, with its portraits of Condé and Turenne; then, in the afternoon, while his father went hunting or fishing and his mother prayed in the chapel, Chateaubriand explored the surrounding meadows and woods. After supper came the dreadful evening routine, which extended until two in the morning. The hall was lighted by a fire and a single candle; while Madame puffed and snorted on a chaise longue, the Comte, in a coarse woolen robe and stiff white bonnet, would pace away into the shadows, disappear completely, reemerge into the glow of the fire, vanish again into the darkness, and continue in this manner until bedtime. Chateaubriand, cowering every time his father veered into the hearthlight, would crouch by the embers and chat in a whisper with his sister.

What passed between the two adolescents has long been a subject for speculation. Ignored by their parents, who had four other children, they began at an early age to adore each other and never ceased to do so. Lucile was four years older than Chateaubriand, a miserable, gawky girl in a tight corset and an iron collar, backward in her studies but temperamentally a poet—he would always regret her failure to develop her gift. He thought her dreamily beautiful, with her pale face, long black hair, and fiery upraised eyes. The pair were confederates in suffering, forever running to each other's succor, but as he later wrote in his *Memoirs*, "Lucile and I were useless to each other. When we spoke of the world, it was of the world we bore within us, which scarcely resembled the real one." Fretting endlessly over actual or imagined slights, bottling up frightful apprehensions, she seemed to him a funereal spirit; sometimes, walking on a path near the château, he would find her on her knees before a rustic stone cross, lost in prayer. The neglected girl had supernatural powers: at the stroke of midnight she could hear the sound of crimes in Paris, and her dreams were verifiably prophetic. One day when the two were wandering in the fields together, admiring the beauty of the solemn Breton landscape, she turned to him and said, "You must tell all this." It was the beginning of his calling as a writer.

As a younger son, bereft of fortune, Chateaubriand served almost two years in the army, then moved at twenty-four to Paris, where he read widely in the literature of the Enlightenment; he also met a number of important writers, including Chamfort and La Harpe. He also got to know Mirabeau, of whom he would render a scintillating portrait in his *Memoirs*. But his days in Paris were numbered. Late in July 1789, shortly after the fall of the Bastille, the Vicomte was chatting in his rooms with Lucile and another of his sisters when a mob of ruffians passed under his windows brandishing two severed heads, one recognizably that of a comptroller in the Finance Ministry. Appalled by these "cannibal banquets," Chateaubriand began to think about sailing to America.

Chateaubriand's journey to the United States, which lasted almost all of 1791, allowed him to try his hand at keeping a travel log in the Romantic manner. The romance of travel writing was twofold: there was the excitement of playing with an open-ended form, of realizing that prose need not be confined to the exposition of preexistent thoughts but could turn into a free quest, whose every sentence was unpredictable as a journey; and there was the option of stretching adventures into implausible or even impossible shapes, virtual trips to the moon, so that the world of fact became mere provender for the imagination. Generations of French schoolchildren have been obliged to offer textual explications of Chateaubriand's lush verbal renderings of the Mississippi River, which are at once highly talented, utterly tasteless, and—as regards flora and fauna—ethologically preposterous. Much later, it was discovered that the Vicomte had purloined some of his more interesting material from William Bartram's *Travels in America*, which had been published in Philadelphia in the year of his arrival. This plagiarism suggests some deep-lying insecurity or want of self-belief in Chateaubriand's character; yet the American writing also offered an early intimation of the techniques he would develop in his mature prose.

NOT LONG AFTER HIS return from the United States, Chateaubriand found himself forced by the Revolution into exile in England, where he lived for seven years in poverty. There he learned of the death of his mother and, overcome by religious feelings, began to write the long, polemical work that would appear in 1802 as *The Genius of Christianity*. This important book revitalized French letters and founded its author's reputation; but its chief arguments are of interest here only for the light they throw on his own character, which happens, however, to be considerable. In the early years of the Revolution, Catholic doctrines were ridiculed, churches closed, and convents suppressed; many artists espoused a return to the models of classical antiquity. Reacting against this tendency, Chateaubriand set out to show that Catholicism was in reality highly favorable to political liberty, elevated taste, and humanistic studies: with its devotional painting and sculpture, its architecture and liturgical music, Christianity was a poetic structure in itself. Drawing on an idea already elaborated by Madame de Staël, he argued that the arts in their modern form cannot be governed by classical rules because our conception of moral responsibility has been irrevocably altered by the Gospels. The ancients, for example, seeing nature as a mere backdrop to the intrigues of man, had never excelled in its representation; yet emptied of its bustling mythological tenants, its demigods, satyrs, and nymphs, the natural realm could be experienced as joyful and consolatory, a fit subject for painting and descriptive poetry. Chateaubriand himself offered several word sketches of North American places, spots that had no classical associations, as evidence that such plein-air meditations could exhibit a votive character. His thesis was generous and liberal-minded, and if *The Genius of Christianity* has since become a "forgotten" book (in the literal sense that most educated French people have at some point been asked to read it, or to read in it, and have then gone on to forget it), that is chiefly because its few really persuasive arguments have been thoroughly accepted and the rest discarded.

Many readers in 1802 felt that Chateaubriand's style was inflated and that only a want of genuine faith could account for this. Since Christianity does not propose itself as poetic truth but as absolute truth, the very idea that it is inhabited by a sort of "genius" was misleading and perhaps even slightly pagan. What pleased Chateaubriand's public in the book, and may still please us, are certain stretches of Baroque evocation. In these passages we find an almost incantatory conjuring up of receding space and dimensional sound, a sort of prose poetry which reappears in his accounts of his journey to Greece and Palestine. The hills and coastlands of Chateaubriand's mind are demarcated by geometrical ruins, broken colonnades, aqueducts stretching away into emptiness, and as he travels about the Mediterranean littoral, he discovers the material prototype for this spiritual scenography. We find him anxiously pacing through roofless basilicas and empty catacombs; he calls out and waits for an echo to reassure him that he exists, and he is overcome with malaise in one abandoned city whose walls refuse to return his voice. Chateaubriand the solitary wayfarer glimpses barbaric figures through shattered arcades, savors the fragrance of unseen women, cranes his neck to view cavalry distantly passing; he ruminates over windblown ruins and the rubble of amphitheaters. The calcified landscape becomes for him an infinitely complicated mnemonic device, a universe existing only to memorialize an earlier universe, and he hopes not only to evoke the past but also to revivify or resurrect it.

Chateaubriand had a great interest in the tender passion, and in those parts of *The Genius of Christianity* that touch on this subject he makes a point of contrasting romantic love with the Catholic sacrament of marriage. The great exemplar of profane affection is Dido, whose unrequited longing for Aeneas, uncomplicated by moral self-scrutiny, can be quelled only by self-destruction. The Christian bride, by contrast, is a creature of discipline, in whose eyes the image of pleasure yields to that of duty; but Chateaubriand also dwells on the importance of memory in the building of a Christian marriage. "Habit and length of time are more necessary for happiness, and even for love, than is commonly thought," he writes. "You do not become truly happy with your spouse until you have lived many days—and, above all, many *bad* days—in his or her company." And striking a blow against divorce (which the Constant character in *Delphine*, Monsieur de Lebensei, vigorously defended) he adds: "No man can be much attached to a property he may forfeit." The brutal economic metaphor recurs in his writing: as married people go through life, Chateaubriand seems to suggest, they pile up jointly owned memories, a little like treasury notes, which divorce would render unredeemable. This curious argument seems based on self-analysis, for in asserting that one of the strong points in favor of marriage is the power of nostalgia, Chateaubriand endows the rest of mankind with his own retrospective bent.

More provocative is Chateaubriand's discussion of the dreamy, unchanneled, and vaguely erotic ennui of modern city dwellers, which he attributes—obviously thinking of Madame de Staël—to the ever-growing ascendancy of women. He tells us that this ennui is a spiritual state that

> fills life with incredible bitterness as the heart twists and turns in a hundred different ways, trying to find a use for impulses that it feels to be useless. The ancients were not inclined to such exaggerations, hopes, baseless fears, such intellectual and emotional fickleness, such perpetual inconstancy—all of which amount to a sort of settled disgust.

Again, there is a good part of self-description in this early image of what we might call existential anxiety.

Chateaubriand himself married at the age of twenty-three. In his *Memoirs* he makes no bones about his abject poverty at the time and the fact that he was traded off in exchange for a dowry of about six hundred thousand francs. The match was concluded in February 1792; he tells us that it was arranged by his sister Lucile, who was friendly with a seventeen-year-old captain's daughter, slender, rather plain, and highly intelligent, named Céleste Buisson de Lavigne. "I sensed in myself not one husbandly attribute," Chateaubriand confessed much later, but he bowed, all the same, to necessity. He was, he insists, an overobliging man, "at the mercy of anyone's whim," and "to avoid an hour's harassment" he would readily "submit to a hundred years of slavery." Even so, he did not tolerate Lucile's match for as long as one year, for a few months later he deserted Céleste, and he would not resume life with her until 1804. She, in the meantime, passed through many mortal perils, including imprisonment during the Terror, quite undefended by him.

"Slavery" is a strong word to use about a marriage, and one senses that it distorts Chateaubriand's real feelings: there is sometimes in his language a perilous skidding toward stretched or sloppy metaphors, and he would never find a natural tone in which to portray this lifelong connection. He says, in so many words, that Céleste worshipped him, that she defended his interests like a tigress, that her character was nonetheless stubborn and contrary, and that her maternal instincts were thwarted by childlessness—he hints that her barrenness may have resulted from infertility on his part, and he never to his knowledge fathered a child. But his writing does not show her in movement or allow her to speak her own mind, and he never mentions the rather extraordinary fact that she penned her own recollections, in a pair of hardbound notebooks of quite respectable size.

For there were in this household not one but two memorialists. Céleste was an amateur writer of undeniable talent, and to set a passage of her writing beside a comparable passage of her husband's often makes for an interesting revelation: by and large she is more auctorially forward, more supercilious, more bossy toward the characters she tries to bring to life. Such juxtapositions also reveal noteworthy aspects of the couple's relationship. At the beginning of this century, scholars noticed that when Céleste wrote about the same events as her husband, her accounts usually seemed to have been composed before his: apparently he recruited her as a sort of living memory aid, a role that gratified her. As we have seen, nothing for Chateaubriand was more pregnant with consequences than the exercise of memory, so he must have reposed more confidence in her than he cared to admit.

Husband and wife had a good deal in common: Bretons both, they were every bit as prosy and unbudgeably opinionated as Bretons are popularly imagined to be, and both, too, were moody, prickly, sarcastic, and allergic to all forms of pretension but their own. Both, too, hitched ambition to religion, he in his cultural criticism and she in a charitable benefice, a hospice for indigent women and elderly priests called the Infirmerie Marie-Thérèse, which she founded and for which she tirelessly campaigned (she was tagged the *"Vicomtesse Chocolat"* on account of the little candy factory she installed on its premises). Yet if Céleste was in some ways dangerously like her husband, stubborn, vindictive, and vain of her reputation, she was in others his temperamental opposite. She never shook off a certain provincial starchiness or high-mindedness, and she never mastered the art of conversational fencing, with its backhanded flatteries and barely perceptible nicks. She wanted to trust and be trusted, and her craving for sincerity must have seemed irksomely naïve to her naturally crafty husband. Above all, their views on the relationship between the sexes diverged widely. He retained the eighteenth-century assumption that love for the male was a matter of self-broadening education, whereas she felt that her loyalty warranted a little self-restraint on his part. Some of her harshness may be attributed to her caged resentment.

It was in England, during the Terror, that Chateaubriand seems to have begun his career as a skirt chaser. Still impoverished and uncertain of his talent, he fell in love with a rural pastor's daughter who apparently returned his affection; but he never declared his love to her or even told her he was married. In London he found simpler attachments: the apprentice celebrity was already beginning to enjoy that large free consumption of women which society had long regarded as the natural right of the world-historical genius. The tempo of these appropriations only quickened when, returning to Paris in 1801, he detached a narrative segment from the still unpublished manuscript of *The Genius of Christianity* and had it printed as a novella. *Atala* became a hit: perfumed billets covered the writer's mantelpiece, and he was launched at last in the salons. He also met an influential and wealthy young woman who would help him get his name struck from the blacklist of former émigrés.

Pauline de Beaumont was the daughter of an aristocrat who had for a while been Louis XVI's Foreign Minister and had been executed in 1792. She presided, in her home in the rue Neuve du Luxembourg, over the so-called Blue Salon, a literary circle whose denizens had whimsically assumed the names of animals: Pauline herself was the Swallow; Chateaubriand, with his ingratiating manner and fluent movements, the Cat; Germaine de Staël, who put in a very rare appearance, Leviathan. Fine-boned, fragile, and piteously thin, Pauline was not good-looking, but Chateaubriand noted that her almond-shaped eyes "burned languidly like light passing through crystal-clear water." She was irritable, impatient, and inconsolably outraged at a respiratory ailment that ravaged her chest and gnawed at her mental clarity: at thirty-two, she was already so enfeebled that she spoke very slowly, and this slowness, which contrasted oddly with her talents as an intellectual hostess, touched a chord in Chateaubriand. He moved into an apartment not far from her home and began, as he put it, to "consecrate myself to her sorrows." She confessed to a friend that he made her feel a "virtual frenzy of love," and that he "played upon all my fibers as upon a clavichord."

Chateaubriand continued to neglect Céleste, who was now living with her people in Brittany, but Lucile apprised her of her husband's improved circumstances. For wherever Chateaubriand went, his devoted sister followed, often in person but always in spirit, stalking him like a Doppelgänger, adoring him, resenting him, living her starved life through his. Somehow Lucile managed to curry favor with Pauline, which enabled her to furnish Céleste with discreet bulletins about Pauline's tie with Chateaubriand. The up-and-coming writer was thus pinned down, perhaps not altogether unpleasantly, by three stricken and predatory women: the slightly demented sister, the slowly perishing mistress, and the banished but strong-minded wife. The situation obviously could not last, and when Pauline lay on her deathbed, in November 1803, she made Chateaubriand promise to honor his union with Céleste—as well he might, considering his religious views.

All this time Chateaubriand was rising in the political world. By the age of forty he had pitched his tent in numerous camps, and many people saw him as a slick opportunist, a charge to which he was sensitive. He would complain later, in his *Memoirs*, that

those who accuse me of ambition and hypocrisy don't know me very well. Precisely because I lack that passion and that vice, I shall never succeed in society. Ambition, especially, could never be anything to me but an outlet for my wounded self-esteem. Though I might want to be a minister or a king for the mere satisfaction of cocking a snook at my enemies, after a day I'd toss my portfolio or crown out the window.

In fact, Chateaubriand served twice as a cabinet minister and never to our knowledge threw anything out the window; his rambling self-defense confirms the slightly paranoid pomposity that we sense in Girodet's portrait. The Vicomte never forgave—or forgot—an insult. At first barely aware that he had been hurt, he would rancorously finger the wound in his mind until it grew unbearably painful; yet he was too proud to acknowledge the pain by openly seeking revenge. He was "singular," he wrote, in this respect—a confidence that suggests how innocent he was of the workings of other minds. Yet his vanity never spoiled his irreverent sense of humor, and he could be surprisingly candid about his failings. Recalling in 1837 the appearance of *The Genius of Christianity*, he wrote that he had "no illusions about the work's intrinsic value" but felt that it had "appeared at the right moment."

There comes a point in many nineteenth-century auto-biographies where the humble writer breaks down and, throwing himself on the reader's mercy, admits to some dreadful defect. So, too, with Chateaubriand. In a chapter of his *Memoirs* entitled "A Flaw in My Character," written in 1822 and revised in 1846, he confesses to being too reserved for his own good and that of his friends. Though insisting that he is by nature "truthful and sincere," he feels unable to tell what is in his heart—except, perhaps, by writing. Oddly, he hates the sound of his voice: whenever he tells an anecdote aloud, it soon wearies him and he drops it. "As I have faith in nothing, except religion, I distrust everything," he confesses, ignoring the fact that religion itself is faith in *everything*—in the goodness of God's creation; and he also regrets that his diffidence weakens his ties with happier, more confident natures. He concedes, a little sadly, that his circumspection puts him at a social disadvantage in that he cannot bear the messy business of repairing a damaged friendship; but then he swerves out of his way to tell us how distasteful such patchings up are, with their "protestations and emotionalism, tears and lamentations, verbiage and reproaches, pettiness, apologies." A squeamish impatience with all human feeling lurks just beneath the hair shirt of Chateaubriand's self-criticism, and in the end he doesn't seem unhappy that the "derisory side of human affairs" strikes him so forcefully. He observes that there are, after all, "scarcely any geniuses or great achievements." Though he is "polite, even admiring" toward those "smug souls" who pose as superior intellects, his "secret derision thrusts [carnival] masks on their incense-wafted visages." These are understandable sentiments, which many of us can share; the problem is that they flatly belie the very truthfulness and sincerity that Chateaubriand has proposed as his chief virtues. All through his writing Chateaubriand reveals this off-putting polarity, this underlying mental oscillation.

CHATEAUBRIAND'S MEMOIRS LEAVE US with the sense that his intimacy with Juliette Récamier was predestined, like a personal providential dispensation; yet he seems strangely unable to remember how they met. The first meeting he clearly recalls took place sometime during the Directoire, an anomalous period when birds who were definitely not of a feather flocked together and sometimes even sang in unison. This may perhaps explain how Chateaubriand—who as an obscure representative of the ruined Breton petty nobility felt at home absolutely nowhere—could have shown up one evening at Juliette's fabulous house (to which, it appears, he had been taken by Anna Lindsay's protector, Christian de Lamoignon). He was petrified by the radiant Juliette and her chic entourage. "Still coming out of the dark forest of my obscurity," he later wrote, "I was unsociably shy. I hardly dared raise my eyes to one encircled by adorers and so remote in her fame and glory from myself." A few weeks later, however, *Atala* came out. It interested Germaine de Staël, who asked to meet him, and he arranged to call on her at her apartment upstairs in the Swedish Embassy. She received him with delicious *sans-gêne*, in the midst of performing her toilette; while her maid Mademoiselle Olive dressed her, she rolled a medicinal twig between her famously perfect hands and orated. She was in mid-phrase when Juliette breezed in, wearing her customary white dress, and sat down on a blue silk sofa. Gazing spellbound at this apparition, Chateaubriand no longer heard the sound of Germaine's voice. Never in his wildest dreams could he have imagined a woman as pure yet voluptuous as Juliette Récamier at that moment, and he felt he had no hope of attracting her; inwardly he cursed his diminutive stature and brooding Celtic looks. A few minutes later she had passed out of his life.

When and how did he begin to see her again? It is not easy to say. Later, when the pair grew close, their love was colored by hindsight: selective memory, especially on his part, re-created the attachment as it ought to have been. In his memoirs Chateaubriand failed to note what is apparent from other sources: that twelve years after the meeting at Germaine's (which is to say, sometime in 1814) Juliette went so far as to organize a reading of passages drawn from his work. This time her white dress fluttered against different paneling and different mirrors, since her husband, buffeted by fortune, had sold the Hôtel Necker and bought a less luxurious residence; but again a distinguished crowd filled her salon, including Madame de Staël, Canova, David, Gérard, Sismondi, Metternich, Talma, and the Duke of Wellington. How could Chateaubriand's prodigious, logarithm-mastering memory have suppressed that glorious evening? Perhaps he and Juliette, who were barely acquainted, had stood side by side without having much to say to each other, and this non-event failed to satisfy his fabulist's desire for a good story; perhaps there was some other, less innocent reason.

In the 1930s, the literary historian Maurice Levaillant pointed out that Juliette and Chateaubriand must already have become quite close friends as early as 1816, and that Chateaubriand's silence about the first two years of their attachment had probably been motivated by considerations both personal and political. Françoise Wagener's well-researched *Madame Récamier*, of 1986, confirms this observation, but neither Levaillant nor Wagener sees anything untoward in Chateaubriand's secretiveness. The gap is disconcerting, however, and only the sheer bulk and antiquity of Chateaubriand's memoirs—their permanence as a feature of the landscape—can explain the two scholars' easy acceptance of so remarkable an omission. Granted, Chateaubriand's great book is not a straightforward autobiography in which events are neatly lined up; yet surely it was odd of him to pass over without a word the first two years of his life's deepest attachment. His negligence is interesting: it suggests a pattern, not only in his work but in the literary registration of the love affair in general, whereby apparently minor inconsistencies—withheld clues, inadvertencies, elisions, distractions—tend to conceal some central, underlying embarrassment.

The facts of the case are these: Chateaubriand, who in 1816 was a cabinet minister in the government headed by the Duc de Richelieu, published a tract concerning the French monarchy which incurred the displeasure of Louis XVIII and caused him to be expelled from the government. Very nearly destitute, obliged to sell many valuable books that Pauline de Beaumont had bequeathed him, he turned for help to an admirer, the influential Duchesse de Duras, and also to her friend Juliette Récamier. Like Chateaubriand, Madame de Duras was both a Breton and a writer, and she harbored proprietary feelings for her countryman; at the same time, Juliette, a believing Catholic, had conceived a deep admiration for Chateaubriand's literary powers and the uses to which he was putting them. One diarist of the period, Madame de Montcalm, noted that Juliette was assiduously cultivating Chateaubriand's wife ("whose character is bitter and difficult"), with the sole aim of winning the writer's friendship and confidence. Juliette's moral support for Chateaubriand was absolute: when the Duchesse de Duras suggested that Chateaubriand should consider retracting some of his views in order to regain his cabinet post, Juliette counseled him against any such compromise of his integrity. Such palpable tension developed between Juliette and the Duchesse that Madame de Montcalm became convinced that the two women were vying for Chateaubriand's affections: in other words, that they were rivals. Though Juliette tried to seem cool and aloof, the diarist wrote that she had more "true passion" than the Duchesse, since

> a complete self-forgetfulness, an absolute devotion, always places Madame Récamier in a position of dependency on the one who inspires it. . . . [She] runs the risk of becoming the victim of anyone she loves, whereas anyone who loves the Duchesse runs the risk of turning into her possession. Though these two ladies were once friends, now their connection has gone by the board. Chateaubriand has remained close to both, but while accepting the devotion of Madame Récamier, he is more swayed by the counsel of the Duchesse—as long, that is, as her advice does not run afoul of his vanity.

Which may be exactly what happened, for Chateaubriand did not apply to be readmitted to the government but put up his house, near Aulnay, outside Paris, for auction.

At this juncture Germaine, ignoring ominous pains in her stomach and heart, gave a dinner in a house she had just rented, in the rue Neuve-des-Mathurins. Too unwell to appear at table, she insisted all the same that the party go on, and Chateaubriand found himself seated next to Juliette. The occasion was doubtless very grim, and as he remembered it in his memoirs, they did not look at each other or exchange so much as a word. "Only toward the end of dinner," he would recall, "did Madame Récamier say a few timid words to me about Madame de Staël's illness. Turning my head to my right, I looked up at her and saw my guardian angel." From this strangely worded passage two circumstances have been deduced. The first is that Germaine had devised the seating arrangement with the aim of allowing Juliette to work her magic upon Chateaubriand; the second is that he must by this time have felt profoundly indebted to Juliette for the influence she was wielding on his behalf at court—hence the expression "my guardian angel." What the romantic language of the *Memoirs* veils is the very unromantic trail of intrigue leading up to this fateful meeting.

How deeply entangled were the pair by this time? We do not know; we know only that Germaine's illness progressed, that she became addicted to opium, and that she died, very painfully, in July 1817. Juliette, of course, was grief-stricken. She had fairly worshipped the great woman, and now Germaine underwent an apotheosis in her mind. Her drawing room, adorned with mementos of the dear departed, became a sort of memorial chapel, and she generously shared her sorrow with all those about her who were saddened by the loss. Among the co-mourners was Chateaubriand, and it is not unreasonable to surmise that Juliette, rendered volatile by the sudden yawning absence in her life, felt especially drawn to the Breton charmer at that moment. His feline manner was certainly seductive—not for nothing had he been assigned the sobriquet of "the Cat" in Pauline de Beaumont's salon—and Amélie Cyvoct was later to remember that he "now conquered the first place in [Juliette's] heart, or, at least, in her imagination." The last part of this sentence gives us pause: did Amélie wish to mark some reserve about Juliette's attachment, to add it discreetly to the list of her aunt's self-delusions? Very possibly, for she goes on to mention that several of Juliette's closest friends, including Mathieu de Montmorency, Adrien's cousin, cautioned Juliette against an emotional voyage that promised, at best, uneven winds.

Mathieu was a devout Catholic and a defender of the Bourbon order. "I am deeply pained and mortified," he wrote to Juliette, "by the sudden change in your manner. Ah, Madame, what progress your lovesickness has made in a few weeks—it causes you to shrink away from your most faithful friends. . . . I implore God from the depths of my soul . . . not to forge an unhappy bond for you." Others among her friends pointed out that Chateaubriand was, under his polished exterior, agitated, moody, and spoiled by women. Their advice went unheeded: Juliette much later admitted to a confidante that "it was impossible for anyone to have her head as completely turned as mine was by M. de Chateaubriand, and I cried all day long." To spare him the sorrow of losing his house, she herself rented it from him for three years, which inspired the priggish but kindhearted Mathieu (who put up half the rental fee) to write her that he counted "upon your perfect discretion in not receiving the house's . . . proprietor too often." Certainly Juliette did receive him often, though just *how* often we do not know—Amélie, who might have told us, had gone off to a convent school—and after a while, her nerves frayed by warring emotions, she repaired to Dieppe, and then to Aix-la-Chapelle, to take the water cure. When this was over she did not return to Aulnay but bought a smallish residence in the fashionable rue d'Anjou, in the Faubourg Saint-Honoré; and in its little garden she and Chateaubriand celebrated, in the autumn of 1818, the first full flame of their love.

In a famous passage of his *Memoirs*, Chateaubriand evokes the deep joy of his visits to Juliette at this time.

> Ah, when one has at last rejoined one's destiny, one feels that one has never gone astray: life, Pythagoras says, is but remembrance. Who, in the course of his days, is not haunted by memories that cannot be communicated? So it is that in Madame Récamier's garden there was a linden arbor where I used to wait for her to appear, and amid whose leaves I would often espy a falling moonbeam. I still feel that this moonbeam belongs to me, and that if I should wait again under those boughs, I should find it there once more.

These words allude, in the euphemistic language of the period, to the beginning of a love affair.

They must have made a curious couple, the balding, bandy-legged lothario and the forty-one-year-old virgin. What transpired between them we shall never quite know, but the veil of mystery was partly rent in 1912, when a French researcher, Ernest Daudet, published a set of documents he had discovered in the archives of Louis XVIII's secret police. The story these documents told was bizarre: After Chateaubriand's expulsion from the government, the King's Interior Minister had assigned to his case, late in 1816, a police spy, who would continue to observe him for about three years. On the lookout for evidence of seditious activity, this agent opened the writer's incoming letters at the post office and bribed his manservant to submit all outgoing letters for inspection; through his snooping we have come to know of the goings-on at the rue d'Anjou and other addresses. What actually took place? On January 7, 1819, the police reported that "for about three weeks Madame Récamier has been sending a carefully sealed letter to Chateaubriand. The Vicomte then hides these billets so carefully that our observer has hitherto been able to see only one." Yet that one letter, penned in Juliette's spidery hand, was inspected by the busybodies in the Interior Ministry, shown to the King, and deposited in the files of the royal police. It is short and to the point:

Love you less? You do not believe it, dear friend. We shall meet this evening at eight. Do not believe in what you call plans against you. . . . It is no longer within my power nor yours nor anyone else's to stop me from loving you: my love, my life, my heart—all are yours.

In itself the billet is perfectly unremarkable; yet coming from one who had so long preserved her virginity intact it is explosive. It leaves no room for doubt that shortly before this day —March 20, 1819—Juliette had become Chateaubriand's mistress.

By initiating a love affair they were breaking their marriage vows—she for the first time, he for the umpteenth—but the deed had a certain redemptive quality. Consider, for a moment,

Juliette's early life: how, barely out of her convent, she had been given away at sixteen to a man of forty-two; how she had passed through a licentious age without losing a feather from her wing; and how, with no authority but that of her astonishing appearance, she had engaged to make Beauty what everybody from the Renaissance onward had implicitly expected it to be: the incarnate face of Goodness. With Beauty alone she had bravely opposed Napoleon; with Beauty alone she had gone into exile with Germaine de Staël. Yet if one must admire her courage in the face of tyranny, one may also question whether in the matter of her stubbornly guarded reputation she had acted of her own free will or as a sort of moral automaton, teleguided by forces beyond her control. In many ways she seems a propitiatory creature, a being into whose limbs a polluted society projected, as though by sympathetic magic, its desperate need for virtue and purity. It was as though people believed, in that age when so many parties were stained with blood, that republican piety could somehow be kept alive if just one person remained uncorrupted. Ancient Rome had had her Vesta, a veiled virgin served by maidens who vowed thirty years' sexual abstinence; is it overly fanciful to see Juliette as a sort of modern vestal virgin, a living warranty that the people of France had not been totally debased by the excesses of the Terror and the Empire? This essentially pagan role was at once her glory and her servitude, and it is to Chateaubriand's credit that he rescued her from a false and idolatrous identity and enabled her to see herself as a flesh-and-blood woman—a woman who was bound, before it grew too late, to know herself as she was and to assume responsibility for her actual emotions and desires.

All this time Juliette's relations with her husband had remained equable but distant. By this period Jacques Récamier had lost his touch at the Bourse—already, as we've seen, he'd come close to ruin—and now she made the mistake (against the advice of that inveterate speculator Benjamin Constant) of entrusting him with most of the modest fortune she had inherited from her mother. Récamier proceeded almost at once to lose all the money she had given him. Reduced to relatively slender means, obliged to sell the house in the rue d'Anjou, she cast about for a way to continue her life without loss of self-respect, and it was at this point, without a murmur of complaint, that she found shelter in the Abbaye-aux-Bois. In retreating to a convent she felt authorized to live apart from her impoverished husband, but she assured him that he could count on her for a small allowance. Amélie was profoundly distressed by their first hours in the abbey annex, where they huddled like castaways in the shadows; yet within a few weeks Juliette had rallied her friends about her, reorganized Amélie's life, found lodgings for her other dependents in the neighborhood, and created, in a dim and uncomfortable room, the most scintillating salon in all Paris.

Her greatest consolation was the joy of lovemaking with Chateaubriand, who was genuinely moved by her devotion. "You alone fill up my life," he told her, "and when I enter your little room I forget everything that has made me suffer." For two years—she would later maintain that they were the only happy ones of her life—she was wholly engrossed in him. Did she know how he spent his time apart from her, this relentless climber who, at fifty-two, was, as one of his friends put it, *un fameux lapin*? One might observe that even her sole surviving love note to him—the one intercepted by the secret police—holds evidence that she doubted his candor: "*Love you less? You do not believe it.*" And if, at this moment of dizzying passion, she already questioned Chateaubriand's sincerity, her friends, who daily watched him pirouette through mirrored antechambers and gilded drawing rooms, questioned it even more. Dismayed by her emotional defenselessness, Mathieu de Montmorency wrote her: "You allow my vagabond imagination to wander amid suppositions that I would gladly reject. Do deign to send me a few words to reassure me that you have not made yourself completely wretched." A little later, he told her: "I cannot grow accustomed to arriving at your doorstep twice in the day only to be sent away by your maid, who tells me fairy tales about your being out so that you may pursue your *tête-à-tête* with M. de Chateaubriand." Mathieu had excellent cause for dismay, since he probably knew, as the police certainly did, that Juliette's lover was at this time paying assiduous visits to a certain Norman manor house inhabited by a pretty young lady. And in January 1820, a police report noted that Chateaubriand "has been writing every day to the wife of the musician Lafont." Rumors were rife of his faithlessness, and inevitably, they reached Juliette.

What the family silver is to other people, Juliette's virginity had been to her. Now it was gone, and she must have suffered terribly in her little room. At once a commemorative chapel for Germaine and a tabernacle of love for Chateaubriand, it was becoming a prison for Juliette. Was there a dual motive, then, in her and Mathieu's efforts, which soon were crowned with success, to obtain Chateaubriand's political rehabilitation and appointment as ambassador to Berlin? On the one hand, this gambit rescued him from royal ill favor; on the other, it caused him to be transported to a distance from which he could no longer harm her. One of her few surviving letters from this period suggests that she had grown wary of his inconstant nature and was trying to suppress her love for him: she wrote to a nephew that although Chateaubriand regularly sent her "sweet" letters, "with a person who lacks truthfulness one can find no way to live, and I am absolutely determined not to expose myself again to such dreadful distress."

Early in 1824, Juliette decided to seek refuge in Italy. This land—compulsively visited and revisited by all her set, who were among the earliest victims of the modern malady that consists in secretly wishing to be (if only by adoption) Italian —was then thought to be a panacea for a great many northern ailments. Juliette's complaint was the *mal d'amour*, which is not generally thought to be climate-related, but in the damp of Paris Amélie had contracted a persistent cough which offered an unimpeachable pretext for the sunny southward journey. Protestations of grief from Chateaubriand followed her all the way, and his unhappiness was probably genuine, for he was deeply, if not exclusively, attached to her. But he never actually pursued her to Rome, and the Italian interlude could be casually passed over were it not for a side intrigue that gave rise to a correspondence deeply revealing of her nature.

EIGHTEEN YEARS EARLIER, JULIETTE Récamier, whose name had figured along with Madame de Staël's on Bonaparte's proscription list, had come to Rome as a young refugee. Now that she was back in the Eternal City, she was saddened by the thought that some of her old friends, chief among them Canova, were no longer alive to greet her: but the Duchess of Devonshire was there, elderly and ailing, and Adrien de Montmorency, and any number of amusing persons both Italian and foreign. She and Amélie enjoyed visiting the ruins and picture galleries, and they grew fond of attending Mass in churches that were great works of art. Before long, Juliette's spirits rose, and she wrote to Mathieu in May 1824 that if she were to return to Paris anytime soon she would only reenter the nightmare that had caused to her to leave. She would be very upset if Chateaubriand failed to welcome her warmly, yet his rekindled affection would only renew "a turmoil I am determined to avoid." She resolved to prolong her stay through the following winter.

Under the Roman sun one could see streaks of gray in Juliette's hair, but with her soft, kind face and expressive eyes she was still delightful to look at. Amélie, who went everywhere with her beloved aunt, was now sixteen, and though not exactly pretty, she had that touching appearance of prettiness which is the patrimony of all young Parisiennes who are slim and fresh and know how to dress. The two were highly desirable females, and presently they found a pair of gentlemen to dance attendance upon them. These were not Italians, as one might have thought, but Frenchmen, and interesting people in their own right. The older, then in his late forties, was the artist-turned-writer Etienne Delécluze, one of whose books, still consulted today, offers precious information on the character and studio practice of David. The younger, who had come to Rome in Juliette's retinue, was Jean-Jacques Ampère, the son of the great physicist and himself a keen student of the humanities; then only twenty-four, he would later make a name for himself as a historian. One might expect that maturity would be drawn to maturity and youth to youth; but as in some cynical opera buffa, it was Delécluze who doted upon Amélie, while Ampère was attracted—violently, hopelessly, and, as time passed, embarrassingly—to the gentle maternal splendor of Juliette.

Beardless and painfully awkward, Ampère had frequented Juliette's receptions at the Abbaye-aux-Bois. One evening at the Abbaye he had broken an antique letter opener made of red marble, and she, to spare his feelings, hid the fragments under a cushion, exciting a wave of tenderness in him. At this age he was "versatile, spontaneous, emotional," as Henry James, an assiduous student of the French literary love affair, would note half a century later, in a review of Ampère's letters for *Galaxy*: "He looked around for a subject and meanwhile fell in love with Madame Récamier." One might say that Madame Récamier *became* his subject, to judge by the profusion of the pages he devoted to her. Rather presumptuously, Ampère saw Chateaubriand as a rival and so took a dim view of the older man's writing, denigrating his "hothouse style" and tendency to "break out in a rash of parallelisms." The boy was transparently in need of mothering, and by living near Juliette in Rome he hoped to triumph over the absent Vicomte and capture her unclaimed affections. He called on her daily at her rooms in the via Babuino and escorted her and Amélie to the

Villa Pamphili and the Villa d'Este; they wandered together through the tortuous alleys of Tivoli, admired the cascade of the Anio, exclaimed at the little Temple of Vesta, peered into the recesses of Neptune's Grotto; much of the time, feeling that Juliette was indifferent to him, Ampère would knit his brow, run his hands through his hair, and stride pettishly back and forth.

Ampère's touchy adoration, which led him to keep a monotonously lovelorn journal about his months in Rome, would be of little interest if not for the reaction of Delécluze, who grew quite fond of him and carefully observed both parties to the dalliance. Widely regarded as a brilliant but difficult person, Delécluze had a grotesquely overdeveloped sense of honor and cherished a fanatical craving for candor in all dealings: Sainte-Beuve called him a "Boeotian," and in one of his own letters he referred to himself as an "ill-licked bear," a French expression denoting one who priggishly rebels against the necessary insincerities of social life. He soon became morosely, even rather self-punishingly, besotted with Amélie, on whom he made advances so proper as not to merit the term at all; he also fell into the habit of slowly sidling, after prefatory remarks on his duty to speak his mind, into supercilious homilies on the subject of love and its responsibilities. Nonetheless, his insights could sometimes be helpful, and before long he grew appalled at Juliette's blithe encouragement of Ampère's infatuation and took it upon himself to reprimand both of them by letter. There is strong evidence to suggest that Delécluze's warm defense of Ampère was dictated by a homoerotic sympathy; even so, his notes to Juliette cast more light on her personality than any other surviving documents.

First, however, he berated Ampère:

Consider, my friend, what lies ahead. Your heart, bruised and battered by the ferocity of passions not all of which have been genuine, has worn itself out in vain attempts to undertake a struggle beyond its powers to carry to a successful conclusion. . . . I have had a long experience of the behavior of lovers. They pour out their hearts to others with a frankness which amounts to indiscretion, but their passion never allows them to say anything to its own disadvantage . . . [and] there is always something about it which the outsider never hears. Now, it is precisely that something which forms the crux of the matter. There is an aspect of the bizarre, even of the puerile, in your strange relationship with Juliette.

Most childish, Delécluze thought, was the artificial chastity of the attachment, which allowed Ampère to mask his physical desire while Juliette dissembled her lingering heartache over the rupture with Chateaubriand. What was worse, Delécluze did not quite believe in Ampère's passion, which seemed positively to demand to be thwarted, and he did not feel that Juliette had developed enough self-awareness to perceive that she was indulging Ampère's self-torment.

Juliette had recently engaged Madame de Genlis, a popular novelist and preceptor of young persons, to teach her niece the art of letter writing. "You may remember," Delécluze wrote to Ampère,

how Juliette, speaking to us of Amélie, said that she was having her take lessons from Madame de G. for the purpose of improving her epistolary style. [Juliette] enumerated, with a certain smugness, all the subtleties of phrase which ought to be used when writing "properly" to persons of various ranks. She dwelt upon the minutiae to which much importance is apparently attached, such as whether one should put the date at the beginning or at the end, etc., and, after running through all the shades of meaning in which the lady has instructed Amélie, added that she felt seriously embarrassed at the idea of this capable woman having to carry on a conversation with Amélie. I cannot tell

you, my friend, the distaste which this way of talking—
seemingly so trivial—caused me.

Delécluze's distaste is understandable: since he at this time was
a prime recipient of Amélie's letters, he could not have been
pleased by the thought that her phrases came out of a tutor's
manual. Yet he was also dismayed by what he saw as Juliette's
insecurity and consequent affectedness, and he decided to set
the poor lady straight.

"You have so far directed your life wisely and successfully,"
he wrote to her, in an astonishingly patronizing letter.

That can have been no easy task, given the advantages be-
stowed upon you by nature, for nothing is, as a rule, more
dangerous than to fill the role of a charming and beautiful
woman on whom Fortune has lavished all its most precious
gifts. . . . I will frankly admit that I began by being antag-
onistic. I had Jean-Jacques's future in mind, and it was not
without uneasiness that I saw him becoming involved in so
indefinite a relationship. It is well that you should know
that I have always regarded the situation as being what, in
fact, it is, and consequently, could not bring myself to believe in any probable or impending issue to this romance of
his. You argued that the whole thing was to his advantage,
seeing that his disinterested adoration of you would at least
preserve him from the follies into which most young men
of his age are prone to fall. You will remember that I coun-
tered this sophistical piece of reasoning with a smile which
brought an answering smile to your lips, and indeed, how
can one reply to that sort of an argument when it comes
from a woman? . . . Jean-Jacques leads, with you, an unreal, an embarrassing, and since the truth must be told,
even a painful existence. Ah! Juliette, nature never relin-
quishes her rights. One may deceive oneself about what it
is one wants, but it always comes to the surface, in one
way or the other, and no man is twenty-four for nothing.
. . . It is with pain that I have watched that young man
caught up in an emotion which gives him ephemeral and

unutterable delight, it is true, but which, fundamentally, leaves him with an emptiness in his heart, a sense of discontent which causes him to fall into moods of ill-humor which perhaps I only can forgive, because I know the reason for them. . . . You are perfectly well aware that all this is true, but you lack the courage to admit it. You turn your back on the truth which presses hard upon you: you maintain, with great difficulty, a false situation which you know for what it is, and which, sooner or later, will be driven into the light of day. Could I sound the hidden recesses of your heart, I might, perhaps, come upon your secret. Who knows but what some leaven of jealousy may not be fermenting in you and encouraging the continuance of a sentiment which is stronger than you thought.

Was Delécluze implying that Juliette, on the rebound from Chateaubriand, was using Ampère's affection as a balm for her wounded pride? This was a pertinent insight, yet one which no gentleman of the 1820s would have allowed himself to pen. In his own way, however, Delécluze knew how to poison a barb. "You keep [Ampère] pure," he went on to tell her, "but he is often sad. . . . I have seen him, more than once, unseen by others, take your clothes and tear them with his teeth, thinking to kiss them. You will agree, Madame, that to drive him to seek such recompense is to do little conducive to his virtue." With these words Delécluze brutally tore away Juliette's mask of impossible goodness, and perhaps his rebuke produced the desired effect, since she presently requested Ampère, for his own sake as much as for hers, to give her a little breathing room.

In an apparent coincidence, Ampère's father, who had just been named professor at the Collège de France, summoned his son back to Paris. The young man's departure pained Juliette, for she needed his sighs, his hand at her elbow, and she later told Delécluze that she had experienced a "hideous feeling of emptiness" when he left. She was terribly lonely, and during her second winter in Rome she finally caved in to her longing for Chateaubriand and invited him to join her. He had in the meantime received, and then been relieved of, the portfolio of foreign affairs, and was now politically idle; but he told her bluntly that her offer had awakened "painful memories" in him and that regretfully he could not accept it. Desperate, her resolve failing, Juliette left Rome shortly after Easter and arrived in Paris in late May.

A few days after Juliette's return, Chateaubriand came to visit her in her little apartment in the Abbaye-aux-Bois. It was a fateful encounter. They had not seen each other for about twenty months, both had aged noticeably, and they must have been full of misgivings; even so, according to Amélie, not a word of reproach was uttered on either side. This is eminently believable. Juliette, for her part, had always had the gift of magically transforming others' desire into friendship, and now, resigning herself to permanent disappointment, she saw that she must work the splendid spell upon herself. She could be his dear friend, his confidante, his âme soeur, but nothing more: to be anything more was hopeless. As for Chateaubriand, we do not know what his sentiments were, but we may guess that his heart was stirred by the chastened woman before him. For Juliette had now become what he loved and had always loved best: she had become—like Lucile and Céleste and Pauline before her—a ruin.

JULIETTE DID NOT TRUST in Chateaubriand's affection, but she trusted in her own, and for her that was enough. As the years passed she let slip phrases that betrayed a smothered sadness ("of true sensibility he hasn't a shadow"; "I do believe he is genuinely attached to me"; "I live only for my friends and have no personal interests"), but their life together had assumed its final, mythical shape. Chateaubriand tried never to leave Paris, and in the last fourteen years of his life, he very nearly succeeded. During his rare absences he wrote to her frequently, and in these letters Amélie remarked "an ever-increasing affection, growing spontaneity, and, in his judgments upon people and events, much less bitterness and severity than he put into his *Memoirs*. He was letting himself be borne away on the current of his true nature, which despite a tendency to boredom and melancholy had rich stores of serenity and sociability." It was true that he continued to give himself airs, but when no one of political or literary note was watching, when he was alone with Juliette and Amélie, he surrendered to his feelings and grew gentle and playful. His talk was entrancing, his jokes hilarious.

In the meantime, Juliette remained on excellent terms with her husband, Jacques Récamier; he died in 1830, to her great sorrow. With Céleste de Chateaubriand her relations were naturally very complex, but in a way that remains unclear, the two seemed to get along well. We find Céleste writing to Juliette on the death of Récamier: "At times of sorrow I do not wish to leave my friends alone; I hope you do not question my tender feelings for you." And once, when Juliette was obliged to leave Paris for a while, Céleste rushed headlong to her door to find out how long she would be away. "What in heaven's name has possessed you?" the wife demanded of the *maîtresse-en-titre*. "What will become of Monsieur de Chateaubriand, with you gone?" They had achieved a workable truce, all three, and their declining years were governed by a calming and amazingly rigid routine. The bells of the Abbaye-aux-Bois rang to matins and vespers; the nuns revolved unfailingly around the cloister garden; Chateaubriand arrived at half past two each day to take tea with Juliette; and, late in the afternoon, he returned to sup with his wife.

Only once do the surviving documents afford a long glimpse of Chateaubriand and Juliette together, and that is during the summer of 1832, when, at the outset of the great cholera ep-

idemic that is spreading unimpeded through Paris, they agree
to meet in Switzerland. She goes to stay with an old friend at
Castle Arenenberg; he leaves his wife with an acquaintance in
Lucerne, then waits for Juliette at an inn in Konstanz. Before
long she arrives, but the inn is decked out for a wedding and
the nuptial preparations fill the pair with melancholy. They
decide to go out on the Bodensee, engage a bark, alight on a
shingle beach; they cross through a willow hedge and discover
a sandy lane winding through manicured meadows and ornamental shrubs. A veil of late summer crocuses covers the grass,
prompting sad reflections in the aging cavalier, and from a
nearby gatekeeper's lodge drifts an enchanting harmony, played
by a harp and a horn, which ceases as soon as they stop to
listen. They sit down by the lake and he reads aloud his recently penned description of the Saint Gothard Pass, that Alpine defile so beloved of the Romantics; she entreats him to
write something in her daybook. He notices that her page is
already half filled with an entry concerning the death of Rousseau, and under this entry he writes: "I do not wish, like Rousseau, to die. I want the sun for many more years, if I may
pursue my life by your side. I hope that my days will expire
at your feet, like these waves whose murmur you love." These
lines determine the spirit in which he will live out his remain-
ing years: in some sense, he will always be hers.

Now all that remains for the triumphant Juliette is one last
turning aside, one last rearward glance at the dead. Late September finds the couple at the gate of Coppet, not far from a
white-capped Lake Geneva; they enter and hesitate before the
tall, deserted château, whose mansards seem to brace themselves against the rushing clouds. The gatekeeper lets them in,
and Juliette wanders dreamily through the light-filled rooms,
seeing her beloved friend as in a dream—Germaine at the piano, Germaine pausing in a doorway, Germaine meditating on
the terrace outside. Chateaubriand watches her, sadly reflecting,

as Proust will do so often in the distant future, that every human spirit contains its own sealed-off world of remembrance.

Then they go out into the park. The wind has died down; they can hear the rustle of a nearby stream and a mill wheel turning, and they walk slowly through a field to a glade surrounded by a stone retaining wall. While Chateaubriand sits on this wall and philosophically contemplates Mont Blanc, Juliette threads her way through the glade until she finds herself standing before the tomb of Madame de Staël; and it is there, amid the fallen leaves, as gracefully bent as a figure on a mourning ring, that we shall leave her.

CHATEAUBRIAND DIED IN 1848 and was buried on the rocky islet of Le Grand Bey, off his beloved Breton coast. His career had been very peculiar. Despite his enormous literary ambition, he had never shown any real talent for fiction, poetry, or drama, nor any patience for sustained history or biography. What he did have was an exceptional gift for the eyewitness report, the travel sketch, the brief life, the pithy vignette— genres that fall under the heading of minor literature and commonly afford important writers no more than passing employment.

To parley these slender assets into a kind of grandiosity was the Vicomte's dearest wish, and to fulfill it he decided to write a huge book brimming with just the sort of tidbits he could pull off to perfection. He succeeded, yet like many of his breed—which is essentially that of the storyteller—he was hampered by problems of viewing distance, what photographers call "depth of field." Brilliant at rendering characters in the middle range, he failed to see faraway people clearly, and his portraits of foreground figures came out blurry and unsure. Thus he could get a good likeness of casual acquaintances, like Mme de Coislin or Mirabeau, but not of people he scarcely knew, like Bonaparte; and he did not succeed in realizing the character of his mother, his father, Lucile, or any of his mistresses—including, most sadly, Juliette. He leaves her voiceless, hidden behind her mask of impossible goodness, and his inability to bring her to life suggests some tragic absence in himself, some astonishing want of reverence for the beauty of his own past.

During the great man's lifetime his wonderful bond with Juliette had elicited both admiration and a certain muted skepticism; after his death and the publication of the *Memoirs from Beyond the Tomb*, the skepticism found a voice. In 1850, in two of his famous Monday essays for *Le Constitutionnel*, Sainte-Beuve, who in 1848–49 had delivered a course of lectures at the University of Liège on the early Chateaubriand, vigorously criticized the memorialist's manner of recalling his private life. The attack was perhaps a little churlish toward Madame Récamier, now a very old lady, since she had liked and helped Sainte-Beuve for more than twenty-five years; but Sainte-Beuve himself felt affronted by Chateaubriand's presumption in rearranging history from the safety of his sepulcher. The truth was that from the first reading of the *Memoirs*, in 1834, at the Abbaye-aux-Bois, until the hour of the Vicomte's death, Sainte-Beuve had resented being forced by the proprieties of salon conversation into stifling his many objections to this autobiographical work.

Sainte-Beuve was the inventor of modern French literary criticism, but his interest in literature reflected an even keener interest in people. One of his great beliefs was that a piece of writing achieves lasting value less through any putative perfection than through its fresh and individual character: it is less a model, one might say, than a friend. Literary style, in Sainte-Beuve's essays, usually appears in anthropomorphic guise, as a sort of figurine or doll of the author in question, and the reader may at times be uncertain whether he's sticking pins in the doll or the man. At his crudest, Sainte-Beuve is an adept of the *ad hominem* attack, yet his most delicate perceptions can suddenly enlarge our sense of a text's personality, and never more than when he has to review one of the many important books of his day—a memoir, autobiography, journal, or volume of collected correspondence—in which life and art are subtly intermixed.

So with Chateaubriand's big book: what bothers Sainte-Beuve in the Vicomte's way of talking about women is at once literary and personal. That Chateaubriand enjoyed sexual privileges is of little moral interest—he was a great writer, and these were his *droits de seigneur*—but his manner of enjoying them offends Sainte-Beuve's notion of how a confident masculinity ought to express itself. There are lotharios and lotharios, and Chateaubriand lacks the high animal spirits and entertaining bonhomie that can make the classic stage seducer a genuinely appealing character. Chateaubriand is cold, self-involved, reptilian. His amours are "ardent whims." What he wants from women is not the tender affection he so often receives but rather an occasion for inner turmoil, steamy reveries, the recapture of his vanished youth, and the worst of it all is that he tries to conceal this erotic sensibility—so evident in much of his writing—by making the virginal Juliette his one truly elevated attachment. "The ingrate!" exclaims Sainte-Beuve at one point: for fond though Chateaubriand is of Juliette, how can he have the nerve to pass over so much touching devotion on the part of other women—people like Lucile, Céleste, and Pauline de Beaumont. The critic goes on to offer a ruthlessly comical portrait of Chateaubriand the Pharisee, a flower in his lapel and walking stick in hand, mysteriously following his afternoon rounds: spending one hour with a certain person, another hour with another person, then having tea with Juliette, and so on and so forth, until he returns home to the rue du Bac, where, subject to the occult power of Madame his wife, he reassumes his role as defender of the Catholic order and dines with creaking royalists and doddering archbishops.

As outlined so far, Sainte-Beuve's attack on Chateaubriand would belong solely to the annals of literary ballistics. But actually it is a specific instance of a general moral aversion, because Sainte-Beuve is above all repelled by the cult of fashionable ennui initiated by the Vicomte.

> Before loving Chateaubriand dreams so much of love that his desire uses itself up, and when at last he is in the presence of what ought to revive and transport him, he has lost the true flame. And so with everything. He has devoured everything with thought . . . his spirit is worn-out and [prematurely] aged, and if his heart still has its needs, immense and vague, nothing is able to fill them.

Chateaubriand's sensibility is overcerebral and too nervously anticipatory: his fantasies drain experience in advance, reduce it to a sort of grisaille.

The *Memoirs*, says Sainte-Beuve, have the "touch and accent of the enchanter," yet they are not very likable. They are bitter and ill-tempered, and even their oft-noted humor is like a shrill laugh rising into a shriek. The "persistent vanity" that leads Chateaubriand to counterpoise himself, absurdly, to Napoleon, "becomes in the long run almost a tic." The chief flaw, however, is the absence of a consistent voice, in the sense that the reader must continually ask himself who is doing the talking. "Is it an actor who, having left the stage, shares with us the secret of the comedy?" Sainte-Beuve demands. "Or is it an actor still on stage, who struggles to convey his character? I believe it is a little of both, for the mask is half-fallen, but the author repeatedly pulls it back up." One might put this another way by saying that the author adopts now an official, pompous tone and now a private, disenchanted one; but this is still only half the truth.

What Sainte-Beuve did not quite see, and what in hindsight we can clearly make out, is the stark disparity between the author as narrator and the author as main character. When someone tells us about himself we expect to recognize the person he's describing, but Chateaubriand the writer, who often sounds gloriously bored, doesn't seem to be the same man as the courageous patriot whose adventures we follow in the book. It gives us pause when he informs us that he has never given a straw about his bloodline, then devotes several pages to his patents of nobility; tells us about his dramatic conversion to Christianity, yet continues to sound like an unbeliever (or, at best, like one who merely wishes to believe). Even if we charitably grant the narrator the right to use several different tones of voice, not one of them can be convincingly attributed to the book's protagonist.

Why this dereliction of autobiographical duty on Chateaubriand's part? Unhappily, the answer is complex, because it has to do with literary verisimilitude. Sainte-Beuve observes a general implausibility in Chateaubriand's recollections, a troubling sense that impressions of recent date have been negligently imposed upon the past: reading his memoirs, one grows convinced that however things may have happened, they certainly didn't happen like this. There are, moreover, many flat factual errors. In one important instance, Chateaubriand accuses Germaine de Staël of not acknowledging, in a book she published in 1800, that she had made use of his ideas, whereas at the time he was completely unknown; he also offers profiles of certain people which do not resemble them and, what is worse, do not resemble his own previously published sketches of them. Readers are left with an uneasy suspicion that they are being asked to accept rather too much on trust.

Chateaubriand's veracity did not go unquestioned in his lifetime. In 1827, for example, the *American Quarterly Review* remarked upon the originality of his having seen parrots, monkeys, and flamingos along the banks of the Mississippi, and subsequent research was to reveal that in his North American voyage he had scarcely left the confines of Pennsylvania, and had never, as he had pretended, met General Washington. Much later, in 1914, an Armenian scholar-priest became interested in Chateaubriand's trip to the Holy Land and discovered that much of his account was plagiarized, inaccurately, from old travel books and geographical descriptions. Down the decades debunking Chateaubriand became a cottage industry in France, and it culminated in 1964 with the publication of Henri Guillemin's *L'Homme des mémoires d'outre-tombe*, whose more than three hundred pages summarize, in a spirit of comic indignation, the stunning breadth and depth of the great man's malarkey. Guillemin, who was particularly interested in Chateaubriand's political role, revealed that he had lied about his lineage (his father was a former slave trader who had purchased his patents of nobility), lied about his resistance to Napoleon (it was wholly imaginary), and lied about his liberal and legitimist beliefs (which were often mere camouflage). There was, in fact, almost no personal claim set forth in the *Memoirs* that did not involve a large component of fiction.

If this is all rather dismaying, even more so is Chateaubriand's willingness to float remarkably tall tales about his deepest personal experiences, especially those involving women. The Vicomte tells us that he became a believing Christian when, as an exile in London, he received a letter from a sister to the effect that his mother had just died; in fact, this sister was then deceased. He tells us he was maneuvered by Lucile into his marriage with Céleste; in fact, he gladly undertook it, deserted Céleste when her fortune proved too small for his liking, then took up with her again when she came into a second inheritance. He depicts himself rushing grief-stricken to the deathbed of Pauline de Beaumont; in fact, he was at the same time pursuing a liaison with another woman, yet dearly hoped (by his own admission in a letter to a friend) to inherit Pauline's fortune. He tells us that he was dismayed, after the death of Lucile, at being unable to discover the whereabouts of her grave; in fact, he knew exactly where it was but did not wish to pay for a funeral monument. Most absurd of all, he composed his defense of the sacrament of marriage for *The Genius of Christianity* when he was married to Céleste yet living in sin with Pauline.

It takes about an hour to read the two portions of the *Memoirs* that are devoted to Juliette, which is not a great deal considering the vastness of this work. We expect, nonetheless, as we reach the first of these portions and come upon an important romantic entanglement, some deepening of tone or refinement of fragrance, some thickening of the very medium in which the most archetypal of tales, that of two people falling in love, is to be told. We find the opposite—an absolute lack of commitment to the task at hand. There is, to be sure, an incantatory presentation of the lady; there is an anecdote about Juliette's compassion for the Italians under Bonapartist misrule; there are other oddments and quotations. But the bulk of this section of the *Memoirs* is eccentrically given over to a verbatim insertion of Benjamin Constant's "Memoirs of Juliette," the already-mentioned work of 1815. It is a long serenade by a rented guitarist, and its inclusion is all the more extraordinary in that Chateaubriand elsewhere permits himself some very derogatory remarks about Constant's character. When we recall the weirdly ventriloquial tone of the little "as-told-to" production, in which Juliette seems to be speaking now in her own voice and now in Benjamin's (and on the subject, it may be noted, of his problems), we marvel even more at its appearance among Chateaubriand's reminiscences.

We actually learn more about Juliette's character from one harsh letter in the hand of Etienne Delécluze than from all the *Memoirs* of Chateaubriand, since he leaves her with her mask of impossible goodness untouched—in that sense, leaves her undescribed. The beginning of the romance, for instance, which requires to be lightly and perceptively told—how, we want to know, does such a deep attachment come about?—is smudged and ultimately bungled. As I mentioned earlier, Chateaubriand declines to discuss their first two years together; then, when we want lovers' talk, mounting emotion, moral decisions taken or evaded, desire granted full franchise, we are offered a ray of moonlight in the rue d'Anjou. As we read along, we continue to feel that Chateaubriand's account of the attachment has altogether too many blackouts and elisions: something in his manner suggests that if elsewhere he is prepared to take you into his confidence, here, regrettably, he cannot, for a wife and a mistress are involved—it would be a breach of decorum.

As it happens, the more tact a writer exercises, the more curious we grow as to what he is being tactful about, and we soon begin to suspect that Chateaubriand has donned the cloak of modesty not so much on Juliette's and Céleste's behalf as on his own; we suspect, in fact, that his chief aim may be to conceal something *from them.* He will not pledge himself to the full truth because he wishes not to deceive and, more especially, not to be found out. Generally Chateaubriand lies to protect his secrets, but in the passage on Juliette the order appears to be reversed: here he is being secretive, we suspect, in order not to have to lie. The option of telling the truth about his former self, about his early, humbling dependence on Juliette's influence at court, his simultaneous cultivation of Madame de Duras, and his later unfaithfulness to Juliette, is inconceivable to him. What would be grist to the mill of a Rousseau or a Constant, those connoisseurs of embarrassment, would entail a devastating exposure for the frailer Chateaubriand.

As a literary genre, personal history has long been felt to be universally interesting. This seems a paradox, but it isn't: every man, as Montaigne famously said, bears within him the entire human condition. Of course, memoirs aren't composed under oath, and we expect a degree of distortion in any such work. Yet intimacy cannot expand into universality if the reader feels that the author falls short of generally accepted standards of honesty, such as those that the reader would hold himself to. Consequently, it is odd that, from the very first, the republic of letters has almost unanimously absolved Chateaubriand of any serious writerly delinquency in prevaricating about his past.* Critic after critic has told us that his lying is a mere peccadillo: if we'd be crazy to trust Chateaubriand, we'd be equally crazy not to enjoy him. Even Sainte-Beuve, who was angry about Chateaubriand's literary successes and jealous of his amatory ones, felt obliged to concede that "a whole age has made itself the accomplice—virtually the confederate—of this writer . . . by declining to pull off his mask. . . . This is because he himself had a sort of weird sincerity which consisted in never much troubling to conceal the fact that he wore a mask." Though Chateaubriand has always been seen, correctly, as a figure on the political right, even Pierre Barbéris, a Marxist scholar, insists in his massive *A la recherche d'une écriture: Chateaubriand*, published in 1974, that the question of veracity is irrelevant to the *Memoirs* as a literary text: "We cannot drag Chateaubriand before some sort of tribunal," he asserts. The *Memoirs*, he says, have an inner coherence of thought and style independent of their relation to fact.

It is true that there are some books which remain uncorrupted by their extensive falsity. The *Autobiography of Benvenuto Cellini* is an exercise in the ancient and honorable genre of leg-pulling; Rousseau's *Confessions* do not seem drastically compromised by his frequent distortions of the record. But Chateaubriand's *Memoirs* are fundamentally different: they are structurally duplicitous, because they depend for their effect on our knowledge of a correlative world of fact, a full half century

* Thus Henri Guillemin, despite the evident disgust that such figures as George Sand and Alfred de Vigny felt upon reading Chateaubriand, claims that he is "impossible not to like"; George D. Painter, in his authoritative volume on the young Chateaubriand, *The Longed-for Tempests*, writes that Chateaubriand in his book about America had "no intent to deceive"; and Roland Barthes, in his superb preface to the *Vie de Rancé*, ingeniously defends Chateaubriand's willful disregard for the facts of Rancé's conversion.

of French literary and political history. Chateaubriand is not an independent creator: he completes a sketch drawn largely by the past, that is, by the writing of other people. He engages his readers' interest by promising testimony about Bonaparte, Talleyrand, Madame Récamier, then goes on to bear false witness and to omit events that might prove compromising to himself. Wanting to both hunt with the hounds of history and run with the foxes of fantasy, he offers not a work flawed by lying but a work that is essentially a lie; and the many critics who have accommodated his duplicity, who have winked at his masquerade, must be placed in the very large category of those who do not mind, and perhaps even like, being lied to. There are many reasons, of course, why human beings, and writers especially, may wish to justify somebody's lying—the most obvious being that their own fibs are thereby implicitly exonerated—but what is striking in this case is that Chateaubriand's expositors have, in their very leniency, recapitulated a fundamental aspect of his relationship to Juliette Récamier.

Listen to Juliette talking to Chateaubriand in the spring of 1819:

Do not tell me that you are sad, tormented. You'll make me lose my reason, I am still suffering but I intend coming tomorrow to the Vallée [i.e., to Chateaubriand's house]. Do you wish to come tomorrow at three or at eight o'clock? Let me know by this evening, I do suffer so and am so tormented, but I feel more than ever that I cannot live without being loved by you and that if need be I shall renounce all the rest. But you love me, you tell me you do, you would not deceive me, why then should we separate? I am as heavyhearted as if I should never see you again. Oh, come tomorrow, I cannot leave with such a sorrowful presentiment.

One of Juliette Récamier's eight extant letters to her lover, this document was found in the departmental archives of the Loiret and published, in 1973, in the *Bulletin de la Société Chateau-briand*. It shows the extent of her mistrust and also her will to overcome it; beyond that, it may also show (though this point is admittedly speculative) that her mistrust acted on her own imagination with the force of an aphrodisiac. The romance of Juliette and Chateaubriand has—at least in its early phase—an almost archetypal quality. He is the Celtic enchanter, plying her with incantatory words; she is the beautiful listener, conscious that the words are not credible but spellbound all the same. There is about him a barely perceptible whiff of Tartufferie, and there is about her, as in a good hypnotic subject, a blank, moonlike receptivity. His brilliant patter is charming, of course, but much of the charm lies in her awareness that it cannot be true. This awareness is exciting because the relation between the deceiver and the deceived is essentially erotic, a sort of restatement, in purely verbal terms, of the relation between the seducer and the seduced. And just as Juliette, in playing along with her admirer, assumes the traditional feminine role, so those readers who enjoy his imposture yield, willy-nilly, to their own feminization. That is why reading Chateaubriand is always a fascinating experience, and one from which the reader is very likely to emerge with lowered self-respect.

One is bound to conclude that the great love affair with Juliette was not at all as Chateaubriand portrayed it. A feminist might argue that she was passive clay in his hands, that she was colluding with an oppressor; but the very idea of collusion begs the question. Juliette's stock was falling in the period 1819–25—she was aging, plump, and impoverished—and if she wanted to find a way of displaying her talents, which were similar to those of a really good present-day talk-show hostess, she was going to have to make a brave forfeiture. Forfeiture is the business of giving up one thing in order to secure another, which is almost a definition of style; and style, eminently, was what Juliette had. The bright veneer, the papering over, would come to hide a multitude of sins, yet who would wish to believe that there was anything truly sinful, or even ignoble, in the long attachment of this masked man and this masked woman? For as the years went by, the bond slowly ripened into what the pair had always claimed it to be—the closest, the most exemplary sympathy. At two-thirty each afternoon the old gentleman, more and more crippled by gout, would arrive at the Abbaye-aux-Bois; he would be carried by his servants up to Juliette's salon; he would be cozily installed before the fire. They would have tea together and chat for exactly one hour; then a wave of visitors would flood in to pay their respects. He would speak in generous, unguarded tones, recalling old friends with a catch in his throat, and as she moved about the room in her shawl and little white bonnet—slowly, very slowly, for she was quite blind by now—he would follow her tenderly with his eyes.

Several months after the death of Céleste, in the winter of 1847, Chateaubriand asked Juliette to marry him. She was overcome with emotion, yet she refused, and none of his entreaties could sway her. "A marriage—why? To what end?" she replied.

Considering our age, can anybody's sense of propriety, however exaggerated, be offended by the care I offer you? If being alone saddens you, then I stand ready to live in the same house as yourself: I am sure that society would justly recognize the purity of our friendship, and would only approve whatever steps might ease my task of filling your old age with happiness, repose, and tenderness. If I were younger, I should not hesitate to accept with joy the right to devote my life to you. But the years, and my blindness, have already given me that right; let us change nothing in this perfect affection.

3

PROMISING LITERARY

MATERIAL

SEVERAL YEARS AFTER George Sand's breakthrough, in 1833, Chateaubriand jotted down his impression of her. He had never seen Sand in any of her famous costumes, in a countryman's tunic or bouffant pantaloons, but he felt that she projected a theatrical aura, what he called "an odalisque's authority." Her dominion was fiercely, insidiously sexual; it troubled him in ways he found hard to express. He was certain that Madame Sand's talent had "some root in moral corruption," but he also conceded that a woman's conscience played no part in her erotic prestige. Voluptuous pleasure, which had never before been treated by a female writer, was yielding Madame Sand an exotic harvest. How should he best describe that harvest? He admitted that he wasn't really sure; and as you read along in the Vicomte's memoirs you can almost sense the moment when words begin to fail him, almost see his pen hand hover helplessly aloft. He has no critical language for a writer like Sand. His native idiom cannot encompass her achievement.

George Sand is now an "icon" of popular culture—we think of her as Chopin's muse. But she first attracted notice during her affair with Alfred de Musset, and it is primarily as Musset's lover, not Chopin's, that the French remember her. While there is no Sand–Chopin correspondence to speak of, the Sand–Musset letters are voluminous and vivacious. Musset was a very great poet; Sand was the nerviest prose improviser of her age; perhaps no attachment in French literary history set heads shaking and tongues wagging for so long a period. The pair's celebrity came naturally, for they pursued their affair in the sunlight of a culture uninfected by puritanism and were perhaps the first literary couple of modern times in which the female partner saw herself as the equal of the male.

Of the Sand–Musset letters it may be said that there are too many of them, that they are too long, and that they are too extravagant. They are also among the most interesting love letters ever written—vivid, direct, and cruelly symptomatic; what they forfeit in composure they gain in the effect of life. Everything—the writers' talent, the Gallic tradition of sexual candor, and the nineteenth-century faith in the power of correspondence—conspired to make them eloquent. They tell their story so well that there is simply no way to tell it better. Though we may smile at the pair's blithe self-worship, we remain astonished that people of a period so long past, so positively ancient with respect to our own, saw the quest for erotic knowledge as a self-evident goal. Here Sand and Musset are quite like ourselves, in the aspect of our personality that we find most essential— and most dubious. As one French commentator has written, these two were the embodiment of "the bad conscience of modern love."

It must also be said there is something melodramatic about the Sand–Musset affair: she is sympathetic, and he is not. She—in the simpleminded moral horticulture to which we all willy-nilly resort—seems the better apple. Yet her sense of her role, of her sexual identity, troubled almost everyone around her. When, several months after the final parting, Musset told a friend, "If you see Madame Sand, tell her that . . . she is still the most womanly woman I have ever known," he knew that his compliment was ambiguous: she might have wondered, like an elephant hailed as "the most elephantine," if it was really a compliment at all. Whatever precisely he meant, however, Musset was sounding the keynote for all subsequent discussions of George Sand. For if undoubtedly she was a great woman, it is precisely *as a woman*, not as a writer or social reformer, that she is thought to have been great. She is remembered for inventing a new type of female, which she achieved, paradoxically, in a top hat, while smoking a cigar.

Even now, more than a century after her death, most people know who lived within those coils of smoke. The ministering angel of ailing geniuses, the scribbler who challenged an emperor, the high priestess of Christian socialism, the Good Lady of Nohant whose funeral cortège was followed by hundreds of weeping peasants—that is the familiar apparition. Like any apparition it frays at the edges; thus we have George Sand the anti-Communard reactionary, and George Sand the pitiless consumer of ink and men, heaping up novels and "unions"— not always quite separable—with the strictest impropriety. Oscar Wilde said that she "had to live her love affairs before she could write them," and the barb gains in subtlety by declining to press home the poisonous corollary that the love affairs, once written, were traded in for banknotes. During much of the last century a fear lurked that Sand was implicitly demanding satisfaction for her sex's long humiliation, insisting that women must "have their innings." Yet just as the prodigious sentimentalist herself, consigned progressively from table to shelf to dustbin in the closing years of the last century, has suddenly been fished up for new uses, so the old indictment has played into the hands of the defense. The suspicion that all her famous brimming over may have been meant to cause a flood has been welcomed, even confirmed, by her party.

Today Sand is accounted an indifferent artist, but this judgment has been made by people who will never read a tenth of what she wrote. She sat up working all night almost every night for fifty years, and demanded, in an open letter to Flaubert published toward the end of her life, "Read me in entirety, and don't judge me on loose leaves"—a Sibyl's cry. We have heard about the bold play of her erotic temperament, about her disdain for male self-esteem; we have heard about her underlying chastity, about her susceptibility to an unsexing maternal compassion with her lovers—and such contradictory traits may perhaps be squared with the lady of fact. The trouble is that when we inquire into the source of this moral Identikit, we discover that it is almost always the lady of fiction, dilating, in her lengthy autobiography and twenty thousand letters, upon her favorite topic. I say "lady of fiction" because the mirror she held up to her face was never, even in "nonfiction" works, the mirror of veracity. It is not merely that there was in this self-portrait something "wrong about the mouth"; there was something wrong *in* the mouth, namely an endless succession of words in which she always came off to advantage. If she was a "magician," as Henry James once said, that is because of the following sleight of hand: we find her unconvincing as an artist, convincing as a great woman—but the great woman was the artist's creation.

IN 1833, THE YEAR that George Sand met Alfred de Musset, anyone making inquiries about her—on the assumption that they uncovered a measure of truth—would have learned roughly the following story: She was actually the Baroness Aurore Dudevant, née Dupin de Francueil, an impoverished landowner from the province of Berry, in central northern France. Now almost thirty years old, she had been living for two years in the capital. Her father, an army captain, had died when she was a young child; there was something embarrassing about her mother's background that wasn't entirely clear. She had not, in any case, been reared by this tempestuous woman but by her father's mother, Madame Dupin, in the little châ-teau—more a glorified farmhouse, really—of Nohant, near La Châtre.

Madame Dupin had adored Aurore's father, a brilliant and witty young man, and was bent on fostering in his daughter an intelligence as virile as the one she inconsolably mourned. So lessons were taken seriously at Nohant. But it was not Eu-clid or ablative absolutes that chiefly occupied the little lady of the manor, for the house was full of the sounds of the spinet and harp, and drawing boards, paper, and paints were often strewn about. Madame Dupin was an accomplished musician, portraitist, and correspondent, and she wished to awaken in Aurore the taste for classic simplicity to which she herself had been bred. Often Aurore would lie on the carpet beside the spinet, marveling at her grandmama's playing and at her way of phrasing some charming old air; Gluck's ideas were ex-plained at length; and later, after the two or three hours of Madame's evening toilette, she would have her granddaughter read to her from some modern writer, perhaps Chateaubriand, never omitting to show where the writing rose to genuine gran-deur or slipped into mere grandiloquence.

With the sole interruption of a spell at convent school, the years passed rapidly; every summer the great chestnuts cast their shade over the lawn; sometimes it seemed as if the asters might bloom forever. Then—all too soon—it was time to start think-ing of a match. But the wise old grandmother sickened and died, and the match that Aurore made for herself left very much to be desired. The fellow was a family acquaintance named Casimir Dudevant, and he was neither rich nor good-looking nor much in love with her—nor she with him. Aurore married him because she thought he would take care of her and also because he was heir to a fortune and a title. He moved into Nohant, and in 1823, when she was nineteen, she gave birth to her first child, Maurice. Her second, Solange, was born four years later, and this time there was some question as to who the father was.

Aurore had no inclination for estate management, and besides, the marriage was unraveling. In 1831, persuading her husband, who had now become the Baron Dudevant, to give her freedom and a modest yearly allowance derived from their land income, she moved with her young children to a small apartment in Paris, determined to try her hand at one of the arts she had dabbled in—perhaps writing, perhaps portraiture, perhaps dressmaking or some form of decoration. Before long, she realized that it was the novel, more than any other form of expression, that held her interest.

In *Indiana*, her first significant try, she used a device that was to become part of her stock-in-trade, namely the sexual transposition of a pair of lovers from a novel by somebody else. In this case it was Julien and Mathilde from Stendhal's *The Red and the Black* whose genders she switched about, while another couple represented the novelist herself and her spouse. "You have the right of the stronger," this wife says to her husband, "but with my will, sir, you can do nothing." It might be thought that only hostility would await such a defiant view of patriarchal society; but the truth was the opposite. This book and its successor, *Lélia*, captured the imagination of Chateaubriand, Madame Récamier, Sainte-Beuve, and many others in the literary establishment.

A heady, static, mythologizing novel, *Lélia* is less about telling a story than about being in the throes of having a story to tell. Part philosophical dialogue, part threnody, part evocation of place, it probes daringly toward the psychic future of womankind. If women are to burn down the house of matrimony, the author seems to be wondering, what form of spiritual shelter may they seek? The sexes are so absurdly ill fitted for each other that one can cherish no hopes for an enduring extramarital union, and sexual nomadism offers very cold comfort.

In one startling passage, the novel's eponymous heroine confesses that her inability to love is conjoined with an "absence of personal satisfaction" so deeply disappointing that her "delirious avidity" can never be satisfied by the "carnal embrace." In different ways, then, both *Indiana* and *Lélia* attest to their author's artistic courage. Though the two novels provide scant evidence of literary genius, they are marvels of verbal talent, their phrases rolling rhythmically forward like breakers cast upon the shore.

By early 1833, Aurore had achieved much of what she wanted, which was to secure her independence and win herself a name in the trade. Yet despite the charm of her new situation, a *succès d'estime* was not enough for her: she wanted a *succès fou*. And here some connection with the theater was necessary. For a writer in Paris during the early years of the Bourgeois Monarchy, the theater, and not the publishing houses or periodicals, whose editions were relatively small, was where things happened. The stage was where you could make money, or at least get into public view.

In those days, the celebrated actress Madame Dorval was nearing the summit of her fame, and could be seen almost nightly in a large theater on the boulevard Saint-Martin (it has long since ceased to exist). The men came there to look at her, the women to look at one another. The theater gown in a taffeta of melancholy tint—"wine-lees," "pigeon-breast," or "pure Ethiopian"—was by now established. Fitted bodices, fluted organdy ruffles, and shawls of silk crêpe were in high favor. For jewelry there was the pearl drop and a wilderness of black jet; here and there a pretty face, pensive or *attendrie*, hid behind a posy chained to a finger ring. The hair was dressed to the top of the head and planted with moss roses, wheat stalks, and lilies of the valley. The off-the-shoulder ruche was all the rage, as were sausage curls and pancake sleeves, and the bosom and throat swooped up out of the décolletage like a great galantine of fowl.

Against this dazzling banquet of fashions an austere but fetching figure in a black cutaway coat began, in the winter of 1833, to stand out provocatively. She was decidedly not on the menu—didn't even seem to want to be recognized—though a few people whispered that she was quite the latest literary sensation. Then came the big shock—or thrill, depending on which party you belonged to. A production of *Le Mariage de Figaro* in which Madame Dorval played opposite her archrival, Mademoiselle Mars, opened at the Comédie-Française, and a week later an article signed "Georges* Sand" in *L'Artiste* tore Mars to pieces and praised Dorval to the skies. Its author, one learned, was precisely that fetching figure in black, though *Le Courrier des Spectacles* (whose counter-attack earned its victim more publicity than her published novels had) announced that "we for our part believe that the author of this article is a nasty man in petticoats."

This vicious comment, ringing an obvious change on the theme of sexual transposition, reveals what raised the hackles of George Sand's coarser antagonists: the black coat itself, the masculine attire. Just as certain critics had once attacked Germaine de Staël as a "hermaphrodite," others now wanted to put Sand down as a freakish monsieur; but she was not a monsieur, and whatever she thought of petticoats, a shrewd logic lay behind her wearing of men's clothes. The cross-dressing advertised her victorious assumption of men's prerogatives, especially the freedom to write about sex. And man-tailored garments were becoming to her, her womanliness gaining distinction by contrast; on this point she was probably inspired by popular engravings of Joan of Arc, and also by the new English riding habit for ladies, a swallowtail with a little veiled topper. Economy also argued for trousers, as did the ominous reintroduction of the corset that was to be worn beneath a dress with a fitted bodice. (There was something reactionary,

* The *s* was soon dropped.

neo-feudal, about this engine of torture, which had been banished during the Revolution.) So Sand wore trousers largely because they were comfortable and cheap, yet her persistence in this dress also showed the nerve of the great fashion innovator. She had, with a sure stroke, invented "the practical outfit for the modern girl"—and, as a by-product, the modern girl herself.

TO SAY THAT THE intimacy of George Sand and Alfred de Musset existed in the mind of Sainte-Beuve before it existed in reality is to fall a little short of the truth—but only a little. We have already met Sainte-Beuve as a writer of criticism and intellectual history, and we have observed the importance he attached to the details of a writer's life. It should not surprise us, then, to discover that the plump little man was a rabid gossip, indeed that he belonged to that large branch of the scribbling tribe who feel that gossip is the essence of literary art.

By 1833, the urge to write poetry and fiction was drying up in Sainte-Beuve; it was being supplanted by another, more powerful urge, the desire to play the part in life of a wise older child. It is not uncommon in a large family for the oldest child to refuse to take part in the romps of its siblings, preferring to be an agent of parental authority, and like one of these children Sainte-Beuve had abandoned the joy of imaginative play. Having made the high resolve to keep his friends on the straight and narrow, he had become, by the age of thirty—he and George were coevals—a distinctly governessy figure, and like all such figures, he had gone into emotional hiding. A founding participant in the so-called Cénacle of young romantics, he secretly disapproved of many of his associates' ideas and tried to find the courage to proclaim what he felt. But he was far too timid, and his reticence gave rise to an accusation that long weighed on him, namely that he had, as he put it himself, a "trick of hinting at things rather than saying them straight out."

George Sand had met Sainte-Beuve a few months before the publication of *Lélia*, early in 1833. From her modest flat on the quai Malaquais, where she lived with her two children, she wrote the critic a note asking for free tickets to a new play by his friend Victor Hugo. Sainte-Beuve obliged, and she invited him to call on her. The interview was a success; she saw him at once as an ally, and a few weeks later she sent him a letter containing the balladlike phrase "We all need our friends to lean on when we suffer." She was referring to her difficulties with men, and this confession of weakness, this plea for support, formed the core of her overture to him. Convinced that the little man could help her both emotionally and professionally, she sensed that he might be wary of her intense need for love and strange taste for unhappiness. For George's spirit, like the nervous system of certain primitive animals, gained a perceptible identity only when irritated—only when tormented into the state she called "demonic suffering."

George's first letters to Sainte-Beuve were a sort of self-presentation. The wounded tone, like that of a person unable to conceal the ravages of a chronic illness, was not affected, for during her already numerous romantic calamities she had developed a valetudinarian attitude. Yet she also had the sensuality of a perpetual convalescent; and as Sainte-Beuve soon noticed, she was always triumphantly "getting over" some personal or spiritual infatuation. George admitted that she was trying to arouse Sainte-Beuve's pity and felt cross with herself for being so selfish and cowardly. But she desperately needed a sympathetic listener, and there was much of the confessor about him: he was the only man, she told him, who did not remind her of the baseness of humanity.

The two lent each other manuscripts of their most recent works, vowing to respond with absolute frankness. He read a draft of *Lélia* and, though inwardly convinced that it represented no more than a remarkable talent for turning the erotic anxieties of the age into popular fiction, wrote back approvingly, in his involuted, diplomatic way. His tact did not deceive her. She felt intellectually and morally inferior to him, and she told him, almost in a tone of reproach, that she believed he was a better person than she. This thought grieved him in turn, and he asked her to peer through the mask of his dignity to the diffidence that lay behind it. "One's affections," he wrote, "are not engaged by one's sense of a person's relative value. You yourself said to me once that even the most exemplary person harbors some shameful secret, and for my part I think these secrets equalize us all."

The epigram betrayed how deeply these "equalizing secrets" interested him, and presently she saw a way to turn his prurience to her own ends. One might say that she saw a use for him, but this would be somewhat unjust, because personal ambition and a warm interest in intelligent men were nearly identical in her. She soon came to regard Sainte-Beuve not only as a confidant, a confessor, an enormous ear, but also as a bullhorn that might publicize her carefully scripted self-revelations to Parisian society.

Since it was part of Sainte-Beuve's job to know all the important people, he at once realized that George was going to be one of them, and he carefully filed her letters away in a dossier labeled with her name. He had serious misgivings about their friendship, however. It was not so much that she obviously had an ulterior motive for securing his goodwill—all Sainte-Beuve's friends had that—or even that she was enlisting him as a sort of press agent. It was something else. True friendship, he felt, was difficult in the best of circumstances between a young woman and a young man. Even if no dalliance was brewing between them, the man was forever adrift between twin shoals: if the woman shared her intimate thoughts with him, he was thrust into the role of neutered listener, but if on the other hand she kept them to herself, he was simply left in the dark. And George, he began to feel, was putting him in the former position: she was getting him to subscribe to some sort of implicit contract that he was still at pains to make out. Her aims were unclear; surely she was not simply the good-hearted creature she proclaimed herself to be.

Then it occurred to Sainte-Beuve that the wisest course might be to attach George to somebody else, for in this way he could retain her friendship while escaping the excesses of her emotionalism. If he remained her spiritual director of last resort, he might pilot her successfully through the new attachment while confirming his reputation as a sage noncombatant, a wise older child. He began by "referring" her—there is really no other word for it—to his friend Théodore Jouffroy, an up-and-coming philosopher then in his late thirties. Unfortunately, George did not cotton to Jouffroy. He was a "finished man," she complained to Sainte-Beuve, and since she was such an unfinished woman, he merely made her feel freakish. What she really meant was that Jouffroy was too unadventurous for her; she said he was like a person who wondered whether some people didn't still engage in cannibalism, whereas she was like a person who wondered what human flesh tasted like. So the philosopher was out. Anyone else? The name of Dumas came up. And then Sainte-Beuve remembered his young friend the poet, Alfred de Musset.

NOTHING COULD HAVE BETTER revealed George's clothes consciousness—which extended even to the finer points of *garniture*—than a touch to the costume she wore early in 1833 to the fateful dinner party at Florestan Bonnaire's where she met Alfred de Musset. The costume—much remarked on, for she was the only woman there—included a bolero; the touch was a small jeweled dagger. Doubtless she hardly suspected, when Alfred asked her what use she had for "that toy," that they would soon be embarking on a romance that was to be transmuted into at least four novels, a published correspondence, and scores of biographical essays.

The dagger, George explained over dinner, afforded the protection she needed when she didn't dress like a man; yet by coffee the weapon had vanished. Later that evening, back home in the rue de Grenelle, the twenty-two-year-old Alfred told his older brother Paul that "a woman of such slight virtue hardly requires so immoderate a weapon." It was his first mistake—his first lapse into literature.

The weapon did not reappear when, a few days later, George received the racy word-child, all gold curls and gold buttons, in her apartment, at the quai Malaquais. Clad this time in the harem costume she favored at home, she was again revealing her taste for disguises. Charmed, Alfred knelt to trace with his finger the thread of gold on one of her *babouches*, but she did nothing to fan his ardor. ("He's a real dandy, we would never get on," she had told Sainte-Beuve. "It is imprudent, I think, to try to satisfy all one's curiosities instead of merely acting on one's sympathies.") They soon agreed on a comradely friendship. She said, "Do not speak to me of love."

A few days later he wrote her a letter. "You know me well enough by now," he said,

> to be certain that the ridiculous question: Will you or won't you? will never escape my lips with you. We are poles apart in that regard—you can give only spiritual love (granting that you wouldn't directly send me about my business if I should take it into my head to ask you for it) —and I cannot give that to anyone, but I can be—if you judge me worthy of it—not quite your friend—that is still too spiritual for me—but a sort of comrade of no special consequence and without any rights, and thus proof to jealousy and quarrels, allowed to smoke your tobacco, to tear your dressing gowns into rags,* and to catch my death

---

* He had torn up one of her dressing gowns in order to make himself a Pierrot costume for a theatrical.

of cold philosophizing with you under all the chestnut trees of modern Europe.

How did she look to him? Years later, Elizabeth Barrett Browning wrote that there was "no sweetness in the face, but great moral as well as intellectual capacities—only it never *could* have been a beautiful face, which a good deal surprised me. . . . Her complexion is of a deep olive. . . . A scorn of pleasing she evidently had; there never could have been a color of coquetry in that woman." But the eyes, soft and "devouring"—the word recurs in diaries and letters—fascinated men. In her portraits, George often resembles Cristofano Allori's *Judith*—she has the same "Oriental" hue, the same tiny mouth and tall nose—but the eyes are unique. Their gaze, all gentleness, is chastened by the sweeping black arches of the eyebrows, as though the latter were a second pair of eyes with their own severe and fervent expression. This double look cast its spell on Alfred. "The men," he later wrote to a friend, "who have been alternately caressed and cursed by those eyes, at once so tender and so terrible, are haunted by them till they die."

The men . . . Alfred was not unaware that she had loved before: apart from her husband, there had been her long attachment to the lawyer Aurelien de Sèze; an affection for the naturalist Stéphane Ajasson de Grandsagne (almost certainly the father of Solange); a serious affair with the novelist Jules Sandeau, from whose name her publisher had derived her own; a notorious misadventure with Prosper Mérimée; and perhaps other, unknown escapades. "There is a black flag in that woman's life," said Alfred's brother Paul; "it warns of a hidden reef." But it was summer now—summer in Paris—and Alfred was not disposed to be prudent. He drew her portrait—he was a gifted draftsman—and sent it to her with a note: "Your beautiful dark eyes, which I yesterday did so little justice to, have been running all day in my head. I send you the sketch, bad though it is, out of curiosity, to see if your friends recognize you in it and if you recognize yourself. Good night. I am gloomy today." In the little time that remained he studied her.

And George Sand studied him. It was a measure she had learned to take after the reviews of *Lélia.* "Learn caution," she had told herself. "Men do not like to be exposed or made to laugh at the mask they wear." The trouble was that Alfred was not wearing a mask—he positively paraded his weaknesses—and as the summer deepened and they walked together under the chestnut trees in the public gardens, she discovered much about him that was captivating, much that was peculiar.

Alfred was six years younger than George—a fact he never for a moment let her forget—and his father had died the year before, in the great cholera epidemic of 1832. He had not yet recovered from his sorrow, which had attached him more deeply to his family, especially to his mother. His father's death had made him a vicomte, and he looked the part—tall, blond, superb in robin's-egg blue and pearl gray—but he had scarcely any income. He had studied, in fits and starts, law, medicine, music, and painting, and had copied pictures in the Louvre, only to discover that poetry, though hardly a profession, was his real calling. He already excelled at it, and at his tender age had written an audacious lyric in which the moon was described as dotting the *i* of a belfry. The Latin Quarter saw him as a genius.

Musset is one of the very few authors whose character can easily be deduced from his writings. His artistic temperament coincides so exactly with his social personality that it seems transparent, and in this resides much of his appeal to his countrymen: the man and the poet are the same. With his exceptional ear for bittersweet effects, Musset hit his poetic stride at about twenty, and unlike many early bloomers, he also foresaw that this blooming itself would be his theme—that he would have no other. There is about his verse the naturalness and indolence of a spring flower, and one cannot exactly say, reading his still-beautiful lines, whether they reveal an active will to fashion some fine thing or a passive submission to his powers. In its morbid fascination with the fragility of youth, Musset's intelligence seemed to shrink from mature manhood, yet the poignancy of his life lay not in his being very taken with himself, which is commonplace, but in his being *hopelessly* so. His self-infatuation was so mingled with hatred that it may be considered a case of unreciprocated self-love.

Much later, Henry James—who remains the most perceptive critic of the Sand–Musset affair—wrote that Musset was the "victim" of his temperament. James saw Musset as the poet par excellence of youth, of youth on the receiving, not the giving, end of experience. "He was the poet simply of a certain order of personal emotions, and his charm is in the frankness and freedom, the grace and harmony, with which he expresses these emotions. The affairs of the heart—these were his province; in no other verses has the heart spoken more characteristically." The notion that the heart may speak not only fondly, or truthfully, or eloquently, but also with its characteristic *accent* of strong inadvertent feeling is the key to all sympathy with Musset. Like a great songwriter, he threw off tune after tune: forms of musical development in which melody acquires a retrospective density, in which it comments or ironizes on itself, remained mostly foreign to his mind. This is not to imply that Musset could not develop an idea, but rather, as James put it, that "the beauty of his verse is somehow identical with the feeling of the writer—with his immediate, sensible warmth—and not dependent upon that reflective stage into which, to produce its great effects, most English poetic expression instantly passes." Yet a man can be wonderfully expressive without being genuinely passionate, and much suggests that George, in falling in love with Alfred, mistook one for the other.

Despite his weaknesses, Musset was just dangerous enough and just funny enough to be really entertaining, especially when he wrote George Sand letters like this one:

My dear George,

I've something simply ridiculous to tell you. . . . I am in love with you. I've been in love with you since the first day I came to see you. I thought that I'd get over it by visiting you as a friend. There are many things in your character that could cure me of you; I've tried to restrain my emotions; but I've paid too high a price for the months I've spent with you. I do well, I think, to tell you what I feel, because I'll recover with far less suffering if you bar me from your house. I had resolved to tell you I was in the country, but I don't want to make a mystery of my doings, nor to seem to fall out with you for no reason. I know what you're going to think, George: *Another awful bore!* But if I'm not just anybody to you, tell me, as you'd have told me yesterday in speaking of someone else, what I should do. Only I beg of you, if you mean to tell me that you doubt the truth of what I say, don't answer at all.

The friendship of George and Alfred, soon greatly intensified, was carried to the Forest of Fontainebleau, where an alarming incident took place. As they were climbing the rocks of Franchard, Alfred, who had tastelessly begun to evoke the memory of a girl he had taken there before, suddenly heard his own echo call to him and taunt him with an obscene ditty. Poor Alfred—was he "losing his reason" or merely slipping back into literature? George may well have wondered, but by now there was no going back.

"I have fallen in love, and this time seriously, with Alfred de Musset," George wrote to Sainte-Beuve, on August 25, 1833.

It is not a whim but a deep attachment, which I shall describe to you in another letter. It would be unseemly of me

to promise that this affection will last long enough to make
it as sacred as the affections to which you are susceptible.
His is a young man's, a comrade's, love, whose existence
I'd never suspected or imagined I'd find anywhere—least of
all in him. At first I denied this affection, I refused it; then
I surrendered, and I'm happy that I did. I gave myself
more in friendship than in love, yet an unsuspected sort of
love did reveal itself to me, without any of the pain that I
thought would accompany it. I am happy; thank God for
my sake. Oh, I still have my hours of sadness and vague
suffering: it is in and of me. If I abjured the difficulties of
my nature, I'd no longer be myself, and might fear that I
should waken to myself again at too short notice. I'm in
the midst of an authentic process of regeneration and consolation, do not try to talk me out of it.

Despite her misgivings, George had faith in the future, and
the future, she and Alfred had already agreed, would be Italy.
She adored music, he painting, and abroad they could pursue
their liaison without offending their respective families. So Italy
it was: Maurice was packed off to a boarding school, Solange was
returned to Nohant, and late that autumn, with sublime protestations of friendship and love, the pair set off for the south.

"I am at Marseilles, and in two days shall be at sea," George
wrote on December 20 to her friend Alphonse Fleury.

[We are going] to Pisa—perhaps to Naples. . . . I have
once again assumed my place in the real life of the soul,
and cannot do otherwise than take it seriously. We only
boast, dear friend, when we claim to have done with the
passions. They flare up the more brightly on the day we
believe we can toy with them. There is only *that thing* in
all the world for certain natures, and one must kill oneself,
or die of boredom, when one's heart is empty.

Italy was then a sort of salad consisting of two Austrian
provinces, four autonomous principalities, a Papal state, and a

Bourbon kingdom. Presently the young genius, to George Sand's dismay, found himself unable not only to keep his currencies straight but even to remember their various rates of exchange vis-à-vis the franc. He gave her his traveling funds to manage, but despite this forfeiture of his majority—or partly, perhaps, on account of it—his loyalty shredded, then snapped. There was a sordid incident with a ballet dancer in Genoa; a depressing amount of drinking; a long sulk in Florence; and in Venice, where the pair decided to settle for a while, he was soon on the prowl again, this time in Byron's enormous footsteps. Winter had come: sheets of rain marched across the Rialto, the riva degli Schiavoni was shrouded in mist. First George caught a head cold and was told that she was a bore; then Alfred fell dangerously ill with typhoid fever, and she found herself nursing him with a certain distaste. The pair grew deeply unhappy, as much with themselves as with each other; they had wished to raise their affection, like Madame Récamier and Chateaubriand before them, to the level of a work of art, only to be forced to confront their own wretched failure of execution.

Alfred, there is reason to believe, had begun to cool to her as soon as she "unveiled the mysteries of her heart"—in other words, as soon as she gave herself to him. But in his morbid fear that she would betray him, he needed the constant reassurance of her tenderness; and craving to make her accept every quirk and kink of his character, he required her submission to his infidelities. His candor was admixed with self-doubt and a great regard for his own misbehavior, as if he were intent on some mischief dreadfully wounding either to her or to himself. Meanwhile, flattered to be of use, she fell in with him; whenever he hummed a melody she would "sing along in the relative minor." He was continually begging for forgiveness, which aroused her pity, but a pity crosshatched with contempt. Now that she saw the feverish bloom in his face, she recalled that he had once made a drawing of them called *Lovers in a Cemetery.*

The stage was set for the appearance of a third party, preferably someone who, in her words, would be "deeply moved at the sight of suffering, and set himself to adore the victims." As it happened, this paternal soul was near at hand, and it was George who unwittingly summoned him. "I beg you, sir," she wrote to a highly regarded young Venetian physician named Pietro Pagello,

> to come and see us as soon as you can, with another good doctor, to judge of the condition of the patient at the Albergo Reale. But first I must tell you that I fear more for his reason than for his life. Since he took ill his brain has been excessively feeble, and often he reasons like a child. He is a man of energy and imagination, a poet much admired in France, but the exaltation of mental work, entertainments, vice, women, and gaming have greatly fatigued him and frayed his nerves. Mere trifles throw him into agitation. . . . He weeps, complains of a malady without cause or name, and longs for his native land. He says he is near death or madness. I do not know if this is the consequence of fever, or overexcited nerves, or the onset of insanity. I believe that a bleeding would soothe him.

Much has been written about George's flighty passion for Pietro Pagello, and triangles being the sharpest of regular polygons, much has been written whose touch is not very sure. No one disputes that Pagello was attractive, openhearted, and fond of his young rival (he had a little brother of his own, just as Alfred had a big brother), and it is generally agreed that he was an uncomplicated man who was pulled into a complicated situation. Pagello's journal and his letters to his father suggest that the moral algebra of the affair resisted penetration by his simple, artless nature. "I am convinced," he would write in his diary, toward the end of his phase as George's consort, "that I have acted as a person of goodwill." But actually his position was not all that simple, though he had reason to present it in a simplifying light. The contrast between the two Parisian artists, wrapped in their private moral twilight, and this man of science, devoted to questions of the operating theater, has drawn attention away from the shadows within his own character.

Certainly Pagello was unusually gifted. The son of an improvident silk merchant from the Venetian mainland and a highly educated Venetian mother, he trained first at the University of Padua, then at the University of Pavia under one of the scientific luminaries of the day, the surgeon Antonio Scarpa. After receiving his diploma, he began a surgeon's internship at Milan, but unable to adjust to life in the Lombard capital, he returned to Venice, where he found a position at the Ospedale SS. Giovanni e Paolo. He was very poor and lived with his younger brother in a small flat whose door, when removed from its hinges, doubled as a dinner table. The brothers loved to hunt in the wetlands beyond the Lagoon, and these forays provided them with most of their more festive meals. Pagello was buoyant, blond, muscular, chubby; when he met George Sand he had only recently extricated himself from a troublesome involvement with a noted Venetian beauty and, by his own account, was not disposed to yield to George's advances. For he would always insist that the first advances had been hers: she had trained those huge dark eyes on him and ensnared him with the "fascination of her genius." "This woman frightens me," he confided to his diary, but his fright did not prevent him from spiriting her away from time to time to his hooded gondola.

George's letters to Pagello reveal a lot about her connection with Musset. In *Lélia* she had written that men and women, so alike and yet so different, are "made in such a way that there is always hate between them, even in their love for each other," and her own feelings about Musset formed an exquisite blend of dependency and repugnance. Life with him was dreadful, she told the doctor one night. She asked for help in being patient: there was so much sorrow in Alfred's face that she felt she owed him whatever compassion she could muster. "What can I do?" she asked Pagello.

I cannot feign a love I no longer feel. The sort of love that he shows me now, which would have given me so much joy two months ago, no longer touches or convinces me. . . . When I was his slave he loved me but feebly, yet now that I regain my rights as a creature endowed with reason his pride is wounded, and he pursues me as if I were a difficult conquest. . . . You are right when you say that once he has subjugated me again he will take unfair advantage of my state: he does not know true love.

The letters of George and Alfred (together with Pagello's communications, his diary, and a smattering of secondary correspondence) constitute the principal record of the Sand–Musset liaison, and thus have historical value. But the time has come in our story to point out that they are not only a record: they are also a fictionalization. The romanticism of the lovers permeates their testimony, bending it in a manner acceptable to both, and that is only natural; but with Sand's next letter to Pagello another kind of falsification slips into the correspondence. Anyone following the exchange would assume, on the basis of its agitated rhythms, that George and Pagello had already become lovers in every sense, and such in fact was the case; but now, strangely, we hear her asserting that they are abstaining from physical relations and so have no reason to feel guilty. Some of her phrases are strikingly out of key with the rest of the writing:

You and I are here to watch over him, and whenever the compassion of one of us dies down, that of the other flares up. Help me to achieve this task: we shall be so happy in

the end, when, dazed with love, we can fall into each other's arms and say that we have nothing to blame ourselves
for!

How, we wonder, can Sand be trying to persuade Pagello that
they have never made love? The explanation is simple: the
correspondence was tampered with at a much later date. Precisely how and why this happened will become apparent further
along, but for now the reader may rest assured that I am
quoting from authentic, undoctored letters unless I indicate
otherwise.

To be caught up in a triangle distressed Sand enormously,
and she agonized over the pain she was causing Pagello.

You hardly know me at all, my Pietro. . . . You have given
yourself to me as a child gives itself into its mother's arms.
. . . You must suffer so much between the two of us; but
that is better than my not seeing you at all. I shall find it
hard to arrange to meet you; you've seen what scenes our
meetings cause; if I'm gone a few hours Alfred upbraids me
for three days and nights together. He never falls properly
asleep, but reawakens after a few moments to continue his
spying.

The surveillance made George's flesh crawl, and at night she
would awaken with a strangulated sensation. She seemed to
hear stealthy footfalls about her bed. "I need a lion's strength
to keep myself from telling [Alfred] how unbearable my situation has become," she told Pagello. "I'll write you a note in
two or three days' time to tell you when I can get away and
join you in the gondola."

Alfred had often spoken as if his and George's love had a pre-
ordained outcome, like a morality play in which the sinner, that
is to say, himself, ends up being punished; what he now failed
to see was that she was suddenly quite ready to oblige. So far
the pair had observed an implicit code which stipulated that

they should always follow their feelings and always be truthful with each other, and though George did not infringe this code by initiating a love affair with Pagello, she certainly did when she failed to disclose it to Alfred. She gulled herself into believing that he would not want to know her secret, that its disclosure would only crush his self-respect; but this rationalization merely dissimulated her ferocious desire for revenge.

George struggled to be honest, and she tried, unsuccessfully, to convince Pagello that they should tell Alfred everything. "Can we be happy and also prudent enough, you and I, to conceal our secret from him for another month?" she wrote Pagello as the winter ended.

> Lovers have no patience and do not know how to hide. If I'd taken a room at the inn, we'd have been able to meet without risking his sudden outbursts. . . . In two or three days Alfred's suspicions will be rekindled, and may turn into certainties; one look between you and me will drive him mad with anger and jealousy. If, as things are, he discovers the truth, how shall we be able to soothe him? He'll hate us for the deception.
>
> I think that the course I favored earlier today was better. . . . In the beginning Alfred would have suffered a lot, cried a lot, but then he would have calmed down and healed more speedily than he will now. I would have stayed away from him until the day of his departure for France, and then I would have accompanied him home.

And then George admonished Pagello himself: "I grow old, my heart runs dry, I may become as ice for you overnight. Take care, take care of my feelings. To preserve my love and esteem a man must hold himself very near to perfection."

George and Pagello continued to hide their entanglement from Alfred, partly out of the fear that it might destroy him. But the situation was intolerable for all three, and it came to a head when the poet, looking up from his delirium-tossed bed, saw a single teacup standing on a table at which the other two had been sitting. Had they been sharing it? He would never know. But that cup, to which his thoughts continually reverted, held a sea of sickening fears, and as soon as he had recovered somewhat, he set off for Paris.

George and Alfred's intimacy did not end there, for they were still in love and would indulge in a *réchauffé* back in Paris that summer. Yet by this point it is abundantly clear that the lofty tone of their association merely masked some more vagabond impulse. This they did not see; but artists that they were, they did see that the thing was growing ugly. For the ugliness they had a remedy, the tradition of an elevated correspondence, and soon the letters flew fast and furious: never had physical passion been so wonderfully extended by other means. There was so much they could do with words: weave a spell, threaten silence, exhibit vast reserves of both chivalry and humbug in a single phrase. Both were so adept at this exercise that one regrets that they ever spoiled their mutual exaltation with another face-to-face meeting. But if their liaison had always needed a few astringent drops of hurt and shame to give it savor, these now began to overpower the balm of affection: there was more vinegar, less oil. Somewhere along the course of this celebrated correspondence love changed to amorous spite.

Alfred fired the first salvo, from Geneva, on April 4, 1834.

I still love you, George. In four days there will be three hundred leagues between us, so why shouldn't I speak frankly at this remove, where there can be no scenes or nervous fits: I love you, I know that you are with another man whom you love, yet I feel calm. . . .
    This morning I wandered about the streets of Geneva, poking into shops for a new waistcoat, a handsome edition of an English book, other trinkets. Then I caught sight of myself in a mirror and recognized the old child. What a mistake you made, my poor darling—this was the man you wanted to love! With ten years of suffering in your heart

and an unquenchable thirst for happiness, you intended to lean on this poor reed! You, love *me*? Poor George! The thought caused me to shudder. I'd made you so unhappy already, and what dreadful miseries was I not about to inflict upon you? I cannot forget your face bent over my bedside, that face grown wan with eighteen nights of nursing me; I still picture you in that fatal bedchamber where so many tears flowed. Poor George, poor dear child, you deceived yourself: you believed you were my mistress when you were only my mother. Heaven had created us for each other; our minds, in their lofty realm, recognized each other like two mountain birds, and flew together. But the embrace was too tight—it was incest we were committing.

George fervently assented.

Yes, our embrace was an act of incest—but we did not know it. We came together innocently, sincerely, and do we have a single memory of our embrace that is not chaste and holy? Alfred, you reproached me during one of your spells of delirium for never having been able to give you the pleasures of love. I wept when you said this, but now I'm glad there was a certain truth to it, glad that those pleasures were more austere, more veiled, than those you will find elsewhere. At least, when you are in other women's arms, you won't think of me.

By means of this rhetoric, with its unerring choice of words (the "glad that those pleasures were more austere" is magnificent) the two antagonists continued to serve as each other's willing victim. Yet in Alfred's mind, if not in George's, the game still had its ground rules, and the most important of these was "truthfulness." Whatever else she did, she must tell him the truth.

"I do not fool myself about any of your faults, but you do not lie, and that is why I love you," he wrote her.

Even if all my suspicions were confirmed, how were you actually deceiving me? Did you tell me you loved me? Was I not forewarned? . . . What I hate most is lying; it makes me a very mistrustful and unhappy man. . . . If it is true that the pleasures I found in your arms were more chaste than those I had found elsewhere, do not tell me they were less intense. . . .

And yet I shall have other mistresses: now a tender green begins to clothe the trees, and the fragrance of lilacs is wafted into my room in great draughts; all is reborn, and my heart pounds despite myself. I am still young, the first woman I shall have will also be young, I'd not be able to trust a "finished" woman. Considering all that I found in you, I have no reason to seek one. . . .

Do you know what charmed me in your letter? It was your manner of telling me about Pagello—of his caring for you and your affection for him—and the frankness with which you let me read your heart. Always treat me so, it makes me proud. My dear, the woman who speaks thus of her new lover to the one she has just left, and who still loves her, accords him the greatest proof of esteem that a man may receive from a woman.

I'm going to make a novel out of it. I really want to write our story: I feel that this would cure me and lift up my heart. I want to build you an altar, if only with my bones.

But behind Alfred's façade of good sportsmanship there was mischief afoot, the to-ings and fro-ings of an ambivalent soul. George could not mistake the vengeful undertone of his letter ("Considering all that I found in you . . ."), and it stirred the banked fire of her jealousy. "Oh, I implore you on bended knee," she wrote, "no more wine or women just yet! It's too soon. . . . Take care of your life, which perhaps I saved with my vigils, my nursing. Doesn't it belong to me a little, on that account?"

Had she ditched him, then, only in order to possess him? Alfred was galled, and this time his reply was brutally curt.

I need a body, a mistress, in my empty arms, since I cannot be a monk. You speak of health . . . but it is you who have opened my veins. . . . So don't tell me to be reasonable; the more I see my world collapse about me, the more I also feel a hidden force that rises within me, rises and arches itself like the string of a bow. . . . But today if my senses were to lead me to an easy woman, I don't know what I'd do—maybe at the climactic moment I'd strangle her with a shout.

Meanwhile, between her epistolary exertions, George made a startling discovery: that her intimacy with Pagello no longer satisfied her. The young doctor had proved a vital support in a time of need, had simplified her life, and had introduced her to many aspects of Venetian culture that otherwise would have escaped her. But he spoke no French, knew little about novels or novelists, and, most important, had no thorn in his paw for her to extract. With Pagello her craving for "demonic suffering" went unfulfilled. She explained this to Alfred:

Beside me I have my friend and support. *He* doesn't suffer, isn't weak, hasn't known the suspicions that gnawed at your heart. . . . He is at peace in his love for me, happy without my needing to suffer, without my needing to work at his happiness. The trouble is that *I* need to suffer—to suffer for another human being. I need to put my surfeit of energy and sensibility to work, to feel again the maternal care that kept vigil over your weary and ailing soul. Ah, why could I not live between the two of you and make you both happy, without belonging to either one? I could have lived for ten years that way. It really is true that I needed a father. . . . We shall meet again next August, whatever happens, shan't we? Perhaps you will already be engaged in a new attachment. This I desire and fear—my child, I don't know what happens inside me when I think about that. If only I could simply give her my hand, and tell her how to care for you and to love you. But she'll be jealous, she'll

147

say to you, Don't ever speak to me of Madame Sand, that infamous woman.

Two weeks later she took up the same line of thought again. "May God keep you, my dearest, in your present disposition of heart and mind," she began—this letter would be a classic performance:

Love is a temple built by the lover to the object (more or less worthy) of his worship; what is grand in the thing is not so much the god as the altar. Why should you fear to trust yourself? The idol may stand for a long time or soon fall, but still you will have built a fine house of worship. . . . Do you believe that one or two failed affections can blight a strong soul? I used to think so, but now I know that the truth is the opposite. The fire tends always to rise and purify itself. Perhaps the more one has searched in vain the cleverer one becomes at finding, the more one is forced to change the more adept one becomes at preserving. Perhaps that is the task—terrible, magnificent, courageous—of a lifetime.

In these letters we can observe George trying out some of the modern girl's dreamier ideas. She cherishes, for a while, the hope that she can be happy, shuttlecock-wise, "between the two of you"—but soon gives it up. Then comes that most literary of fancies, the notion of passion without jealousy. She describes Alfred's love as a temple; what is "grand in the thing" is "not so much the god as the altar." One pictures a doghouse in the garden, with its successive occupants; and no sooner are there signs of new occupants than she will rail: "Your conduct is deplorable, impossible. . . ."

IN EARLY AUGUST, George Sand returned to Paris, and on this homeward journey Pietro Pagello was, in Henry James's immortal phrase, "no inconsiderable part of her luggage." Once back, she consented to two meetings with Alfred, which were almost as painful for her as for him. Devastated, he tore off to Germany, to Baden-Baden, where after ten days he regained some semblance of self-mastery and wrote her a letter. He wished to control his impulses, he wrote, to address her as gently as possible, but it was evident that he had relapsed into a violent passion for her. His metaphors grew hackneyed and self-pitying; he told her that her coldness had damaged his attachment to life, that he was "flooded" with love and she was watching him drown.

George received this letter at her house in Nohant. Upset by its fierce reproaches, she walked some distance to the skirt of a wood, where, sad and exhausted, she sat down and penned a reply. "What, alas, is all this?" she lamented.

> Why must you always forget that your feelings were sup-
> posed to change into something innocent . . . ? Ah, you
> still love me too much, we mustn't see each other again.
> What you're expressing here is desire, not the sacred en-
> thusiasm of your good moments. . . . For you're losing
> your way, and *he, too*! Yes, he, too, whose Italian speech is
> full of images and protestations that would seem hyperbolic
> in French; he who according to their custom kisses his
> friends virtually on the mouth—which I say without mal-
> ice, the grand and pure boy that he is; he who addresses
> the beautiful [soprano Madame] Crescini as *tu* without
> dreaming of an intimacy; yes, he who composed for his . . .
> sister . . . verses and romances full of *amore* and *felicità*—
> behold this poor Pietro, who after speaking so often of *il
> nostro amore per Alf.* reads a part, I don't know which, of
> my letter to you, the one written on the day of your depar-
> ture, and imagines God knows what—perhaps that I was
> complaining to you about him or about my sadness and
> declining health. . . . Although everything was clear to him
> in Venice, as soon as he set foot in France all his ideas
> changed, and now he has lost heart. My every word

wounds or vexes him, and—must I admit it?—he is leaving, he has probably left already, and I don't intend to restrain him, because I'm offended to the quick by what he writes and because I can clearly feel that he has lost faith, and thus also his love. . . . I loved him like a father, you were our child, yet now he has become a weak creature, suspicious, unfair, quarreling like an ape, and dropping stones on one's head, shattering everything! As for me, I must no longer think about living. Ah, how unhappy I am, I am not loved at all, and I do not love! I have become an insensitive being, sterile and accursed!

And Pagello? No longer a part of George's luggage, he had packed his own. He felt that he'd come to know her too well, *la George*, with her Gallic superiority and fears of sexual subjugation, and that she was frightened of what he knew. He also continued to feel that his conduct had been perfect. Yet the fact remains that he was a doctor who had taken that oath whose first clause is the promise that one will "cause no harm" and which forbids entry into a house for purposes of seduction. Something about Pagello is not entirely convincing, not entirely real, as though he had ceased to believe in the reality of his own life, in its geometries of cause and effect.

His father, the silk merchant, guessing that something was amiss and fearing that this unserious attachment might soon bring discredit on his son, wrote him anguished letters from Venice. Pietro, whose mother had died a few years earlier, was very attached to his father, and his tortured replies made no attempt to parry the paternal arguments. Perhaps he held the traditional Latin view that passion cannot be effectively resisted and should be allowed to run its course, like a fever. This, it appears, was his secret diagnosis, as he attempted—at first haltingly, then more successfully—to rid himself of the illness that had invaded his soul. By late October he was gone.

George all the while was trying to free herself from Alfred's icy embrace. "Poor unhappy man, I loved you like a son," she wrote him.

It's a mother's love, and I'm still bleeding from it. I feel compassion for you and forgive you everything, but we must leave each other alone. I tell you we simply must recover from this—Sainte-Beuve says so, and he's right. Your conduct is deplorable, impossible. My God, what sort of life am I abandoning you to? Drunkenness, prostitutes, over and over again! But since I can do nothing to restrain you, why prolong my shame and your torture? . . . And why must you babble on about Pietro, when I expressly forbade you ever to mention him? What right have you, besides, to cross-question me about Venice? Was I yours, at Venice? From the first day, when I fell ill, were you not put out, and did you not say that a sick mistress was wearisome and boring? Did not the beginning of our rupture date from then? My dear, I don't want to add my recriminations to yours, but you really must try to remember all this, you who so easily forget what actually happened. I've no interest in telling you how badly you behaved. I never accused you of anything, never complained of being abducted from my children, my work, my affections and duties, to be carried off three hundred leagues and dropped with offensive remarks and for no other reason than my having a migraine —than my showing, with stricken eyes, the deep sadness into which your indifference had cast me. I never complained, I hid my tears. And then, one evening I shall never forget, in the Albergo Danieli,* you uttered the dreadful words "George, I've been deceiving myself. I beg your forgiveness, but I do not love you." If I hadn't been ill, if I hadn't expected to be bled the following day, I'd have departed forthwith. But you had no money, I didn't know if you'd accept any of mine, and I couldn't leave you alone and penniless in a foreign country whose language you didn't understand. We closed the door between our bed-

* The same as the Albergo Reale. (See page 139.)

chambers and tried to resume our old life as fast friends, but that was no longer possible. You grew bored, you vanished in the evenings, and one day you announced that you were afraid you'd contracted a social disease. We were sad. I said, "Let's go. I'll take you as far as Marseilles." And you answered, "I think that would be for the best, but I must do a bit of writing here, since this is where we happen to be." Pietro came and tended you, it never occurred to you to be jealous, and it certainly didn't occur to me to love him. But when I *did* start to love him and be his, can you tell me what I owed you? You who had called me the personification of boredom, dreamer, fool, nun, and I can't remember what else? You hurt and offended me, and I told you, "We don't love each other anymore—we never really did." And now you want the day-by-day chronicle of my relations with Pietro, but I don't recognize your right to interrogate me. I'd only debase myself by allowing myself to be confessed like a woman who had deceived you. Think whatever you want in order to torment me and yourself, but there is only one thing you've a right to know: that I did not love Pietro from the first day, nor even immediately after your departure. When I told you that I "perhaps" loved him, that it was "my affair," and that since I wasn't yours I could be his "without telling you anything," he himself was still somewhat entangled with several former mistresses, a ridiculous and disagreeable situation that made me hesitate to consider myself under any engagement to *anyone*. My sincerity you may vouch for yourself, indeed your own letters corroborate my good conscience in the matter.

Much here rings very peculiarly (like the idea that Alfred somehow owned his side of the correspondence), and the reason is that this letter is inauthentic. Though untruthful, it chimes with what George was telling Alfred in the summer of 1834; but the sudden invocation of material that Alfred had no way of consulting suggests that it was written much later and destined for the general public. Modern research has proved that it is a bogus document, yet most of it makes psychological sense, which suggests that it must be based, at least in part, on a genuine—that is to say, a lost or destroyed—original. We have no trouble, for example, believing that the George Sand of 1834 actually wrote its conclusion:

> Never at Venice did I permit you to inquire into the slightest detail of my life; and though on certain days we kissed each other's eyes or brow, I forbid you to enter into a phase of my life when I had again put on the veil of modesty, and rightly too, in your presence.

THE ACTUAL MECHANISM—one is tempted to say the plot device—whereby George and Alfred separated again, in the autumn of 1834, is worthy of a talented novelist: it heightens the contrast between her freewheeling instinctuality and his patrician restraint. Though Musset's father had managed to reduce his family nearly to penury, the son retained an aristocratic cast of mind, and one thing he aristocratically refused to do was to hide his nature or apologize for it. But he was more than ready to apologize for his conduct, to take all the blame on himself, and that is just what he did in his eleventh hour with George. (Much later Matthew Arnold, who had studied the pair's correspondence *Chez Sainte Beuve*, called Alfred "a gentleman of the first water.")

The facts are these: for some weeks, Alfred conducted an obsessive investigation of George's behavior in Venice, and in October his inquiries bore fruit. It turned out that before leaving Paris, Pagello had blurted out to a third party the whole story of his intimacy with George; this secret got abroad, and presently Alfred heard the dirt being dished about George's carefully concealed double cross during his bout with typhoid fever. It is hard to believe that he was doing anything more than discovering what he had always secretly known, but whereas private suspicions do not involve a point of honor, public exposure does, and Alfred, first-rate chap that he was, demanded an explanation from the man who was maligning his mistress. It was then, to prevent unnecessary bloodshed, that George confessed to him, and he, horrified to be associated with her, broke with her completely. Technically, of course, she had lied to him; but doubtless she felt full of smothered truth, a truth known only to a woman's heart, for she was what one might call, without irony, a sincere liar. Her deceits usually sprang from genuine affection, a desire not to hurt or be hurt, whereas, paradoxically, Musset's unfailing truthfulness stemmed mostly from ambivalence or a positive wish to wound.

So at the very moment when the wandering cadences of George's letters attested to her reawakened passion for Alfred, he finally decided that they'd had a good long run and that the curtain should come down on their romance. But the sad story was not quite over. In January 1835, Alfred would yield to George's desire for a resumption of their intimacy, yet this final act was unplayable, for they had lost every scrap of faith in each other, and on March 6, 1835, they parted forever.

It is difficult to see how George in this adventure could have made her way forward without duplicity, for she was playing two roles at once. Her letters show her taking on her lover as an equal, an audacious act in her day; yet when the chips are down she willingly abuses the presumption of feminine tenderness and vulnerability. What's worse, she seems driven by a morbidly competitive sensibility that refuses to let Alfred feel more than she feels—she has to insist constantly on the sincerity, spirituality, and sheer artiness of their affair. She wants to convince the world of a perfectly reasonable notion, that free love is truer than the indissoluble bond of matrimony; yet what does her fling with Alfred show but the misery a *dissoluble* bond can cause?

Sand and Musset liked to refer to their liaison as a "novel," but the author of this novel—or at least of its initial outline

—was neither Sand nor Musset but Sainte-Beuve. Most of the inspiration had been his; then the two characters embraced their destiny, and he filed away his outline in the back of his mind. Now that they were back in Paris and obviously unhappy, he was overcome by an access of remorse and took steps to scotch the tale he had helped to create. After visiting a distraught George sometime in November 1834, Sainte-Beuve called on Alfred and found that he had gone out, so he scribbled a message on the back of a visiting card:

My dear friend, I came to see you to beg you not to see or to receive the person whose affliction I have witnessed this morning. I gave you bad advice when I urged a reconciliation—the time was not yet ripe. Do write her a kind word, but don't see her, it would hurt both of you too much. Forgive misleading counsel.

Despite Sainte-Beuve's good offices, Sand's relations with him were no longer of the best. They had begun to cool much earlier, soon after she first met Alfred, and though the reason is somewhat mysterious, it must probably be sought in the confidential nature of their discussions. Sainte-Beuve had been right to suspect that he could not entertain an innocent friendship with a woman like Sand: in accordance with the logic of intimate conversation, whereby the beans spilled by one party inexorably call forth some equivalent spillage from the other, Sainte-Beuve had begun by late summer of 1833 to leak to her a secret of his own. What was that secret? We do not know for sure; we know only that George wrote to him in August that "all your confessions only increase my veneration for you; and now, more than ever, I trust in you, because like myself you love." She speaks of "confessions"; confessions imply sins. Had Sainte-Beuve formed an attachment that he, like George, might later have cause to regret? Was he then not quite the wise older child that he gave himself out to be? He must have realized that it was a mistake for a superior person like himself to reveal to a professional teller of tales his great shame—his one "equalizing secret," as he himself would have put it.

Sainte-Beuve's initial solution to this problem, in the fall of 1833, was to curtail his visits and letters to George. She waited weeks for each missive, feeling increasingly hurt and forsaken, and by the time she left for Italy he was scarcely writing to her at all; the correspondence was not revived until she had returned to Nohant and was trying to get over Alfred. By this time Sainte-Beuve could presume that she had lost interest in his indiscretions, and besides, he felt genuine compassion for her; so here was an opportune moment for him to dress up again in his wise older child costume. Gently he counseled her to show some simple pedestrian caution, to seek a route to happiness that skirted "precipices and volcanoes." One of his letters especially moved her, and for a while she pored over it every day at the hour when she went outside to inspect her beds of hyacinths. It was a bitter moral pill sugar-coated with flattery, and her vanity delighted in some of his phrases, even as her conscience was stung by others. She reflected awhile, and then wrote him a long letter.

"I now see clearly that my error, my unhappiness, stems from blind pride," she said.

> Everything in the world . . . called me to a life of presumptuous carefreeness and shameless heroism. . . . Living only for myself and risking only myself, I offered and exposed myself always as a free being, isolated, useless to others, and mistress of herself to the point of doing herself in for the sheer joy of it and the tedium of every alternative. . . . Now I should like to be only a respectable old mother to my children.

Never had she been more affectionate or clear-sighted. One of her first letters to Sainte-Beuve had expressed her misgivings about trying to satisfy all her curiosities; now she had grasped, intellectually at least, that a "contempt for the normal conditions of happiness"—her phrase—was bound to be checked and reproved. If her heroism seemed to her "shameless," as her need for suffering had felt "demonic," that was because the struggle for self-knowledge ran counter to the only real reason for living, which was to love and be loved. Her oxymoronic pairings expressed the painful abrasion between her Diana-like appetite for the chase and her equally consuming need for the hearth.

"Your genius, or your devil if you will—your Satan—is to be forever young," Sainte-Beuve wrote her. But his high-minded phrases sounded hollow now—unearned. By going to Italy with Alfred she had risked her reputation, the custody of her children, her very felicity: what had *he* risked? Always in their debates Sainte-Beuve claimed the upper hand, yet her humility gave her strength, and soon the worm turned: the very circumstance that had once afforded her so much pleasure, his telling everyone about her, began to seem offensive and intolerable. "In your conversations with people," she wrote him, late in 1835,

you remember rather too well the privilege of . . . confidence that your friends have accorded you, but not enough of their weaknesses and miseries, which have need of the veil of discretion. You dispose rather too completely of their souls . . . [and] to call a spade a spade, you prattle rather too unguardedly about those you care for. . . . Really, a man like you, called to perform so serious a role by those who know him or seek him out, should have less wit, less memory, or less of an audience. . . . I know this is the first time I've permitted myself to scold you back, but the rarity of the occasion only adds to its joy—I've been wanting to tell you all this for ever so long. . . . It's just that I love the truth, whatever people say, and I cannot nurse a grudge against my friends. To be frank is my way of telling them how much I need their affection, and how highly I value it. . . . Understand that I am still terribly unhappy—also that I love you.

This was not the tone in which Sainte-Beuve wished to be addressed, and her letter remained unanswered. He did not pick up his pen to write to her again for five years.

GEORGE SAND AND Alfred de Musset were born legend creators: they intended their affair to be convertible into literature, and they advertised it as literature almost from the start. Soon after leaving Venice, Musset began to speak of them as "mountain birds" or "wounded eagles," totemic creatures flying beyond the range of ordinary mortals; a little later, at a time when the two were scarcely talking to each other, he wrote her that theirs was a "sacred marriage . . . a chaste and imperishable marriage of the Intelligence," and that "future generations . . . will perhaps bestow their blessing on those who rapped on the door of liberty with the myrtle-wand of love." He promised that he would not die before writing a book about their attachment, and swore that only the "purest lilies" would grace her tomb. Alfred began this book, *The Confession of a Child of the Century*, in the summer of 1835, only a few months after their final rupture; but she had already outpaced him with her three first "Letters from a Traveler," open letters to Alfred published in the *Revue des Deux Mondes* in the spring of 1834. Though her references to their interlude were conventionally vague, it was quite apparent to literary-minded Parisians that she was offering a stylistically correct example of the modern love affair (how opportune, here, was the Italian setting!) while conveniently boosting her fame.

Even after the final breakup, George's notes to Alfred conveyed a desire to assemble their sacred correspondence and preserve it from the hands of the ill intentioned. He obligingly returned her side of the exchange, unconcerned that her intentions might prove less than benign. When she died, in 1876, the bundle of letters remained unpublished, but she had heavy-handedly redacted the entire collection and instructed her secretary to release it. The process of publication was highly irregular—the letters were not printed in a single volume until 1904—but as they jumped in fits and starts before the eyes of a fascinated and mildly appalled public, nobody doubted that they represented the last testament of Madame Sand or that the shadows they threw on her character appeared with her express permission. What they showed about her disloyalty to Musset wasn't entirely clear, but by this time only her most intransigent partisans still believed that she had been faithful to him during the episode of typhoid fever in Venice. That tale was unbelievable on its face and there was plenty of evidence against it, some of which could be traced back to her. It wasn't, however, as if the world much cared. Her conduct, after all, had been understandable if not exemplary, and she was of very little interest to most people anyway by the turn of the century. It was not until the rebirth of feminism after World War II that her life and writings began to receive more attention.

Chief among those at work in the suddenly revived field of George Sand scholarship was Georges Lubin, who in the 1960s was entrusted by Garnier with the task of assembling and editing her complete correspondence for the Pléiade editions. As Lubin grew familiar with her handwriting and began to prepare the material for Volume II, which was published in 1972, he discovered that a number of her letters from the Musset period, that is, 1833–35, were written in a hand that she developed only after 1856. The inescapable conclusion was that she had recopied them and destroyed the originals. There was, as Lubin suggested in his commentary, every reason to believe that most of the material in the recopied versions was authentic—for one thing, Musset's answering letters addressed numerous points raised by her. But considering that these letters had precisely to do with George's Pagello phase (several of them were *to* Pagello), there was also every reason to believe that some of the material, perhaps the most crucial part, was fabricated.

Lubin pinpointed six recopied letters—six *forged* letters, if you will—whose overall linguistic register is in keeping with the rest of Sand's letters of 1833. They are, nonetheless, adulterated, which we know with certainty because they have George writing things to her correspondents that neither she nor they could possibly have believed but that might have convinced a casual readership. Of the six forged letters, I have already quoted from two. The first, from a letter to Pagello, contains the telltale sentence "We shall be so happy in the end, when, dazed with love, we can fall into each other's arms and say that we have nothing to blame ourselves for," which sounds like George trying, absurdly, to convince Pagello that she has not yet gone to bed with him. The second, from a letter to Alfred, intimates just as falsely that Alfred contracted a venereal disease in Venice and all but dismissed George as his lover; and it again asserts, baldly this time, that its writer "did not love Pietro from the first day, nor even immediately after your [Alfred's] departure." From such phrases one must conclude that George, having fibbed to Alfred during much of their intimacy, refloated the same fib for her followers some twenty years later.

Sand's biographers have all but passed over the discovery of the counterfeiting of her letters, but it's a stunning revelation all the same. In its light, an erotic contest long interpreted as a sort of power struggle, as a woman's doughty challenge to the male double standard, takes on a different complexion: it seems also to involve an inauthentic posture, a refusal to admit to one's public, and perhaps to oneself, who one really is and what one's real circumstances are. Consider what George was doing here. To falsify someone else's letters is a rather drastic step; to falsify one's own, even more so; but to falsify one's own *love* letters is extraordinary. The perjury, if it weren't so comical, would be outrageous; that she had no intent to wound anyone—Alfred having recently died—only makes the corruption seem more gratuitous, like an apple welcoming a worm.

But of course it was not gratuitous. Madame Sand's way of viewing the past may best be expressed by an image: her life was like a painting that never dried, and anytime she wanted she could paint into it, wet-in-wet. She knew just how to touch up the picture in order to give it a fine moral force, and if, as in the present case, she was not above forgery when the past required it, one must imagine how she probably regarded that old bundle of letters: as "first-rate material," as a grand old tale in which her name almost coincidentally figured. Why ask her, if she was going to be good enough to preserve it from the flames, to submit to double jeopardy? Hadn't Alfred tortured her enough? Hadn't he already forced out her confession?

The discomfited observer is bound to observe that Madame Sand's conception of her life story seems—like Chateaubriand's—insufficiently pictorial. A person's history isn't like a half-finished painting; it is bone-dry and unretouchable, and the obsessive attempt to rework it betrays disrespect for the intrinsic beauty and usefulness of the past. Memories, for most of us, are like pictures that project themselves into our minds unbidden and unalterable. One doesn't own one's past; and though this obvious truth has always been accepted by the world's simpler folk, it was not accepted by Madame Sand, who could never strike a truce with her experience and arrive at the moment that we call letting go.

HENRY JAMES'S ALERTNESS TO George Sand's character has not been matched by any subsequent critic. In the annals of the last century's presentiments—those things that were known before they were known or that happened before they happened—his questioning of Sand's veracity is among the most surprising. But what first fascinated him when a portion of the Sand–Musset letters was published, in the *Revue de Paris*, in 1896, was merely her breathtaking freedom from reserve. The scandal itself struck him as "antediluvian," and we can share his impatience with the old biographers' endless speculations as to George's sexual identity—that she was "mannish," that she was "exclusively maternal," or that she was somehow both, as if her failing pity for her sick and faithless lover and lightning seduction of the nearest handsome Italian were not proof of the everyday woman in her. No: the great interest for James was that she had told everyone about it, that she had bullhorned her love life to the world.

Despite his affinity for indirections, for undertow, the American novelist felt a real attraction to the blatant surf of Sand's prose. Above all, he admired her command of the "grand manner." This term is generally reserved for painting, but by it James seems to have meant the sweeping representative story, the primacy of passion as a driving force, the close analysis of emotional states, and, not least, the importance accorded to questions of the artistic life in the spinning out of the intrigue. And it was in this last connection, he felt, that the Sand–Musset correspondence made a real contribution to literature. He mused in *The Yellow Book* for January 1897:

> Were the letters given to the world for the encouragement of the artist-nature—as a contribution to the view that no suffering is great enough, no emotion tragic enough, to exclude the hope that such pangs may sooner or later be aesthetically assimilated? Was the whole proceeding, in intention, a frank plea for the intellectual and in some degree even the commercial profit, to a robust organism, of a store of erotic reminiscence?

This, as it seemed, was the possible gain; the loss was to the sense of discretion, to our feeling that many of the things in this world are simply none of our business.

The standing argument in defense of discretion is that the revelations of the indiscreet person, the tattler, necessarily entail so much oversimplification that even when free of malice, which is scarcely ever, their value is seriously impaired. The dizzying atmosphere of the parliamentary chamber, the divorce court, and, nowadays, the television talk show, engulfs and confuses the tattler, so that even his expression of his own heartfelt feelings fails somehow to convince. Fantasy has a wonderful way with memory, and when the tattler starts talking, he usually falls victim to one of the many agreeable selves that jostle in his head. This was why Henry James distrusted Sand as an autobiographical novelist; he said that her brand of self-exposure produced the effect of a trial witness who is "eager to tell more than is asked" of her, who offers testimony that is untestable, unassimilable, and which the fair-minded juror is reluctant to receive.

Like Benjamin Constant, though for different reasons, James suspected that the broadcasting of certain private matters is, in the attendant distortion of context, really a sort of mendacity. Yet he also felt that something could be said for the growing culture of self-revelation and that everything could be said for publishing Madame Sand's letters. As the champion of a woman's right to meet life "at first hand," Sand had

> put a premium on all passion, on all pain, on all experience and all exposure, on the greatest variety of ties and the smallest reserve about them. . . . Say that we are to give up the attempt to understand [such intimate episodes]: it might certainly be better so, and there would be a delightful side to the . . . arrangement. But in the name of common sense don't say that the continuity of life is not to have some equivalent in the continuity of pursuit, the renewal of phenomena in the renewal of notation.

The truth was that Madame Sand could give pretty precise readings of a state that even British writers on the level of Austen, Scott, and Dickens were not equipped to record, namely sexual passion. So much the better, then, that Sand and Musset had been "naked in the marketplace" and had "performed for the benefit of society": their letters revealed the process by which "private ecstasies and pains are transmuted into promising literary material."

With his phrase "the renewal of notation" James put his finger on just what drove Madame Sand as a writer: her need to interpret her immediate past. But he also admitted his unease at some indefinable falsity in the texture of her prose, which he tried to explain with reference to her belief that passion is an improving experience. This explanation, taken on its merits, is persuasive—any attempt to grab the high moral ground will tend to pervert the storytelling impulse—but that far James needn't have looked if he'd known that George, more than twenty years after the Venetian triangle, had cold-bloodedly doctored her letters to Alfred and Pagello. Renewal of notation indeed!

In James's opinion, Sand lacked most of the conventional womanly attributes, but there was one she possessed in abundance, and that was her "immense plausibility." She was incapable of admitting that she had been in the wrong; her fluent outpourings "floated her over the real as a high tide floats a ship over the bar." James wistfully observed that if most people are restricted to saying for themselves what they can, "she said—and we nowhere see it better than in her letters to Musset—every thing in life that she wanted." Of course James's feeling that women (and most especially French-women) do not really value the truth or, rather, that they "do not value the truth for its own sake, but only for some personal use they make of it," is merely a Victorian bromide, of no special interest to us now. What is of interest is his awareness of the mythomania of this particular woman and his sense that her "lightness with the truth" was a necessary condition of what he called her "serene volubility": to have forced Madame Sand to tell the unvarnished truth would have been tantamount to robbing her of her gift. The sublime style of the Sand–Musset correspondence was a "wonder and a force" precisely because its subject was so sordid; and the real lesson of George's letters to Alfred was that "the tone, when you are so lucky as to possess it, may be of itself a solution."

IT IS THE FASHION nowadays to hold that George Sand found her "voice," her integrally feminine tonality, in her late twenties, as an aspiring novelist in Paris. It is also the fashion to deplore the public's continuing interest in her love life at the expense of her lifework. What smuthounds all those biographers and moviemakers are, her partisans exclaim, to be endlessly pawing through her laundry, when her many wonderful novels still go unread; but the smuthounds' instincts are sound. That George Sand was brave enough to write her trailblazing novels is certainly a prime historical fact, but it doesn't mean they're worth reading: they remain what they have always been, *des histoires à dormir debout*, and there's no use pretending anything else. But if she is to be granted any talent at all, and her talent was considerable, then credit should be given where credit is due—to her superb work in "nonfiction." This word may make the reader wince, since it seems curiously anachronistic in this context and unsuited to one who seldom deserted the comforts of the fictive. And yet that is precisely the point. Sand's nonfiction—her chronicles, memoirs, letters, and travel correspondence—were far ahead of their time and also the truest expression of her gift for fiction.

The subject of George Sand's nonfiction was always, in one way or another, George Sand: the myth of herself was her only truly artistic creation. We can trace the emergence of a distinctive nonfiction style in her fine early letters, in the landscape meditations of the *Letters of a Voyager*, in *A Winter in Majorca* (which, though exhibiting the usual defects of travel writing—the dyspeptic complaints about the weather and the food, the bigoted attacks on the lazy thieving natives—remains a classic of the genre), and in that neglected little gem "A journal of the coup d'état." In this crisp daguerreotype of Louis Napoleon's counter-revolutionary putsch of late 1851, she shows the gifts of a reporter of genius, yet as she reels through a Paris thundering with the wooden shoes of the working classes, boards a southbound train, and lurches down to Berry, she also fills her account with a sense of her own physical motion: we're watching the apostle of Christian socialism make a mad dash out of the combat zone and back to—well, to the family château! Never was narrative structure more precisely aligned with personal salvation, and if a certain silliness peeps out from among the wonderful descriptions, it only adds to their charm.

George Sand's inability to suppress symptom—really the outcome of a desire to give it play—is just what James reproached in her novels, which he felt to be oversuffused with the author's own voice. He meant not only that the characters all sound the same but also that the narrator speaks in too personal a manner. Her voice is too eager to invest itself in everything, too unwilling to stand back and let situations bloom with the force of their own genius: there is always too much consciousness in the climate. But in 1854, when her autobiography began to be serialized in *La Presse*, this voice, which had always sounded so natural in her letters, found an ideal subject. For in this affecting reminiscence she set out, free of filial scruples, to chronicle her relationship with the mother who had abandoned her (here, too, there was a plethora of doctored letters). The title of the autobiography was revealing: she called it *Story of My Life*, the absence of the definite article suggesting that if it was indeed a "story," a fiction, it was not the only one her history might entertain: any number were possible.

In his preface to the Pléiade edition of this work, Georges Lubin discusses the falsifications she squirreled into her text, some of which actually enhance its vivacity. *My Life* also contains many events so stereotypically Romantic that they must be classed as the purest blarney: whatever the equivalent of the Brooklyn Bridge was in Paris in the mid-1850s, George Sand was ready to sell it to you. Despite all this, that voice of hers —touchy, humorous, indulgent, often compassionate, always vain of its own social usefulness—triumphs; it's a more mature version of the tone she had tried out in her letters to Musset and Sainte-Beuve. Because of her deep identification with her grandmother Madame Dupin—the only family member who had troubled to care for her in her youth—George Sand has always had the air of someone waiting to become a grandmother herself, and at the age of fifty she suddenly discovers that every one of Madame Dupin's gowns fits her—she can ditch her other identities. Béatrice Didier has written movingly of the chapters in *My Life* devoted to Sand's apprenticeship in Paris, and certainly the young woman from the provinces with the two noisy children and the rain-soaked shoes, wandering starry-eyed up Grub Street in the mad hope that somewhere an inkwell has her name on it, makes a suitably edifying ancestress for Colette and Simone de Beauvoir. Yet these chapters, which are of merely middling quality, do not form the core of the book, and anyone seeking the precise moment when the famous voice finds itself—that is, the moment when it finds something desperately worth saying—will have to turn to the pages devoted to the bitter three-way struggle between little Aurore, her mother, and her grandmother.

George Sand made no bones about the fact that she did not like women—that she wanted to play, as an equal, with the boys. There is nothing to wonder at in this, for she had suffered terribly at the hands of the women in her family. Her childhood consisted of one long struggle between her plebeian mother, a reformed courtesan with flawed maternal instincts who "pecked off her chicks like a hen," and her pseudo-aristocratic grandmother. Sand's account of the mutual backbiting of the young woman and her mother-in-law, as mediated by Aurore's watchdog tutor and seen through the eyes of the little girl herself, is the tenderest and most daringly handled subject in the book. When French readers first came on her account of her grandmother's senility and her mother's descent into mental illness, they must have realized they were in the presence of a kind of writing that was not only totally new but also spiritually indispensable. To look back unflinchingly and capture so much meanness and bitterness was an extraordinary artistic achievement, and if some of the narrative creaked and swayed, that was only because Sand's "lightness with the truth" was indeed "the condition of her supreme volubility"—the facilitating agency that made her writing possible, and which we readily forgive because her characters, unlike most of Chateaubriand's, exist only here and nowhere else. It is in the light of Sand's autobiography that we must judge her forgery of those letters to Musset and Pagello. For the truth is that even before she was a Romantic she was a romancer: her absolute identity with her fictions is the secret of her power of enchantment.

THE SAND–MUSSET LIAISON probably occasioned more writing, including more published volumes, than any other of the last century. Heavy with recriminations and apologetics, these are books that—as the French so charmingly put it—"fall out of your hands." Still worth reading are the delightful letters, and also several of Alfred's productions. The latter are not vendettas decked out as art but the precious stuff itself, and they so clearly transcend the author's personal experience that no one would care to consider them in the deceptive light of biography. Foremost among them is the great poem "May Night," first published in the *Revue des Deux Mondes* for June 15, 1835; in our present-day parlance we might say that this piece completely "reprocesses" a love affair, rescues it from the impure mental space in which art and biography intersect.

So much cannot really be said of *The Confession of a Child of the Century*, which appeared a year later. The problem is not that this novel slavishly rehashes the George-and-Alfred thing, which it doesn't—the book has a genuinely invented quality, and some psychologically probing pages—but that it shoots itself in the foot with long passages of sophomoric moralizing. Like Constant with *Adolphe*, Musset wants his *Confession* to be a cautionary tale, but whereas Adolphe's story is genuinely tragic, because he proposes to share his life responsibly with a woman and fails, that of Musset's hero, Octave, is merely puerile: Octave, like Musset, is basically frivolous, so what befalls him feels more like a comeuppance than a calamity. And Musset's intrigue feels too pointedly plotted: in making his *Confession* a lesson to himself, he resembles Saint Augustine composing the first part of his autobiography, showing himself as really wicked, preparing everything for the moment of rebirth.

Musset's novel gives us the queasy sensation that in mounting his high horse to conquer someone as experienced and resilient as George he was willfully riding for a fall—willfully exposing his persistent childishness and mortal fear of women to some devastating reprimand. Perhaps he was trying to grow up too fast: Sainte-Beuve felt that Musset never really recovered from the affair with George, that it pushed him into alcoholism and did him in as an artist. In a review of the *Confession* that speaks directly to us, the critic complained that the underlying assumption of the book, which is that libertines grow tired of their women, marked a significant retreat from the premise of Constant's *Adolphe*, which was that *men as such* grow tired of their women—that they aren't emotionally or physiologically cut out for monogamy. Sainte-Beuve questioned whether Musset should have tried to build an articulated plot, a moral trajectory, out of his messy love affair with George; wasn't that trying to wrench more out of life than life had to offer? With beings who had arrived at such experience and sophistry, and who had shown such imagination in the diversification of their love lives, nothing argued that the tale should conclude in any particular way. There was, wrote Sainte-Beuve, "no foundation on which to rest a moral concern." What, he asked, does the analysis of a passion, that ruthless exercise reinvented by Constant, have to do "with this fatigued and exalted, factitious and physical something-or-other?"

Was that all it was, then, the George-and-Alfred thing—a *something-or-other*? Here Sainte-Beuve sounds a contemporary note, hitting on the anxious, amorphous, essentially aimless quality of the modern love affair. Today we might express his point somewhat differently: we might say that in failing to become drama, in failing to achieve the structure that can be imparted only by moments of irrevocable decision, the Sand–Musset liaison presaged a twentieth-century narrative format—the soap opera. In the soap opera, as in everyday life, people do the same things over and over, until their mounting misery or a fortuitous accident or the blasted boredom of it all causes the situation to change. It's quite possible, of course, that no real-life situation exists for which some dramatic form cannot be found, and it's perfectly supposable that this one, in the hands of a Chekhov or a Proust, could have been transmuted into more than a something-or-other. But neither George nor Alfred was a Chekhov or a Proust.

PART TWO

IRON
FINGERNAILS

"As if the things of love could ever be put to
rights, as if human creatures could ever love each
other without fingernails, teeth, cries, and
bites, without fury and without hatred."

". . . all the iron fingernails of jealousy . . ."

ANATOLE FRANCE,
TO MADAME ARMAN DE CAILLAVET

4

THAT LITTLE

DROP OF ACID

AS ONE READS ABOUT the great love affairs of the last century, there may come a point at which one feels a need to sort through or to categorize the styles of romance. The human brain, with its craving for logical arrangements, wants smoothly plotted curves, crisp dichotomies, recognizable "stages of development." But France is a nation devoted to Eros in all his guises; and a glance at the large Gallic literature of love (so much of which, even to the most occasional pieces—the wry letter to the editor, the brief critical notice—gives an inkling of a vast hinterland of worldly intelligence) should be enough to convince us that this isn't possible, or, if it is possible, that it isn't advisable. The mind, trying to grasp this or that style of courtship, is like a spotlight playing over a fashion runway, where every design is in continuous movement and disappears at once into the wings. Unlike old gowns or gloves, however, which can be found in costume museums, the grand love affairs of nineteenth-century France have dematerialized, leaving only words behind them. Foxed diary pages, third-person reports, yellowed press transcripts, beribboned bundles of *billets doux*, mildewed novels with broken spines that no longer mean anything except as records of self-exposure—only from such fragments can we assemble a notion of those ancient passions. In our thoughts they solidify, acquiring the density of myth, but myths are immune to vogue, which they are not: by Flaubert's day, for example, the lachrymose, suicide-threatening lover of the Romantic age was already over the hill.

The modern French tradition of the literary liaison seems to have been defined not so much by positive as by negative reflection, by what Benjamin Constant called "hostile sensibility." To borrow an analogy from the art of sculpture, the process was more like carving than like modeling, more like cutting away material than like building it up. In learning what one didn't like in people's behavior, one discovered one's own appetites and manners, one's own individuality. This negative mode of self-definition is perhaps most keenly felt in Balzac's reaction to other writers, especially to Sainte-Beuve. Balzac resented Sainte-Beuve's criticism and sneered at his attempts at imaginative writing, and partly just to humiliate him he reworked the theme of Sainte-Beuve's autobiographical tale *Volupté* into a smaller but much stronger fiction, which he titled *The Lily of the Valley*. A few years later, Balzac got excited by *Adolphe*—he'd been reading the preface to the Charpentier edition of 1843—and he decided to recycle Constant as well. In *Muse of the Department*, he invented a heroine, Dinah Piédefer, who has read Constant's novel and thought hard about its characters; stuck with an ambivalent lover of her own, she decides that she will do anything to avoid becoming Ellénore and eventually walks out on the man. Dinah is more believable and also more interesting than Ellénore, and in featuring her Balzac modernizes Constant's plot, making it end not with a tragic bang but with a naturalistic whimper. In real life, Balzac thought, people didn't die of a broken heart; when love petered out, which it did all the time, that was usually on account of disgust or bad habits.

To be put down by Balzac might have flattened a lesser man than Sainte-Beuve, but the critic thrived on such attention. While Balzac spun out his imaginary romances, Sainte-Beuve continued to push his way into many of the real love stories of his own and even the preceding period. His role varied— it might be that of matchmaker, spectator, or retrospective chronicler—but whatever he was doing he always left his mark. In the words of André Maurois, Sainte-Beuve "enjoyed perching on the edge of other people's nests," and his ghost still haunts us, nattering on about everyone he met in life or on the printed page. By the time Sainte-Beuve died, in 1869, his diction and usage had burrowed into many minds, including some that deeply resented the incursion, and later his voice reappeared, as if by metempsychosis, in the accents of several of Proust's characters.

Sainte-Beuve saw himself as a moralist in the great tradition, that of Pascal and Racine. As such, he passed judgment not only on written works but also on authors and entire social circles: his enterprise was in some measure a sublimation of the scandalmongering instinct, a transformation of gossip into the criticism of mores. He excelled, as has often been noted, at the miniature, at portraying the secondary figure, and this practice allowed his own gifts to upstage those of his subjects. It has to be said that Sainte-Beuve was, and still is, amusing to read. He is not objective, his style is irritating, and his sense of literary value is unsure, but he has a raptorlike ability to carry you with him wherever he wants to go. Fundamentally a raconteur, he shows immense patience in the quiet parts of a story, especially in what used to be called the "painting" of character. Applying many coy, coaxing touches, he hovers over the halftones and the subtler shadows, and though his portraits are often malicious, you can't but enjoy their high finish and wit. French people who love their national literature often have a tattered copy of his *Lundis*, his Monday-morning essays, lying within reach: if they want to find out about a bygone writer and have to choose between Sainte-Beuve and some more recent and responsible historian, they will usually go for Sainte-Beuve.

He did not merely observe the drama he wrote about but was a character himself, and a lurid one. The true Sainte-Beuve of history—the tiny, fat, bald, blubber-lipped, hand-rubbing, sexually promiscuous Sainte-Beuve of the back alleys and brothels—was an apparition to wake the dead. You wouldn't deduce this from his critical writing or even from most of his extant letters, and though he tended to employ rather dodgy expressions, he wasn't embarrassed about being who he was. It was simply that the writers of his period were inclined to generalize the personal: even a free spirit like Sand, when she wishes to talk about beds and lovers, resorts to phrases about altars and gods. Partly it's because lust, especially in the fair sex, is considered indecorous, a little bestial, and people want to humanize the beast; but that's not all there is to it.

In French, a language that tends to make abstraction a condition of any seriousness of thought or feeling, the old love parlance is often puzzlingly vague—it's as though the writer has decided to honor his or her experiences only if they can be expressed in generic terms. Even in intimate letters, even in the routines of everyday life, the concrete, the tangible, the bumpy is avoided: a woman putting on her red dress is "making her toilette" and a man tossing off his shoes for the night is "retiring." But the upshot of this distance between word and act isn't at all what one might expect. Far from seeming dainty or refined, people's actual conduct, when we come face-to-face with it, can seem glaringly, almost surreally, vulgar; and so it is with Sainte-Beuve.

His image—the image that has come down to us in other people's memoirs and letters—has a dreamlike horridness. It seems tailor-made to satisfy our most hackneyed vision of his role as public scold. Consider, for example, his appearance as he received visitors in his study—the dumpling-shaped torso in its folds of dressing gown, the shiny, bandanna-coiffed head, the shifty eyes, the orange complexion: is this not how a critic, a dream critic, should look? No writer with a red-blooded hatred of reviewers should deny himself the solace of picturing Sainte-Beuve seated at his worktable during the spring of 1856, his mouth drooling slightly in its uncontrollable way, as he pores over *Madame Bovary* and tries to contain his amazement that somebody has written a novel that doesn't seem autobiographical, a story in which the author can't be found. Sainte-Beuve was always on the lookout for concealments, for secrets: there was something charlady-like about him, and something priestlike. He was fond of saying that he should have been a cardinal (presumably a Borgia or a Richelieu), but one of his acquaintances remarked that he was "born defrocked." Completely faithless, and also unhappy about it, he is best met in his own writings, each one of which amounts to a profile of himself. "Sainte-Beuve," he once observed in his notebook, employing the honorific third person, "never makes a portrait in which he does not preen. Every critic, in the favorite types that he draws together, only stages his own apotheosis." He frankly admitted to bestowing perfidious praise. "Do not," he warned, "try to get to the bottom of my soul."

One of the most sensitive appreciations of Sainte-Beuve is the short biography by Harold Nicolson, who admired his work and took him as a guide to something elusive in the French spirit, a certain mixture of reason and reticence. Nicolson was writing in the mid-1950s, a low period in Sainte-Beuve's posthumous repute; trying to muster some fellow feeling for Sainte-Beuve as a man, he noted that his subject, while having few real enemies, had been "much disliked by his friends," and that the reason for this animosity was his envy of all imaginative talent. Sainte-Beuve had thrown in the sponge as a poet and novelist, and considering his ability, one had to wonder why. Nicolson thought it had something to do with flawed self-belief and poor stamina: referring to a distinction that Sainte-Beuve himself had drawn between voluptuousness and passion, Nicolson argued that "the literary talent of Sainte-Beuve was, as he himself would have said, 'voluptuous' in the sense that he possessed creative intelligence without creative tenacity. His inventive faculty was, so to speak, parasitic: it needed some external theme or character from which to draw its sustenance and over which, with delicate and prehensile tendrils, it could creep and climb." He was, Nicolson felt, the great intruder.

Sainte-Beuve achieved supreme vulgarity in his greatest act of intrusion as a man—his affair with a poet friend's wife. It is this transgression which almost certainly explains George Sand's letter to the critic, written late in the summer of 1833, where she speaks of his many "confessions."* The subject of these confessions was not disclosed, but it was almost certainly what Sainte-Beuve called his "underhanded duel" with Victor Hugo over the affections of Hugo's wife, Adèle. Thousands of pages have been devoted to this tussle over a notably brainless and sexless woman, but its monumental triteness cannot be grasped until it is boiled down to its skeletal elements.

Like many of the episodes in this book—the story of the Don Juan who's interested only in changing his prey's no into a yes and then gets stuck with an Amazon for fifteen years; the story of the man who counterfeits both his life and his great love and is therefore elected the spokesman of his age; the story of the mature author who finds a younger man on whom to lavish all her sensibility, only to discover that he's totally ungrateful—the labyrinthine history of the "underhanded duel" is fashioned around a tiny, ludicrous plot. Its basic ingredients are a famous, supervirile artist, his neglected wife, and a cringing little critic; throw in an illicit affair with lots of secret meetings in churches, add some chatter about "allowing Madame to decide for herself," season with an unctuously dishonest correspondence, and there you have it, ready to serve—the *plat de résistance* of all French literary scandal. Here experience is reduced to the bare bones of cliché, as when the envious

* See page 155.

little critic writes the he-man poet: "I could gladly kill you, murder you—and for those horrible thoughts you must extend to me your forgiveness."

In the land of literary cliché the story of the artist and the critic is always that of the beauty-contest winner and her mother, of the derby winner and his jockey, of Pollux, who was born immortal, and his brother, Castor, who wasn't; more darkly, it is the story of Abel and Cain. The difference between the artist and the critic is a difference of sex, of procreative voltage: the artist is hot and the critic is not. That is why Sainte-Beuve had to hate Hugo, we tell ourselves, wincing at the ease with which we resort to such stereotypes, and that is also why he had to sleep with Hugo's wife. The fact that Sainte-Beuve, who had rather standard heterosexual desires, was commonly regarded as androgynous, or perhaps impotent, and is still believed to have arrived at some of his assignations with Adèle disguised as a woman—this satisfies the perennial view of criticism as an effete, unmanly occupation. It corresponds to what John Updike has called the "deadly auntiness" of the book world's arbiters. In *Picked-up Pieces*, an essay collection, Updike speaks of "the something intolerable about a literary establishment—any literary establishment," and goes on to lash the critics' "worthy intelligence," "complacently agonized humanism," and "inability to read a book except as a disappointing version of one they might have written."

Of course, Updike's "auntiness" is meant as metaphorical kidding: it stops short of wanting to be taken literally, of actually making fun of anybody's aunt or of implying that male critics have a sexual defect. Sainte-Beuve, however, did have such a defect: it is known as hypospadias. A recent edition of *The Merck Manual* describes it as follows:

The hypospadiac urethra in the male opens proximal to its usual position, presenting along the shaft of the penis, at the penoscrotal junction, between the scrotal folds, or in the perineum. Usually, there is an associated ventral curvature of the penis (*chordee*) caused by a fibrous band along the usual course of the corpus spongiosum. Also present is a "dorsal hood" formed by incomplete foreskin development. The principal complications are meatal stenosis, the patient's inability to direct the urinary stream, and sexual disability in later life.

Hypospadias does not by itself cause impotence, and Sainte-Beuve was no more plagued by this disability than his illustrious, skirt-chasing hypospadiac predecessor Louis XV. But he was, like other sufferers from this handicap, keenly embarrassed by it (its psychological consequences may be so severe that modern urologists advise its surgical rectification in most cases). His sexual unhappiness probably had some psychic bearing on what Harold Nicolson identified as his lack of "creative tenacity," and it offers some ground for sympathy with this pitifully unattractive man.

Sainte-Beuve didn't invent the love affair as an art form, but he virtually invented (or reinvented) its critique. And the remarkable thing, considering his own involvement with Hugo's wife, is that he showed so little imaginative leniency in his judgments of other people, that his sanctimony never faltered. Chateaubriand, Sand, Musset—none measured up to his lofty ideals, and the publication, in the summer of 1849, of Constant's rather fascinating letters to Madame Récamier only afforded him the pretext for another moralistic tirade.

These missives, long kept from the public eye, had recently become known because Madame Récamier, in May of the same year, shortly before her death, had entrusted them to Louise Colet, who had then turned around and sold them to the newspaper *La Presse*. This outraged Madame Récamier's niece Amélie Lenormant—the same Amélie, née Cyvoct, to whom Etienne Delécluze had pitched woo in Rome some twenty-five years earlier—and she forthwith filed suit to stop publication. Madame Lenormant's action resulted in one of the most celebrated trials of the century, but its practical results were inconclusive, and Sainte-Beuve was able to read and to write about Constant's letters.

What he said was unsparing of both Juliette and Benjamin, and it may stand as a perfect representation, like a salesman's bottled sample, of his critical personality. Though it was "painful," he gloated, for him to have to impugn the testimony of so fine a person as Madame Récamier, the truth was that her reason for releasing the letters to a journalist was

> typically that of a woman, and amounted to saying: "Benjamin Constant loved me, therefore he was a man of sensibility." But from the fact that a man has been in love with a woman, desired her ardently, and written her a thousand lively, witty, and seemingly passionate things, in order to appeal to her tenderness and possess her—from all this what can one reasonably deduce about the sensibility of the fellow? It is not what one writes *before* [a seduction] that matters. Wishing to please, the desirous male fluffs up his plumage.

All the ingredients in Sainte-Beuve's poison—the contempt for women, the envy of men, the *ad hominem* vehemence, the debonair logic—are distilled in this passage. But Sainte-Beuve conveniently forgot to give credit to the inventor of the before-and-after calculus, who of course was . . . Benjamin Constant.

AT THE BEGINNING OF this book, I said that I wanted to write about two phases in the evolution of the literary liaison. But before the curtain goes up, so to speak, on the next act of the drama, I feel I should point out that the scenery has been struck, that the action now has a new backdrop. Between the end of the Sand–Musset affair, in 1835, and the year 1887, in which our story resumes, Baron Haussmann, the great Prefect of the Seine, changed Paris so greatly that the second part of this book is set in a section of the city that simply did not exist during the years spanned by the first. Haussmann wanted to develop a network of traffic arteries offering unobstructed passage to firemen, riot police, ambulances, and other modern services, and through the quarters around the Place de l'Etoile he cut a series of radial thoroughfares whose grandiose apartment blocks, ornate cafés, and other street-level amenities were intended to attract upper-middle-class residents. The nearby Bois de Boulogne was redesigned and relandscaped, and a delightful public garden, the Parc Monceau, was conjured out of a domain that had belonged to the Duc d'Orléans.

The modern lodgings available in these new neighborhoods appealed to many artists, musicians, and writers, among them Arsène Houssaye, a former associate of Sainte-Beuve's and a popular novelist and chronicler. Houssaye bought and for several years lived in the townhouse at 12b, avenue de la Reine-Hortense, a Renaissance-style structure whose otherwise mediocre façade was enlivened by three tall, south-facing windows on the *piano nobile*. After the fall of Napoleon III, this street, soon to be renamed the avenue Hoche, became an increasingly desirable location, and in 1878 Houssaye sold his house, which had been reassigned the number 12, to a very wealthy and rather pretty woman named Léontine Arman de Caillavet, who soon took possession of it together with her strapping husband and plump little son.

Madame de Caillavet is remembered, along with two or three other hostesses, as the last of the true race of the salonnières: in this house, every Wednesday for almost thirty years, she held a salon attended by some of the cleverest men and prettiest women in Paris (clever women making no noticeable appeal to her sensibilities). She was known in her day as "the Récamier of the avenue Hoche," and her house came to serve as a sort of incubator for some of the most important literary tendencies of the period known as the fin de siècle. It was there, in 1890, in a quiet room away upstairs, that Anatole France installed his copper-cornered writing table, his books and journals; it was there, too, at roughly the same time, in the drawing room on the *piano nobile*, that France met Marcel Proust, then an aspiring writer of nineteen who was finishing his military service.

Léontine Arman de Caillavet was forty-two in 1886, the year in which she launched her salon. Her features were dainty and piquant, her eyes gray-green and of so pale a shade that she dyed her hair auburn with no discordant effect; she also had the sort of tiny hands that excite protectiveness in the male. Yet Léontine's gaze was direct and her repartee often devastating, and she felt herself entitled to talk about any subject provided she found the right way to do it. She was famously quick to find people boring, and her quips, some of which may have been borrowed from friends or lifted from literary reviews, made the rounds of the salons. (When a lady of fashion held forth to her once on the certainty of an afterlife, she replied, "I see you perfectly, Madame, arriving in Paradise. Saint Peter will offer you his arm and escort you to the buffet.") Aware that her bluntness might intimidate certain people, Léontine wore her hair in corkscrew curls and received her guests in dresses trimmed with gathered lace and silk moss roses; she was also a stickler about hats (and toward the end of her life wrote a novella about a milliner). Fond of beautiful things, she had tried in her youth to paint, then given it up, but she haunted museums and antique shops, went shopping for herself and her friends, and arranged fittings with the finest couturiers. Still, she remained a literary woman, not regarded by anyone as a person of exceptional visual taste.

Léontine's memory *was* exceptional. Well-read in the classics and in French literature, she ornamented her correspondence with references to ancient mythology; she also had some English and Italian and spoke fluent German, which she had learned at home, since her parents were Austrian émigrés of Jewish extraction. Her father, Auguste Lippmann, a dashing, gray-haired man of Semitic aspect, keen on women, parties, and balls, had gone into banking and parlayed his wife's dowry into a fortune. He doted upon his beautiful daughter, and she in turn upon him. Léontine's mother belonged to a family that had been ennobled by the Hapsburgs; like Germaine de Staël's mother, she seems to have been left somewhat out of the picture. She was no longer alive by the time Léontine founded her salon, and the widowed father, never known for marital fidelity, had unblushingly thrown himself into the life of an elderly *viveur.*

Despite her many advantages, Léontine had not made a good marriage. Her husband, Albert Arman de Caillavet, was the son of a Gironde shipbuilder who had proceeded to go bankrupt almost immediately after the wedding. By 1887 Albert had almost nothing to his name: even the title to his small wine-producing property of Capian, in the Gironde, was made over to Léontine after she paid off his creditors to prevent foreclosure. Albert burred his *r*'s in the Gascon manner, generally botched up his business dealings, and was naturally jovial and tolerant, if easily put out of temper. He lived on his wife's money—she didn't so much dip as scoop into principal—and pursued fervently his chief interest, which was very big boats. Under the name Jip Topsail, he covered regattas for *Le Figaro*, an employment that occasioned much mirth among his literary acquaintances, though his clubbier friends found it a madly good yachting column; later, in 1892, he bought himself a sloop, the *Cymbeline*, in which he and his wife and their guests would sail across the Channel or go island-hopping in the Mediterranean.

Léontine and Albert were not, and had never been, especially close—it was rumored that she'd married him on the rebound, after an unhappy romance—and following the birth of their child, Gaston, in 1869, she led her private life unimpeded and unexamined by her husband. Such wifely freedom was perfectly respectable in the Paris of those days, on condition that one showed respect toward one's husband and observed the "forms," which Léontine did, more or less. She had one affair, by all accounts not very intense, with a fellow named Gasson (his first name has slipped into oblivion), a handsome huntin'-and-fishin' type who owned an estate near the Caillavets' little château in the Gironde. And she had another with Victor Brochard, a gifted scholar who'd distinguished himself in Paris with a book about the Greek Skeptics and who figures, radically altered, as the pedant Brichot in Proust's *Remembrance of Things Past*. The only shadow over these attachments was Léontine's rumored difficulty in cutting her lovers loose, which led to a period in which she may have been the mistress of both men at the same time. This indulgence might have besmirched her reputation in a stuffier milieu, but one can hardly imagine the habitués of Léontine's salon—people like the younger Dumas, the worldly naval officer and writer Henri Rivière, the critic Jules Lemaître, and the satiric playwright Edouard Pailleron—feeling moralistic outrage about the way she pursued her affections. She was a loyal friend and an attentive hostess, and she answered a vital social need.

Léontine's strongest attachment was to Gaston, who turned eighteen in March 1887. Dark, oval-faced, and much given to the verbal deflation of himself and others, he had early developed an intense interest in children's theater, charades, costumes, balls, tennis parties, and fireworks displays—anything dramatic or suggesting some departure into drama. Exuding gaiety and high animal spirits, he was popular at school and with Léontine's servants, who moped whenever he left on vacation. Yet his mother was greatly concerned about his real or imagined shortcomings as a student. "You may have won first prize in French," she wrote to him in the spring of 1887, during one of his absences, "but you still have a prodigious amount to learn before you can claim to write properly. I hope you understand how urgent it is for you to apply yourself in that direction. . . . And do begin by sending me more presentable letters. Your handwriting stampedes across the page like a herd of wild animals." Léontine was extremely close to her son—her taking him to task was part of that closeness—and Gaston missed her terribly whenever they were apart.

Léontine de Caillavet is one of those historical figures whose role, long obscured and distorted, has become clear only with the passage of decades—a posthumous fate caused largely by the typically French habit of squirreling away family archives, forgetting that they ever existed, and then rediscovering them. In his *Marcel Proust: A Biography*, George D. Painter observes that some of Léontine's superficial traits were inherited by Proust's character Madame Verdurin, the salonnière of *Remembrance*. When Proust writes that evening wear was banned at Madame Verdurin's soirées in order to avoid any resemblance to "the society of the bores," we know that he's recalling Léontine; likewise with Madame Verdurin's manifest petulance toward anything—whether a relative, job, country house, or illness—that might keep her "faithful" from her side. But Painter overstresses the resemblance, because Madame Verdurin is far more snobbish and insecure than Léontine was; and when Proust tells us that his fictional hostess didn't like to throw very large parties, we know that he can't be thinking of Léontine, because that lady held a general reception every Sunday afternoon in her drawing room, to which scores of people were invited.

So Madame Verdurin is anything but a simulacrum of Léontine, and most of our knowledge of the latter's salon comes not from Proust but from two other sources. One of these is Jeanne Pouquet, who in 1893 became Gaston's wife. In 1926, Jeanne published a reminiscence, *Le Salon de Madame Arman de Caillavet*, which (like its prototype, Amélie Lenormant's pious memoir of her aunt, *Souvenirs de Madame Récamier*) coasts along between undigested quotations, most of them drawn from famous men's letters to Léontine. In 1928, another book appeared, slightly more personal and substantial, *Quelques Lettres de Marcel Proust*, largely devoted to Jeanne's memories of the great writer, who had died six years before.

The second, and far more engaging, source is the late Michelle Maurois's *L'Encre dans le sang*, which was published in 1982 as the first volume of a trilogy devoted to the Caillavet family. Michelle Maurois was the daughter of the biographer André Maurois and his first wife, Janine de Szymkiewicz; after Janine's death, Maurois married Jeanne Pouquet's daughter Simone, making Michelle Simone's stepdaughter and thus the stepgranddaughter (if there is such a thing) of Jeanne herself. In time, Michelle Maurois inherited a share of the Pouquet château, in Périgord, and when she was obliged, with her fellow legatees, to sell and vacate this property, she discovered a huge quantity of family papers piled high in steamer trunks, armoires, and boxes, including numerous letters penned by Léontine, Jeanne, and other Caillavets. As a writer, Michelle Maurois had a need to come to terms with her stepmother, to understand the forces that shaped this unsolicited parent, and this need often conditioned her writing, making it superscrupulous, taut with abstention. Not wanting to judge Simone, Maurois found it wiser to judge no one, leaving us with a group of people whose darker motives we feel free to speculate about.

Michelle Maurois tells us that Léontine was rather fond of Louis XVI chests of drawers and girandoles ornamented with gilded flowers. Although her chronicle and Jeanne Pouquet's memoirs are sometimes at variance, the two sources agree that Léontine held her soirées in her dining room, on the ground floor of the house on the avenue Hoche. Its dimensions were small and so, in consequence, was the table, which allowed places for about twelve guests, who would generally partake in the same conversation. The table was decorated with Dresden china flowers and pink candles under coral-tinted lampshades; the walls were hung with tapestries and the chairs upholstered in red silk. Léontine had an extensive Limoges service whose pattern was derived from an earlier Sèvres design composed of a turquoise marli, or raised rim, flanked by a Greek-key pattern in whose midst could be discovered the entwined initials L.A.C. (Léontine also signed her letters with these initials, dropping the pretentious particle *de*, which her in-laws had only recently affected.) At dinner she offered excellent fare, prepared by a trusted female cook and orchestrated by her husband, who was a gourmet and also an oenophile—it was his family, of course, that had originally owned the viniferous property of Capian (whose vintages may be found to this day under the label Château Caillavet). One gathers that Albert Arman de Caillavet went about with his thumb stuck in old cookery books or in Dumas *père*'s gastronomic dictionary, and that he was known to haunt the kitchen for whole afternoons and to weep tears of blood over flopped concoctions. He liked pheasants in white sauce and cassoulet toulousain, and one memorable day he induced the cook to prepare Carême's version of a sixteenth-century recipe for salmagundi of hoopoe.

Among other things, Léontine was a staunch opponent of electricity. Researching this abhorrence, Michelle Maurois discovered that electric light was then considered bad for women's skin and eyes, and that young girls were advised to open their parasols when standing under illuminated globes. In addition to these cosmetological objections, Léontine also believed that electricity was a fire hazard. Her dining room was consequently lighted by gas, which heated the air to such a degree that the pink table candles often melted by dinner's end and the ladies' makeup ran in rivulets. Too engrossed in talk to pay much heed to the general discomfort, Léontine, once alerted, would throw open a pair of double doors, letting in a blast of frigid air, which roused the gentlemen from the somniferous effect of Albert's ancient Armagnac. We are given to understand that the party would then troop upstairs.

Dumas seldom visited Léontine, and in about 1887 a new

star rose in her salon. This, of course, was Anatole France. Léontine was in the process of luring him away from the salon of Madame Aubernon de Nerville, an older woman who, unlike Léontine, was neither comely nor rich nor a capable judge of food. Madame Aubernon was a capable judge of people, however, and presided so forcefully over her table that sometimes she would silence the "bores," those bogeymen of the late-nineteenth-century salon, by ringing a little bell. There was a standing story that Léontine became embittered against Madame Aubernon because of the latter's patronizing airs: whenever visitors complimented Madame Aubernon on Léontine's elegance and wit, that hostess would reply, "Of course, she is my creation." (Léontine's and Anatole's eventual abandonment of the older dame would be widely compared to Julie de Lespinasse's analogous elopement with d'Alembert from Madame du Deffand's circle in the previous century, and it suggests that a salon is often, if not always, founded on a primordial theft: one recalls Madame de Staël snatching Constant from Madame de Charrière and Madame Récamier wooing Chateaubriand away from Madame de Duras.)

At this time Anatole France's ambition was rising. He had spent the first two decades of his adult life in relative obscurity, but by the early 1880s his sensible and humane newspaper articles, together with his novel *The Crime of Sylvestre Bonnard*, had won him a large following in Paris, and Léontine made him the sacred monster not only of her salon but also of her Sunday receptions. Immediately recognizable by his long nose, pointed beard, and trademark walrus mustache, France would loiter uneasily by the door or beside the fireplace; the mustache was of the variety we have come to associate with Third Republic military officers, but on a man of such slumping posture and unmartial bearing it was decidedly unfortunate, and one visitor described him as resembling a provincial stationmaster presiding over a waiting room.

More than one of Léontine's familiars felt that the oddness, the misplaced look, of that mustache was a clue to France's personality. Though it advertised its wearer's claim to manliness and his wish to throw himself into the hurly-burly of social competition, actually France was one of the most bookish men who had ever lived, and he knew it. In fact, he gloried in it. At this time he already sensed that he didn't have Maupassant's toughness, Loti's panache, Zola's powers of observation; whatever his gifts were, he couldn't line them up and display them as they could in the literary marketplace. Lacking self-confidence, France was continually beset by doubts and reservations, and he had very nearly wilted in the climate of late-nineteenth-century positivism: at forty-four, he already had the bent spine of the perpetual student, the writer who finds inspiration less in his own intuitions than in other people's books. Except for a stint in the military in 1870–71—the siege of Paris and the Commune had scared the wits out of him— his experience of life was confined to libraries, bookshops, cafés, and the offices of newspapers and literary magazines; unlike many popular writers of his day, he knew nothing of his country's new empire, nothing beyond the exotic flora and fauna in the Jardin des Plantes, a favorite haunt. France liked to thumb through illustrated magazines and ethnographic encyclopedias, and one pictures him gazing with wistful resignation at their oversize wood engravings of painted peoples and pagoda-studded cities.

Anatole France may be unique among major French writers in being the son of a bookseller. His father's name was François-Noël Thibault, but because his shop was called the Librairie de France he had received the moniker "Monsieur France," which his son inherited. Anatole, like Léontine, was born in 1844; for the first nine years of his childhood his family lived in the jumble of buildings at 19, quai Malaquais, where George Sand had dwelt at the period when she met Alfred de Musset. (She moved out in 1836.) The elder France ran a so-called *librairie à chaises*, in which you could fling yourself down and bury your nose for hours in some scholarly study, perhaps a multivolume work on the colonies or an ancient quarto tome, full of tipped-in, hand-tinted plates, on the lore of the French Revolution—these two subjects being Noël's chief specialties. Little Anatole loved to frequent the place, and so it came about that the old-time bookshop, reimagined as a sort of archetypal landscape, gave him an image of sheltering warmth: those canyons of embossed morocco would remain his native habitat.

This was, in a way, a wonderful advantage—a sense of home is a gift of the gods—but being a bookseller's son had its drawbacks. It situated you squarely among the petite bourgeoisie, among people whose clothes were cheap and whose French was bad: Anatole's father, despite his admiration for scholarship and his stabs at self-education, had never learned to write grammatically, and his son was mortified by his letters. When Anatole was thirteen, the Goncourt brothers, who often browsed in the Librairie de France, made a dandyish note in their *Journal*:

> We went into the shop of France, the honorable Legitimist
> bookseller. His son is at the Collège Stanislas. Instead of
> having, like his father, an independent and remunerative
> trade, offering some leisure time and enough money to rear
> his children, this bookseller's son upon finishing his studies
> will doubtless become a proud bureaucrat with 1,800 francs
> a year. . . . Education is the modern plague.

It's hard to guess just how grievously such snobbery aggravated France's bitterness—he had all sorts of reasons to be bitter—but a certain mean-spiritness was often to surface in his spats with other writers.

Anatole married Valérie Guérin de Sauville, a bureaucrat's daughter, in 1877. She was about thirteen years younger than he, with little education, and he never felt strongly drawn to her. The match was suggested by Valérie's aunt, a certain Mme Vervoort, who had insisted, according to a letter Anatole wrote to a friend at the time of his engagement, that the two were made for each other. "That I doubt," Anatole conceded, "but I want to change my life—my present one is stifling me. My parents still treat me as if I were fifteen years old. I am thirty-three. It is time to throw off this heavy yoke. Mlle Guérin is very young and very white, a river of milk. Let's hope she'll be as sweet." For a while the ménage functioned smoothly, and in 1881, after the birth of a daughter, whom they named Suzanne, the couple used Valérie's dowry to buy a small house in the rue de Chalgrin, in Neuilly. On a wall in his study Anatole hung a pencil portrait of Benjamin Constant, who seemed to look down on him with an "exquisite and miserable" expression.

Until the watershed year of 1881, France had been a pugnacious bantamweight, awkward, ill spoken, and generally frustrated. His long years of poverty, of writing ill-paid articles for journals and newspapers and of being rebuffed by young women, had scarred him for life. He had the late-blooming writer's secret spleen, and it may be surmised that his journalistic attacks on superior talents—Verlaine, Mallarmé, and Zola among them—had only aggravated his small readership's perception of his deficiencies. It was during the late 1870s, though, as a writer apparently destined for obscurity, that France made some interesting personal discoveries.

One of them—perhaps not the chief one but a valuable key to his temperament—was his realization that he was incorrigibly bookish. He saw that if he was candid about being what is known as a bookworm he would at once gain complicity with many of his readers, who themselves were probably bookworms, too. And his candor would yield other, more valuable dividends: it would be a way of professing his faith in the imagination, and it would give him the charm of modesty, the right to coast cautiously forward on the mazy current of his scruples and qualms. Above all, the bookshop as a setting, along with its cognates the library, the bindery, the print shop, the artist's or architect's studio, and the naturalist's private museum, would help solve the problem that bedevils so many half-finished writers: "What world do my people naturally inhabit —what environment is thoroughly known to me and to me alone?"

In the beginning, Léontine was not very attracted to France, though she recognized that despite his weakness as a conversationalist he had much to say and was not one of those ghoulish bores who polluted her life. It is probably also true, as Jeanne Pouquet suggested in her memoir, that Léontine was grateful to him for his inclination to quit Madame Aubernon's salon in favor of the one she was in the midst of launching. Certainly such gratitude would help to explain why, in the face of her lukewarm feelings for France, she invited him, Valérie, and Suzanne, in September 1887, to spend some time with her at Capian. After some deliberation, the Frances—the "Anatoles," as Léontine called them—accepted her invitation; and as she had not yet left Paris, they looked in on her one evening in advance of the trip, France distracted and tongue-tied, Valérie all peaches-and-cream but also, in Léontine's estimation, bossy and insensitive. "I saw the Anatoles yesterday evening," she wrote to Gaston, who had preceded her to Capian, "and he still trembles and stammers before his domineering spouse. The husband worked out a little plan for their departure, and the wife then instantly demolished it." Léontine's rather dim view of the couple's marriage did not improve on their arrival at Capian. The wife, she thought, was perversely fastidious, a woman who enjoyed triumphing over other people; the brilliant but mousy husband was securely under her thumb. As long as he could not be pried away from Valérie for a bout of literary conversation, the pair made dreary houseguests. Nothing seemed to presage an intense affection between Léontine and the tall writer with the sloped shoulders, anxious eyes, and stationmaster's mustache.

IF THIS IS THE image of Anatole France that we get from Jeanne Pouquet's memoir and from several of Leontine's surviving letters, it is not the only one that history has to offer: a subtle, and much-discussed, portrait may be found in the earlier volumes of Marcel Proust's *Remembrance*. What fascinated Proust, and what has always fascinated his readers, was the disparity between Anatole France as the youthful Proust had imagined him—or, rather, as he'd deduced him from his writings—and the real man. In Proust's masterpiece two writers preside like benevolent caryatids over the entrance to the temple of literary art: one is the fictional Bergotte, a writer closely resembling Anatole France,* and the other is the historical George Sand, who is referred to by her real name. This might seem a curious pairing, but to a word-child of the 1870s and '80s, enchanted by vocabulary and the rhythms of prose, Sand and France, however dissimilar, would have seemed to share certain qualities. Late Sand is often countrified and folksy, early France erudite and humorous, but both are skilled musicians of language who use many exotic and evocative words. Their usage recaptures a dimension of the past, and to a boy who had yet to perceive that the central strength of good French prose is its psychological acuteness, this romantic quality must have been highly seductive. Proust's protagonist, whom scholars usually call the Narrator, speaks of the "hidden harmonic surge" or "inner prelude" that animates Bergotte's rhythms; he praises the "brusque" or "hoarse" accent, the affecting dissonance, of its more melancholy passages. When

---

* And also other writers, including (as George D. Painter has argued) John Ruskin.

Bergotte describes certain things for which the boy as yet feels no affinity, for hail showers and pine woods and the alexandrines of *Phèdre*, they "explode" toward him in all their difficult beauty.

The adolescent Proust idolized Anatole France. In May 1889, when a Paris newspaper ran an unfavorable notice of France's recently published novel *Balthazar*, Proust wrote France an anonymous fan letter declaring:

> For four years I have read and reread your divine books, to the point of knowing them by heart. . . . You have beautified the universe for me, and I am so much your friend that not a day passes without my thinking of you several times, though I have some difficulty imagining your physical presence. With the memory of the hours of exquisite delight you have given me I have built, deep in my heart, a chapel filled with you.

Yet the young Narrator in *Remembrance* is also put on guard against Bergotte by a certain Marquis de Norpois, a pharisaical old diplomat who actually knows the novelist. The captious Norpois does not like Bergotte's writing; and he also does not like the man. What's wrong with the writing is the damnable habit of unexpectedly juxtaposing opposed words or sounds, of contriving little musical sensations independent of a larger artistic plan. Norpois grants that such tricks are chic and hard to pull off, but as for Bergotte himself, he is not chic at all. He is a vulgar bonhomme who seems to have been created as living disproof of the thesis that you may tell a man from his works, and vice versa—the thesis of old Sainte-Beuve. Bergotte is pretentious and solemn, and he sounds like a book—a book written not by himself, more's the pity, but by some untalented dullard.

And then in Proust's novel comes the moment when the Narrator actually meets Bergotte at a dinner party. He is not, as he should be, a white-maned old gentleman, but a vigorous lout in his mid-forties, "coarse, broad-backed, and nearsighted, with a red nose shaped like a snail shell, and a black goatee." The Narrator is seated near his hero, and from this vantage point he observes that Bergotte seems to pursue his ideas backward, confusedly, dragging out inessential words and elaborating his images in a tiresome monotone. The Narrator is miserably disappointed; and "drop by drop" the entire Bergotte of his imagination melts away, "like a stalactite." It's a comical mental event, and except for the description of Bergotte's nose, Proust's profile of France the loquacious diner chimes perfectly with those penned by others. As is usual with Proust's caricatures, there is nothing personally vicious about it—it is about as objective a characterization as a writer could hope for—and the comicality is calculated to undermine not Anatole France, whose character emerges as engagingly flawed, but Sainte-Beuve, or, more precisely, Sainte-Beuve's facile assumptions about the intimate correspondence between personal character and literary style.

The real-life meeting between France and Proust took place in 1889, when Marcel was eighteen. His asthma was then in abeyance; having recently joined the army, he had been attached to a regiment stationed near Orléans, but often returned to his parents' Paris apartment on weekends. During one of these short leaves he was taken by somebody—we don't know who—to an afternoon reception at Léontine's, and with his flowery compliments he at once took the salonnière's fancy, and she presented him to Monsieur France. The great encounter was obviously a letdown.

What Proust had no way of knowing that day was that Anatole's painful speech patterns were the consequence of his thoroughgoing makeover at Léontine's hands. The older writer was overpolite, even obsequious, but the most evident sign of his lack of self-assurance during the early months with Léontine was a stammer that caused him to hesitate at the beginning of certain words. In a milieu that tended to view wit as the sole index of a man's worth, this stammer might prove socially crippling, and Léontine knew it. She also knew, partly because she had studied the art of conversation and partly because she had studied Anatole, that there was a way out of this predicament. It was to train him to speak slowly, with a somewhat stentorian delivery, and if he *must* halt for a moment, he had to learn to do it before some select word, a word that showed his curious learning or his taste for arresting epithets. Léontine's coaching worked, and Anatole mastered his lesson. But he never mastered it as well as she thought he had, and because she encouraged him to talk incessantly, something remained of the old stutter, a dwelling on irrelevant words, a chantlike tone, a cramped forcing of the tongue that could drive some listeners to distraction.

We have no idea how Léontine and Anatole became attached to each other, or how they experienced the earliest stages of their involvement. From the period starting in September 1887, when Léontine still regarded Anatole with circumspection, to July 1888, when the pair were already exchanging ardent missives, no letters have come down to us (on the assumption that there were any). The Léontine–Anatole correspondence, which fills a middle-sized volume, was first published in 1984, by Jacques Suffel; we owe its existence to Léontine's custom of leaving Paris each summer, which obliged the lovers to keep in touch by post. Léontine was incapable of staying in town during the dog days; possessed by the demon of tourism, she would drag Gaston, her maid Eugénie, and anyone else who'd betrayed an interest in her destination on exhaustive, culture-seeking visits to some storied region of France or Italy. On these jaunts her demon drove her relentlessly: she took notes all day long and missed nothing of interest—nothing, that is, but lunch, an oversight that often distressed her companions. Day after day, the chubby, half-famished Gaston was forced to slog through sunbaked cloisters and sepulchral museums.

Scarcely less taxing, in their aqueous way, were the cures that Léontine took at Saint-Gervais-les-Bains, in the Haute-Savoie, ostensibly for the purpose of purifying her kidneys but really in the hope of preserving her looks (for if, like many petite women, she retained a youthful appearance, her short limbs revealed the slightest tendency to embonpoint). With Parisians of this period Saint-Gervais-les-Bains was a popular spa. To get there you caught the early-morning southbound express at the Gare de Lyon, then changed at Lyons for the overnight train to Geneva, where, the next morning, you boarded a diligence—a horse-drawn omnibus—that took you all the way through the uplands of Haute-Savoie to Saint-Gervais. It was a trip of several hours, and you knew you'd arrived when a massive, ornate châlet, flanked by a pagoda-like tower, loomed before you. This châlet was the spa's world-famous thermal establishment, with its bathing cabinets, showers, clinic, library, games room, billiards saloon, and ballroom; the tower's top story afforded dramatic views of Mount Dolent, Mount Joli, and the shimmering aiguilles of Warens. Conscientious patients were expected to take a water cure of at least twenty-five immersions; but for the vacationing Léontine and her entourage, Saint-Gervais also meant the roar of a mountain stream, a fringe of deep-green conifers cut out against the bright blue sky, and *table d'hôte* dinners with the inevitable assortment of bigots and bores. Since her own favorite topic was now the writings of Anatole France, she hoped that a stray France fan might be seated within her oratorical range.

Gaston accompanied Léontine to Saint-Gervais in the summer of 1888, but he returned early to Paris, leaving her and her maid alone with the roaring torrent. He was now almost twenty and in need of a little time by himself, but the mother and son soon missed each other sorely, and she wrote to him every day. He had recently taken an important examination whose results, published in the Paris newspapers several days after his departure, alarmed her: his standing was not what she had expected. She had brought him up to respect his intelligence and to love good books, but now he had lost the habit of reading and spent his free hours sauntering up and down the boulevards. The handwriting of his letters appalled her— it still looked like a stampede of cattle sweeping across the page—and his attempts to sound literary, that is, to sound like Victor Hugo, were wince-provoking. She did not enjoy nagging him, but the truth was that she'd allowed him to slip away from her lately, she'd left him too much to himself.

Léontine's and Anatole's letters of that summer give us our first inkling of the fury of their mutual infatuation. Though Léontine felt that she'd been neglecting Gaston in favor of her new lover, Anatole was heartbroken that she'd left Paris without him. The distance between them sharpened his feelings, and he asked her to write him more often and sketch more amply her Alpine surroundings. He was interested in her description of the deafening torrent, how it drowned out the loudest human speech; couldn't she send him a pebble from its bed, to confirm that her thoughts were with him? White with foam, veiled by drifting spray, bounding downhill with a clamor that silenced all attempts at speech and seemed, as she put it, "to hear only itself," the torrent became the emblem of their deaf roaring passion; she told him in a tone of feigned offense that she could never send him a *small* stone from such a prodigy of nature, where every rock fragment was a menacing boulder.

And then, all at once—it happened only a few weeks after they'd said farewell to each other—a metaphorical boulder came crashing down on her: her husband wrote to tell her that M. France had been seen at the window of his house with his arm about Mme France. Whether or not what he said was true, whether or not it meant anything, Léontine suddenly felt sickened by the thought of one window framing both Anatole and Valérie. "The very idea . . ." she wrote France, "is odious to me. . . . To accept [Valérie] as my rival, to embark on a struggle that would only degrade me—that is impossible! It's already hard enough for me to forgive you for attaching your life to someone so common." After lecturing her son on his epistolary style, Léontine had lapsed into the sort of language that a girl in a farce might have thrown at her married lover —the leveling, democratic invective of spite.

By this time Léontine was well into her course of hydrotherapy. Inside the Saint-Gervais establishment were two bath courts, the second of which was surrounded by a quadrangular three-story building containing thirty-two bathing cabinets for women. It was there, one gathers, that Léontine began the cure to which she frequently alludes in her letters. Though she never describes it, the procedure was fairly standard: the hot springs of Saint-Gervais offered five qualities of salt or sulfated water, which was piped in at its natural temperature of 38–42° C, and you bathed and showered daily in whatever succession of waters was indicated for your complaint. The baths were recommended for skin inflammations, especially eczema, the showers for "catarrhal asthma," and a regimen of frequent drinks from a spigot dispensing chilled water was advised for indigestion, kidney problems, and "uterine catarrh." Yet even as Léontine purified her bowels she was poisoning her spirit, for her correspondence with Anatole reveals that a venomous collusion had grown between them. They had arrived at an explicit agreement—justified as obedience to the despotism of desire—never to forgive any pain that one might inflict on the other. For passionate people like us, they seemed to be saying, clemency is out of the question.

The first of the pair to strike was Léontine. Ignoring the thoroughly suspect origin of that image of France and his wife at the window, she told him that he had committed an "unforgivable crime" against their affection, and that if the allegation was true, she would be "unable to bear further contact with him." On August 8 she declared:

I can no longer write, I am all dried up, desiccated. I fret my heart and flail about and suffer. Why did you write me that you go out alone with [Suzanne], why that precaution? I know very well that the three of you go out together, I'm resigned to it, I see you as a group, at least your daughter is between the two of you then. Ah, you've made me fall out of heaven and I soil myself now in the filth of the gutter. I'm ashamed of my pain and it's not because of you, you know very well that I place you above everything on earth. As I wrote you the other day, I am a Semite, ruthless in pursuit of life's delights, I am of the Old Law, I know nothing of the sweetness of pardon, and the wounds I am dealt will bleed forever and always.

But already an outraged letter was on its way from France to the Semite concerning "this absurd window business." In a cascade of short-winded, almost stammering sentences, he chose to see her accusation not as a warrant of her attachment but rather as a rank breach of trust.

For two days now you have been offending and tormenting me with the most craven and unworthy suspicions. . . . You are unforgivable. You have committed the only fault that could make you ugly in my eyes. I can no longer behold myself in you without disgust. You have debased and besmirched my image, which you bore in your breast. . . . You are unworthy to receive the gospel of my love. I have very little confidence in your clear-sightedness. Your soul is a broken mirror shattering all that it reflects. But I love you and I want you.

By August 11, Léontine realized that she'd been taking the "window business" rather too seriously, and she apologized to France. She'd passed a sleepless night, she told him, then spent the whole morning walking off her agitation, first visiting the little church of Saint-Gervais, where she knelt to commune with her memories of him, then wandering disconsolately about in the flowering churchyard. She confessed that her sense of proportion was weak, and she asked him if he couldn't indulge her a little on that account. For the truth was that France had begun to worry her a little. He seemed ready, she lamented—conveniently forgetting her own proclaimed contempt for pity—to judge her by the dictates of something like criminal law. It was true that she'd been unfair and absurd, but unfairness and absurdity were part of love, indeed they were *le propre de l'amour*. The real problem was separation. Like night, it magnified things, even to monstrosity. France's astonishing phrase "the gospel of my love" passed her by unremarked.

All this while the weather held serene. One morning a tide of brilliant sunlight washed into the gorge of Saint-Gervais, and Léontine, out exploring, discovered a fir wood "less majestic and austere" than the other evergreen forests about her, which allowed a "wild tangle" of foliage and scrub to display itself against a millefleur carpet of wildflowers and moss. "Ah, if only I could dash with you under the great trees, wander with you along the brooks—what a dream that would be." Her descriptions of the gorge delighted France—he found the passage about the fir wood "saturated" with nature—and he wondered briefly whether she shouldn't enter on a literary career.

France's letter of August 13 has an odd ring: "Are you quite aware, Madame, that your letters are marvels of taste, good sense, criticism, and irony." This form of address (and also the use of the formal *vous*) alerts us to the fact that this is one of France's many ceremonious or "feigned" letters, which mimic the reticent tone of a mere family friend; France had such letters delivered by hand to Albert with the request that he forward them to Léontine, whereas he enclosed his genuine love letters in nondescript envelopes with no return address and then posted them himself. The obvious consequence of such shifts and devices was that the epistolary Anatole became two-people-in-one; his writing became structurally duplicitous, hinting at a fissure within the man himself. As if this were not confusing enough, she in the midst of their storms would occasionally beg him to send her cables dictated in advance by herself ("PARDON GRANTED," etc.), whose impersonal wording was necessitated by the irksome fact that the Saint-Gervais telegraphist was situated in her inn and knew her by sight. When we recall that the pair used not only the postal service and the telegraph but also the Paris pneumatic tube—a citywide message-delivery network operating on compressed air—and, a little later, the first public telephone lines, we are bound to conclude that never had so many forms of human communication been so resourcefully employed by people who did not believe in the possibility of human communication.

It is a bedrock truth of the epistolary craft that letters tend to reflect the strains and anxieties of absence, and the extant correspondence of Léontine and Anatole is no exception to this rule. It mostly dates from the period 1887–89, when the two were often apart and still plagued by frequent fits of disbelief in their mutual devotion. Whatever the letters ostensibly concern, their very syntax often verges on the hysterical; yet we have to remember that it reflects periods of stress and so may offer a misleading picture of two reasonably self-possessed and socially successful people.

As her fears quieted, Léontine felt inundated by a new tenderness for France. On August 17, under a baking sun, she ran a long errand on foot, and when she had used up her energy she sat down beside a "murmuring spring in a meadow strewn with pink wildflowers." Soon she would be nearing the end of her cure, yet she felt that the peace in the woodlands about her had failed to take root in her soul. Was her anxiety a premonition of what was to come? It is impossible to guess: her love at that moment felt so powerful that she could not contain it, and it overflowed as from the lip of a pool.

On or about the same day, France, who was in an entirely different mood, penned Léontine the following fateful letter:

I can no longer live without you. When I'm far from you everything wounds and irritates me. I can think only of you, and I am torn by all the iron fingernails of jealousy. Yesterday I went alone for a walk in the cool wet Bois de Boulogne. The leaf-covered lanes were all a-tremble. Not a soul passed my way. What I suffered was indescribable. Consider, my beloved, that for me to be happy I must forget you, and that I can only forget you by submerging myself in you. To not be able to think about what I love— that is a torture I cannot imagine. Dearest, I am desperate. In the horrible state that comes over me when I imagine your past, I do not feel that I have the right to desire you. What place have I in your life? One hour. And the other hours—oh, listen, your love appalls me! I cannot forget you for a single second, and I cannot think of you without torment. Oh, I want to die! We met each other too late, too late! . . . Forgive me, I feel my blood rising against you, you who are nonetheless irreproachable—the anger of a brute, the hatred of a chronically unhappy man. Forgive me, I am jealous as I thought no one could be. I bite my fists until they bleed.

On receiving this letter, Léontine dispatched a cable to France: "WICKED TO TORTURE SO. COURAGE FAILS TO WRITE." And again, a day later: "NO LONGER UNDERSTAND. REPLY BY TELEGRAPH IF YOU WISH TO SEE ME SATURDAY MORNING." Cutting short her course of hydrotherapy, Léontine packed her bags and tore out of Saint-Gervais on August 23. She probably arrived in Paris late the next day, still in the dark as to what had prompted Anatole's fury.

Only a few weeks earlier, France had deemed Léontine's

doubts about the exclusivity of his love to be unforgivable. Yet now he gave proof of doubts far more pervasive than hers. Jealousy, in the catalogue of the sins, is generally considered a contortion of envy: one envies a person who has something one wants, one is jealous of a person who may take away what one has. But what was Léontine (or anyone else, for that matter) about to take away from Anatole? *Her* earlier jealousy had had a cause, however silly or ephemeral, whereas his seemed completely unfounded. He had no rival for her affections, and her conjugal relations with her husband had ceased long ago. What, then, was he so upset about? The source of his anguish was a mystery to her.

The two were able to patch up their quarrel in Paris, but their armistice lasted only a few weeks. Léontine left again, this time for Capian; shortly afterward she invited the France family, who had in the meantime come south to Bordeaux to visit a friend, to spend a few days with her. They accepted; though this was their second visit to Capian, it was France's first as Léontine's lover, and it was probably at this time that he conceived his great affection for the little estate. The Caillavets' château was an oversize farmhouse, long and low, roofed in terracotta tiles; two modest wings reached out on either side to embrace a small forecourt, whose carriageway encircled, in the classic fashion, a roundel planted with ornamental shrubs. Once the Frances had settled in and unpacked, Anatole went out walking. The city boy in him was fascinated by the purple tint of the fruit-laden vines and by the picking and treading of the grapes; with somewhat self-conscious politeness—for he'd been deeply offended by Zola's brutal depiction of agricultural labor in *The Earth*—he began to question the harvesters about their tasks and kept at it for hours. He also liked to watch the wheat harvest—the dray horses turning around the threshing machine in the early autumn heat, the urchin whipping away the flies, the gnarled men in berets bringing in huge sheaves for the barefooted women in great straw hats to feed into the noisy thresher. Yet despite the charm of such rustic spectacles, the France family as a whole was very ill at ease, and it is small wonder that Valérie chose to avoid a reprise the following year. (She would never return to Capian.)

To leave is to wound, and Léontine felt deeply wounded when France and his family left, via Bordeaux, about October 6. "Dear Madame," France's next letter to her began, "I wish to tell you what grateful memories of enchantment," etc., etc.—it was one of his dreadful ceremonious notes, and her soul filled with bitterness. Two beings seemed to struggle within her, one gentle and resigned, the other violently sexual, even cruel. *Her* memories, she wrote him, in her most bravely unforgiving vein, were of "keen and smarting sensual pleasure, with no trace of sweetness mixed in." And though she had once felt that their love was a "great and beautiful garden, in which one could wander forever," it had now become a "hovel exposed to all the winds, where one hears the howling of beasts." Yet outside, in the slopes all about her, the vine harvest went forward under a cool, clear, azure vault: every morning the sun rapidly drank up the last night's dew and picked out brilliant hues on the vine shoots. Léontine understood that the more recent of the estate's two plantings, the one whose roots hadn't struck very deep, was in danger of being damaged by the dry spell. She and Albert, their vintner and field hands would gaze up at the sky, praying for showers to come and swell the grapes, but under the Indian-summer heat millions of wildflowers sprang up unseasonably and the butterflies danced "in amorous pairs," unaware that the north wind would soon blast them away. "Well, isn't such improvidence the happy privilege of lovers?" she asked Anatole in a letter. "There are moments when I hate you to death, when I'm all but deranged in my anger. You see, we two suffer from the same malady. . . . The thought of the past, of the joys it has separately brought us, becomes unbearable, and seems to us a kind of defilement."

None of the couple's letters from the first half of 1889 have survived, but their amorous spite does not seem to have abated during this period. By early August, Léontine found herself back in Saint-Gervais for another water cure, lodged beside "our acquaintance of last year, the torrent." Already on arriving she felt full of woe. "It's extraordinary how restless one can grow," she wrote France, "beside an Alp all black with fir trees, and that bald head of a rock dome, and that pale green patchwork of meadows, and those little chalets for decoration. What wretched taste and how annoying." Never without a certain practical lucidity, however, Léontine also grew aware of something else. Letters arrived at seven in the evening and were picked up at one in the morning, so if you wanted to reply right away you had to do so after dinner, at night, and then "you don't know what you're saying anymore and must throw yourself on the mercy of your correspondent." She preferred writing the following morning, but this led to most of her letters crossing France's on the way to Paris. She was always receiving an answer, not to what she had just said but to what she had said a few days before, with the consequence that she experienced an ever-renewed overlap or double exposure of emotions; which he, for his part, did also, with even more devastating results. Their recent past was being constantly regurgitated—they simply couldn't get free of it—and neither of them ever seemed to answer to the point. Under these circumstances, there was no way for them to allay their mutual suspicion.

Her first letter to him that summer (or the first that we possess, since after her death Gaston burned a portion of her correspondence) entailed, in the slightly sadistic brand of poker they were playing, a raising of the ante. "I have never been loved except physically," she declared, bluntly rejecting any elevated rhetoric of the Sand–Musset ilk. She asked France if he was even conscious of the disdainful irony with which he tended to address her, "for you are cruel, my sweet poet, when it pleases you to be so; you are deliciously cruel because everything in you is exquisite, and the needles you thrust into my heart are of gold." He had by now become a deity for her, and on page after page she wafted him with incense, telling him of the sacred tremor she felt in his presence, of his perfection and radiance, his occult power, and so on and so forth, until by degrees he came to half believe it, until he came to depend on her praise. Yet all the while the divine one went on helplessly raking up the past and dragging what he found there into the cruel light of day. Could she feel in her solitude, in her dark fir wood, how all her reassurances and her "little way of putting things to rights" was making him die minute by minute?

As if the things of love could ever be put to rights, as if human creatures could ever love each other without fingernails, teeth, cries, and bites, without fury and without hatred. My dearest, I entreat you in the name of my love to spare me your tact, that is an insult I do not deserve. . . . You have been hiding something from me, forcing me to suspect everything in such a way that there is not one moment of your life that I can peacefully consider, not one safe place in your soul where I can let my own repose. And I love you. So rest easy. You have lied to me, yet I love you. . . . Today, my beloved, I have dragged myself wearily through the dust of the streets and I've seen nothing, nothing but the spectral black firs of your letter. And then, finding myself on the avenue Kléber, I went up in the balloon they keep moored there—it's silly but delightful—and I saw like an immense field of boulders the city where you were not. What's exquisite is the softness of the ascension, the feeling that one is dissolving in the sky. At one point I had the prodigious impression that I was escaping from myself and almost from you—that I was free. I forgot the mooring and the rigging, and the network of your caresses and your lies. . . . "Don't be wicked," you said in your letter. . . . But not to be wicked in love is the supreme disaster, don't you see? You who have not been wicked in love have done nameless things, without any possible sense or virtue, without even the virtue of a decent whore, and all this because you were not wicked. But I am wicked, I acknowledge it, and the volume of hatred in my heart is incalculable.

Here France overstepped an implicit limit, for Léontine, despite the thrill she felt at arousing such a lurid erotic commotion, was afraid of what he called his "hateful love." Yet her intuition told her that a violent letter, like an access of rage or any other kind of emotional flare-up, does not necessarily reveal the "true man" but only how the man acts under the influence of an uncontrollable passion; and France, by and large, seemed a reasonable fellow, skeptical, decent, and circumspect—a creature, most often, of *controllable* passions. What stood between them, she saw in optimistic moments, was not any real sin of hers but simply the excessive pain that her imagined sins caused him. Her real quandary was that the only balm she had for his wounds was the tact he forbade her to use.

There is one form of tact that most people accept, and that is an old-fashioned apology. She wasn't sure what to apologize for, but she figured it would all come out in the wash, along with her absolution. She told her lover that the fault was all hers: yes, it was "odious" the way she'd first given herself to him, just lightly falling into his arms, but actually she'd had her reasons at the time, and what difference did it make now —now that she was so madly in love with him? She reflected, with some bitterness, that he seemed to have appointed himself "the guardian or curator" of an inert past, a past she no longer recognized, since her memories of him crowded out everything else. Even a brisk walk through the gorge at Saint-Gervais gave her no solace, "for all those thoughts I had thrown to the wind, all those dreams, desires, and anxieties—it seems to me now that I find them again. Asleep in the hollow of a bush or the turning of a road, they awaken; they rise up as I pass and live again, unchanged, in their old forms."

Scarcely had she penned this apology when she received a letter from France, dated August 8, stammering out that he did not trust in the sincerity of her affection.

> All that I can tell you is: I do not believe you. It is a gift in you: you cannot inspire belief. It is your genius to remain forever doubtful. You speak of laying our ghosts. But what am I but a ghost, the most ethereal of all? And what do your words matter to me? I have seen your tears. Why do you lie? But I, too, am at fault. I asked the impossible of you, I frightened you. I brutally destroyed the little arrangements of your heart. After all, you had told me, "Do not ask me his name," and then I indiscreetly demanded it . . . I beg of you, do not lie to me again. You know very well that you can no longer deceive me.

These words give the first concrete indication of what it was that was eating Anatole. It appears that earlier that year he had managed to browbeat Léontine into revealing the name of her previous lovers, and then, Musset-style—it's here that the story begins to feel like a variation on a theme—he had asked enough questions of his acquaintances in Paris to reconstruct the story of her connection with Gassou. And, again like Musset, he'd discovered (or managed to convince himself that he'd discovered—there is room, this time, for serious doubt) that for a while she had been simultaneously both his and another man's mistress. Fabulist that he was, he easily reconstructed (or simply imagined) the entire story of this phase when she had supposedly been lying to him, and just as Musset had agonized over a shared teacup, France now remembered that the year before, when he had visited Léontine at Capian, he had seen her post a letter, with apparent casualness, in the nearby village of Cérons. But why had she gone to the trouble of posting it at Cérons, rather than giving it to the postman at Capian, unless it was a clandestine missive? And to whom—*to whom*—was it addressed? "Never, never again," he wrote her,

> will I be able to imagine you alone. . . . I have seen his portrait, I even know the names of his horses. . . . And the other, whom I do not know.* Oh, why have I loved you, and why was I born? And all this is nothing compared to the idea of seeing you again, you whom they have ———. Listen, Léontine, from now on I have only one feeling in my soul and my body, I hate myself and I hate you infinitely.

The next day France received a brief note from Léontine proposing that they stoop to being ordinary people and forgive each other their mutually inflicted wounds. He wrote back angrily, asking what he had done to require *her* forgiveness; the possibility that his continued cohabitation with Valérie might pain Léontine completely escaped him. He had obtained "proof" in the most unexpected way, he told her, that she had "shared herself" for some months with him and another man and, worse still, that she had not voluntarily broken off the earlier liaison.

Was there anything to France's "proof"? It's impossible to know, though there may have been a particle of truth to it. But whatever had happened, it lay in the past, at a time when Anatole himself was not yet committed to divorcing Valérie; and Léontine, half despairing, returned to Paris, where in a secret flat in the rue Washington she managed temporarily to convince France that none of it really mattered, that all her previous affections were by now null and void. She sensed that his morbid self-torment was in large measure a complication of simple loneliness, which only her physical presence could assuage. For one week, "*chez nous*," as they liked to say, they were happy; and there would be nothing to add to this story

* A reference to Victor Brochard.

if, unhappily, Léontine had not earlier made a promise to spend two weeks at the Grand Hôtel de Biarritz with her frivolous father, doing frivolous-father things like going to balls and promenading by the sea. This meant another long separation—a serious blow to the pair's mutual trust—and after Biarritz the autumn would be at hand, and the vine harvest at Capian would again be upon her, with its nervous interrogations of the sky, its days of grape pressing, cask filling, and reviewing of the vintner's ledgers.

That September, back at Capian, Léontine did something astonishing. She added insult to injury by offhandedly inviting Victor Brochard, who happened to be passing through Bordeaux, to spend a few innocent days with her. This visit never took place—having contracted a sudden, opportune illness, Brochard did not turn up—but in the meantime she sanguinely reported the invitation to France, adding that she could foresee no objection to it on his part. But France had learned of her affair with Brochard, so one can hardly imagine a more provocative act. Was she angling for an expression of France's absolute trust, or was she merely probing his mind, measuring the extent of his jealousy and thus of his desire? It's conceivable that she was merely being unintelligent. France had every objection in the world to Brochard's reappearance, and he didn't hesitate to let her know it; yet what begins to become apparent in his letters of that autumn is the unmotivated nature of his jealousy. It seems to have only recently struck him that a woman, even an educated woman, might commit adultery, or engage simultaneously in several love affairs, pretty much on a whim; there was no reason to think that women were more moved by men than men by women, or that the love of one good man necessarily inoculated a woman against enjoying herself with any number of others. Might not Léontine want to eat the whole cake of pleasure without having one crumb of the cake of virtue? Nothing, to his mind, excluded the possibility; and the possibility was enough to torment him.

Anatole brooded over the last words Léontine had uttered in the Gare de Lyon before boarding the train to Bordeaux. "I want to be at peace," she had told him. "If I cannot be at peace with you, then I shall be so without you. I want love to be a pleasure." In a letter of September 16 he asked her to "admit that this remark had not the same tone as your letters, and that it sounds emphatically more sincere. You knew what you were doing, my darling, when you let fall that little drop of acid. I shall bear its mark for a long time."

When she insisted that France was the only real thing in her life, that all the rest was "mere smoke," he was ready with a caustic reply:

> Come now, my beloved, you are too charming to impose metaphysics upon love. I know how you love: you told me in a moment of perfect sincerity. You love in order to enjoy a delicate pleasure. "Understand," you said, "that I insist that love must be a pleasure for me." You possess in the very highest degree the sense of the possible.
>
> But as for me, what tempts me most in love is the impossible. I love you in an unbounded and painful way. I want to suffer. I am your distraction. You are my religion.

This now becomes the leitmotiv of France's side of the correspondence; we sense the approach of the fin-de-siècle female, the Delilah- or Cleopatra-type whose free-floating lust can pull down the world. But this vision of Léontine exists primarily in France's head, for each time he quotes her remark in the Gare de Lyon, he remembers it a little differently. As the reader has probably noticed, on September 16 it is "I want love to be a pleasure"; on September 23, "I insist that love must be a pleasure for me"; and in a triumphantly self-lacerating letter dated September 24, he recalls her saying, "I want to love for my own pleasure. If not with you, then with somebody else."

"My God but you're a quibbler!" exclaims Léontine upon sustaining this final tantrum. For the plain sense of her words was merely that their love should be enjoyable, that it should not be a torture, and here he is indulging in the grossest distortion of what she said in haste in a railway station. "You're abominable," she writes. "If I didn't adore you, I'd hate you." She calmly explains the nature of her former attachment to Brochard (a dry man, she says, incapable of "abandon"), then lectures Anatole on the perils of a jealousy that "verges on derangement"; but already the tempest is over. Adroitly—for her love has suddenly illumined France, she has mentally encompassed every vagary of his spirit—Léontine changes the topic: as far as she's concerned, there has been enough of fingernails, of bites and scratches, in this particular tussle. It has to be stopped or it will end in tears. Like a mother distracting a toddler from some perilous interest, she tries to nudge their epistolary chats toward Anatole's literary projects. All along, their mutual fury has been growing like a wave gathering height and weight; at last it crests and breaks and is no more.

"Forgive my past doubts and rages, oh, forgive me all that I've been," he begs her, dead tired. "I was born when I loved you—my [cries] were a baby's." His jealousy is at last beginning to ebb; but Léontine fails to see that this is not, with Anatole, an auspicious sign.

BY LATE 1889, MARCEL Proust had begun to frequent Léontine's house in the avenue Hoche. The tonic effect of his months in the army had put a new spring in his step, and his lively (though probably innocent) comradeship with the undemanding peasant boys of his regiment had bolstered his confidence. Léontine was amused by his punctilious courtesy and extravagant adjectives, and soon she introduced him to her son, who had preceded him by two years at the Lycée Condorcet and whom he may already have known by sight.

Gaston's wit, his warmth, and his vaudevillian's ear for *la gouaille parisienne*, that nasal music of wisecracks and put-downs, delighted the young Marcel. He would later recall that Gaston had

> an esteem for my intelligence that I did not deserve; his let-ters were not only admirable in feeling, he also put a real coquetry into them. . . . He long maintained this friend-ship, born virtually in our correspondence, and he did so with a kindness, an infinite gentleness, that I'll never forget. . . . The heart melts with such memories, how can one re-live them without tears? His merit in persevering in this friendship, at least for some time, was all the greater in that I was detested by almost all his companions. . . . My friendship for Gaston was immense, I talked about him constantly at the barracks, where my batman, the corporal, etc., saw him as a sort of divinity, so that on New Year's day they sent him, by way of homage, a formal salutation.

Gaston may have been the first young man of Marcel's acquain-tance who extended him an unquestioning friendship. Marcel was not only a "special" or, as the French say, a "particular" boy, he was also unusually fragile—thin skinned, susceptible to mockery. His sensibility and courtliness often irritated other boys of his own class, and two of Gaston's chums from the nearby avenue de Messine, René Lévi-Alvarès and Frédéric Grunebaum, found him absolutely insufferable. But the buoy-ant Gaston had confidence to spare, and his arm often casually fell around Marcel's shoulders, just as Saint-Loup's would fall about those of the Narrator in the early phase of their associ-ation in *Within a Budding Grove*.

Toward the end of his weekend leaves, on Sunday after-noons, Marcel would usually turn up at Léontine's. Foundering in an easy chair whose heap of frilly cushions gave his brass buttons and stiff collar an air of comical displacement, he would let his head loll back on a shoulder; though he was in excellent health, his asthma had already given his frame a slightly cramped or squeezed-together look, as if it were braced against some imminent blockage of the respiratory organs. The face was moonlike, the eyes a little sad, yet the extraordinary teeth, which are praised so often in letters and memoirs, illumined his face when he talked. He and Gaston and Léontine would chat and laugh awhile, and then, all too soon, Léontine would be loading him down with sandwiches and pastries to tide him over on his trip back to his barracks, and he would struggle not to drop his armful of parcels as Gaston drew him toward the door. Always he lost track of the time and had to make a mad rush of it: he would tumble downstairs with Gaston to the cab waiting by the curb, and Gaston would try to calm his nerves all the way to the Gare d'Austerlitz, where the two would dash to the platform, juggling cases and packages, breathless, pursued by the cabman calling for his fare.

A born farceur, Gaston de Caillavet was already writing revues when Marcel met him. Before long he succeeded in getting them produced by a group of young amateurs, in the drawing room of a stockbroker's apartment in the rue Miromesnil, not far from the avenue Hoche. The troupe's star was the daughter of the house, the fifteen-year-old Jeanne Pouquet—the same who would later write two short memoirs about Léontine and Marcel. Jeanne was informally engaged to a cousin who was expected to come into a fortune, but Gaston himself had fallen headlong for her, an emotion that he confided to Marcel. Marcel soon joined the troupe, and it was probably during his introductory visit to the Pouquets' apartment that he had his first vision of Jeanne. It was a moment he would never forget: she was looking impossibly lovely, and he paid her such effusive compliments that she bashfully turned her back to him, revealing the dark-gold braids that fell to her waist. Words never failed Marcel, however, and he asked her in a bantering voice if she had twirled only so he could admire her tresses. Jeanne was, or affected to be, put out by this remark, but

Marcel, like Gaston, was smitten. He was to finger those tresses in his mind for two long, painful years.

LÉONTINE DE CAILLAVET'S MANY efforts to further Anatole France's career have often been recounted; not least was the offer of that tranquil upstairs room in her house, where he was able to pursue his labors free of his wife's intrusions. For the sad truth was that he now found life with Valérie virtually impossible. Frightful scenes took place in the house in the rue de Chalgrin, the most notable culminating in the henpecked writer's defenestration of a wicker dressmaker's mannequin woven to match Valérie's opulent shape. Finally, on June 6, 1892, as a wretchedly hurt and disappointed Valérie burst into Anatole's study for the umpteenth time, the writer, who was in the midst of working, rose from his desk, slammed his paper and inkstand on a tray, and, still in dressing gown, slippers, and skullcap, marched out of the room, downstairs, and into the street, where without breaking the movement of his writing hand, and with the cord of his gown trailing after him on the pavement, he continued to scribble briskly until he reached the Hôtel Carnot. Life with Valérie was over; and so, too—more fatefully, and far more problematically—was life with Suzanne. The divorce would go through in August 1893, with France forfeiting both house and daughter—and also the portrait of Benjamin Constant.

It was in the midst of his struggle to break up with Valérie that France received an offer, perhaps not altogether coincidental, to write a preface for a new edition of the greatest breakup novel in French literature—Constant's *Adolphe*. Some forty years after the scandal of *Mme Lenormant v. Louise Colet and La Presse*, the perennially troubling little tale had become the subject of renewed scrutiny in Paris: between 1889 and 1891, both the novelist Paul Bourget and the critic Emile

Faguet wrote fresh evaluations of Constant. In his preface, France implicitly distanced himself from the negative view of Constant expressed by Sainte-Beuve at the time of Amélie Lenormant's lawsuit. Sainte-Beuve had died in 1869, and his critical method, historically important though it was, had long ago ceased to appeal to France, whose own complex feelings about the relation between life and art had emerged during a visit to Flaubert. Calling on the great Norman writer in his little apartment in the rue Murillo one Sunday afternoon in the fall of 1873, at the period of the Flaubert–Sand correspondence, he had been greeted by an amiably apoplectic Viking who trotted out all his pet peeves. The visitor sat aghast: the nonsensical notion of artistic "impersonality" had filled Flaubert's hairy head, and France came away from the meeting convinced that the only real news Flaubert had ever broken to the world was news about himself—"He can scream as loud as he wants about his absence from his work." All any writer ever talked about, France was now certain, was his own life; but that didn't legitimate Sainte-Beuve's prying. In his own book reviews France provided only the briefest biographical information about the author, and he occasionally complained, much as certain critics do today, that writers were becoming better known for their baldness or their bad debts than for their achievements.

Declining to pass judgment on Constant's personal behavior, France ended up reading *Adolphe* with much more sympathy than Sainte-Beuve had. Whereas the pundit had seen Adolphe's contradictory sentiments as evidence merely of bad character, of a soul that gave back, "as from a broken mirror, nothing but piecemeal traits," this psychic fragmentation interested France: for him it was self-portrayal of the grittiest sort. Innately skeptical, France doubted that people are ever as consistent as they claim to be, and he was happy to discover that Constant had made no pretense of consistency. The natural comparison here was with Chateaubriand: whereas the great memorialist had "indulged in a superb comedy" of self-impersonation, a peekaboo act using mask upon mask, Constant had never learned "how to practice the art of make-believe"; he'd had the nerve to admit that he lacked a certain integrity, and largely for that reason his novel had worn well. Mercifully, too, *Adolphe* did not "smell of the lamp"— it was free of the literarisms that had so marred Chateaubriand's style. (France felt that the Vicomte had botched the portrait of his lost sister Lucile: despite his desperate struggle to recapture her likeness, he had drawn her "smudgily—in the light of a cruel and tender selfishness—and not such as she was.") All of this is passably perceptive, but France's interpretation of *Adolphe* was actually more eccentric even than Sainte-Beuve's, and it says more about himself than it does about Constant. France began by contrasting Chateaubriand's view of the character of Ellénore with that of Jean Simonde de Sismondi, the economic historian, who like Chateaubriand had known both Benjamin and Germaine and had written an appreciation of *Adolphe*. For Sismondi, France noted, Ellénore was indisputably Madame de Staël; whereas for Chateaubriand she was the spitting image of Anna Lindsay. The disparity between these two eyewitness identifications perplexed France, and re-examining the text of *Adolphe*, he concluded that the problem resided not in the testimony of either observer but in the novel itself. For the truth, as he saw it, was that the character of Ellénore changes, and changes implausibly, as the story develops.

There is a want of unity [France wrote] between the woman of discretion who figures at the opening of the book and the loud-mouthed victim whose despair overruns all bounds, to end only in her death. We may see where, at a given moment, when the situation becomes acute, the truth breaks its way through the fiction that should contain and hide it. . . . The first vision, that of a mistress resigned and touching in her appeal, vanishes altogether before that other whom we see quivering with rage, armed with the Fury's torch, and vengefully pursuing the man who loves her no more.

All at once we make out how widely France diverges from all previous views of the novel, including Balzac's in *Muse of the Department*; France fails to see any vanity in Adolphe's catalogue of his sins, any sense in which he might be showing off his cruelty like a curiosity in a cabinet of wonders. One need hardly add that this was not Constant's own view, since the moral he tagged onto the end of his book, in the form of a fictional "Publisher's Reply," indicates that he was fully conscious of Adolphe's inwardly self-cherishing tone. Yet France's whitewash of Adolphe is far less bizarre than his condemnation of Ellénore. Although the novel clearly explains Ellénore's death as the consequence of an ailment contracted during an episode of despair, France deems it a vindictive suicide: in his reading, Ellénore consciously chooses to die in order to saddle Adolphe with eternal remorse. "This lover whose heart is dead within him," France writes, "this unhappy prisoner standing amid a love laid in ashes, appears to us a very martyr to his own compassion and patience, and soon our undivided pity is for him and not for the tyrannical figure who stifles and oppresses him." And so France turns Adolphe into that most tedious of beings, an edifying hero, while Ellénore becomes a waxwork villainess.

What can explain France's weird failure of perception? Curiously enough, there's an old, apocryphal tradition (upheld by Jeanne Pouquet, Charles Maurras, and, in fictional form, by Proust) that his preface to *Adolphe* was actually written by none other than Léontine de Caillavet. In her memoir, Jeanne recalls Léontine mentioning at this time that she had already written a preface under Anatole's name for a new edition of *The Princess of Clèves* and was engaged in writing another for *Adolphe*.

In fact, some of the phrases that Anatole devoted to the character of the Princess—like the statement that the world must have seemed to her a "fine, well-lighted salon, which one must walk through with dignity and nobility," or that "sometimes it takes more courage and firmness of spirit to smile during a ball than on the field of battle"—do suggest Léontine's influence, if not her hand. Two circumstances are worth noting: that France was not usually disposed to write so ungallantly of women as he did of poor Ellénore and that the preface to *Adolphe* was composed during a period of tremendous tension between Léontine and Valérie—that same Valérie whom Léontine had once described as a "person who enjoys triumphing over others." It seems possible, then, that the preface bears the stamp of displaced jealousy, with Léontine using Ellénore as the butt of her own fury against Valérie. (It's also tempting to see Léontine in the role of the lady juror, proverbially more harsh toward a female defendant than a male would be in her place.) For all that, one cannot easily imagine Anatole France the freelancer farming out to his mistress so juicy an assignment as an essay on *Adolphe*. What's more likely is that the verdict on Ellénore was collaborative, reflecting the couple's shared resentment of a Valérie whom they regarded as vengeful and obstructive. (Léontine saw nothing untoward in the ease with which Anatole knocked out this flippantly aggressive essay.)

If one reads France's preface with any knowledge of Constant, one's memory is instantly tripped. One is put in mind of the discussion that took place way back in 1801 between Constant and his friend Julie Talma about his recent split up with Anna Lindsay. Constant had admired Julie for her grasp of this exquisitely wretched situation, for her ability to console Anna and make her accept the inevitable; now, some ninety years later, and almost on the eve of female suffrage, France insists on pushing what you might call the aesthetics of the breakup one step further. Women, he seems to be saying,

should learn to accept rejection not only sensibly but also gracefully. No ranting, no weeping, no runny makeup, please: Thou
shalt not make a hysterical fuss over being dumped.

THE IMMEDIATE LITERARY PRODUCT of Anatole France's ongoing affair with Léontine de Caillavet was the novel *Thaïs*,
which was published in 1889 (and which later served Massenet
as the source of his opera of that name). The tale belongs to
the historicist genre most famously represented by Flaubert's
The Temptation of Saint Anthony, and though it has lost whatever appeal it may once have possessed, it has a certain biographical interest; as Marie-Claire Bancquart has explained in
her impressive *Anatole France: un sceptique passioné*, the plot
of *Thaïs* is nothing less than a heavily intellectualized, fancy-
dress version of France's emotional awakening to Léontine's
embrace. It is, as Bancquart writes, his "novel of carnal blos-
soming, of the liquidation of the haunting memory of sexual
defeat" occasioned by his youthful desire for a succession of
unattainable women and by his failed marriage to Valérie. Yet
France's infatuation with Léontine inspired only one work of
compelling artistic value, and that is *The Red Lily*. Because of
its violent, somewhat sinister portrayal of the carnal impulse,
this novel conveys the impression that it was written in the
heat of passion, but actually this wasn't the case. By the time
Anatole began work on it, in the middle of 1893, his sentiments for Léontine had palpably chilled, and in composing it
he was merely stirring up the embers of a once-bright blaze.
The book won immediate commercial success in its day and
remained a popular favorite well through the 1950s: it was the
sort of novel one could always count on finding, battered and
bruised, in some *bouquiniste*'s stall by the Seine.

The Red Lily is an example of emotion recollected in tran-
quillity. The idea for the story seems to have been Léontine's,
for despite Anatole's increasing coolness toward her, her fond-

ness for him had only grown, and to induce him to write a fictional account of the early phase of their attachment seemed a means of rekindling his affection. At the same time, she suspected that the illicit nature of their bond would be distinctly appealing in the current literary climate. Adultery formed the subject of some of the most challenging and popular writing around, in particular that of Maupassant and Paul Bourget, and France himself, in his recent criticism, had responded with interest to the "mood of disenchantment," the "failure to believe in the goodness of things," that marked his contemporaries' novels. Always warmly ambitious for her friends, Léontine had prevailed on France to strive for election to the Académie Française, but his wispy tales, scholarly journalism, and personal reminiscences did not bid fair to qualify him for an Academician's uniform: some more robust work, such as a full-length *romain mondain*, or "society novel," would have to figure among his accomplishments. France's friend Bourget was the reigning master of this newly rediscovered form, and though it's hard to believe that France was blind to Bourget's coarseness and superficiality, he clearly felt that he could open the society novel on deeper psychological perspectives than any it had yet commanded.

It must also have been Léontine who decided that the city of Florence would provide a suitable ambiance for France's new novel. Italy, as we've seen, was the preferred backdrop for a love story of exemplary intensity; besides, the pair were already familiar with the country in a touristy sort of way, and Anatole felt that a colorful backdrop would spur his invention of scenes and dialogue. When the two arrived in Florence, in June 1893, Léontine spoke constantly of the novel-in-progress, jotting down descriptions of piazzas and churches with the repeated exclamation "Another great setting for a scene!"—whereupon Anatole, increasingly alarmed, would groan, "A novel in ten volumes." Michelle Maurois has astutely noted that Léontine was occupied in the spring of 1893 with a pregnancy of sorts, for *The Red Lily* would be her and Anatole's only child, and in fact the novel was finished in about nine months. It was first subjected to Léontine's ferocious editing—she toned down the steamier love scenes and insisted on better disguises for certain too-recognizable characters—and then passed around to interested readers for their comments, one of these being the very young Colette. It was published, by Calmann-Lévy, in July 1894.

In his preface to *Adolphe*, France had spoken of a "truth which breaks its way through the fiction which should contain and hide it," a phrase reflecting his tacit assumption that fiction is merely a thin foil hiding a world of fact. The novelist had never concealed his lack of imagination as an inventor of stories, and *The Red Lily* is indisputably a *roman à clef*: it doesn't, for the most part, have a made-up feel. Its heroine, lovely, gray-eyed Thérèse, is the daughter of an ambitious financier named Montessuy (in France's first draft, Krantz), who by degrees has acquired enough wealth to buy a historic château. Though he has already settled enough money on Thérèse to make her rich in her own right, she allows him to marry her off to a certain Comte Martin-Bellème, a rather dull politician for whom she feels no genuine inclination. The couple have a townhouse in Paris overlooking the pont de l'Alma; they are childless and morose, and for three years Thérèse has been pursuing a secret affair with Robert Le Ménil, an ardent sportsman who is frequently away in the country. Thérèse and Le Ménil have furnished a love nest not far from the Comte's house, and it is there that we find them, at the outset of the story, quarreling bitterly. In a callously offhand manner, Le Ménil (who resembles the real-life Gassou) has just let it be known that he plans to be absent for a while during the fox-hunting season, and Thérèse, despite her reproaches, realizes that she will not really miss him. Her affection for him, which has never amounted to anything but gratitude for being loved, has simply dried up.

"I am harsh and obstinate [she confesses to Le Ménil]. It is in the blood. . . . I am a parvenu's daughter, or a conqueror's daughter, it's all the same. We are people of material interests. My father wanted to earn money, to possess what he could buy—that is, everything. I wish to earn and keep —what? I do not know—the happiness that I have—or that I have not. I have my own way of being exacting. . . . Love must be a pleasure, and if I do not find in it the satisfaction of . . . my desire, my life, my love, I do not want it; I prefer to live alone."

It seems to her suddenly that her adventure with Le Ménil has really been happening to another woman, a stranger whom she doesn't admire, and she walks away with a melancholy conviction that she will never again enter the secret room that has witnessed her most intimate moments.

Le Ménil departs, and partly in response to his selfish absence, Thérèse decides to spend the winter with her friend Vivian Bell, a Pre-Raphaelite poet living in Fiesole. She brings along her friends Mme Marmet, an elderly archaeologist's widow, and Choulette, a middle-aged bohemian poet and self-proclaimed follower of Saint Francis of Assisi. France's talent for caricature was perfectly suited to the task of depicting artist types who are at once estimable and ridiculous, and Miss Bell and Choulette, who are loosely based on the historical figures of Vernon Lee and Paul Verlaine, provide much of the comic interest of the novel. Yet these two, like a number of other droll personages, play no integral part in the story. What happens to Thérèse is that she meets, at Miss Bell's home, a moody, dilettantish French sculptor named Jacques Dechartre, who is staying at his little garden lodge in Florence in order to pursue an informal study of Tuscan art. Dechartre, who is the novel's Anatole character (France's mother came from Chartres), reveals a flattering sensitivity to Thérèse's manner of dressing, then whisks her off to the Brancacci Chapel, where, in front of the fresco of *The Tribute Money*, he conjures up for her the spirit of Masaccio. His talk grows so animated that he seems to inhabit "the soul of those magnificent forms," and Thérèse inwardly determines "never to give him up," for she is convinced that only he can acquaint her with what is truly artistic, and also voluptuous, in her being. For several days they wander together through the streets of a wintry, crystalline Florence—in the alternation of the city's glitters and glooms the reader can sense the pair's moods of joy and despair—until, as they round a corner of Orsanmichele, Thérèse comes upon a postbox into which she rapidly thrusts, with apparent casualness, a single letter. And now despair wins out over joy, at least in the mind of Dechartre, since he has previously observed that Thérèse leaves all her outgoing letters in the hall tray at Miss Bell's and accordingly must have some special reason for concealing this missive from her hostess: it can only be that she has a lover. And indeed, this is true—the envelope is addressed to Le Ménil—but what Dechartre doesn't know is that it contains a note of dismissal.

This letter will haunt Dechartre till the end of the book, yet still he presses Thérèse to give herself to him, for

> she had to know that he was in love with her—not with vague tenderness, but with cruel ardor. . . . And then it seemed to him that they might have joys which should make life worth living. Their existence might be a work of art, beautiful and hidden. They would think, comprehend, and feel together. It would be a marvelous world of emotions and ideas.
>
> "We could make of life a beautiful garden."
> She feigned to think that the dream was innocent.

But soon Dechartre begins to trace within himself the growth of a stifled, half-stunted hatred, to which at times he gives "stammering" expression; stammering and breathlessness being generally linked in France's writing to carnal rage. Dechartre's love for Thérèse is hopelessly compromised by a sense of diminishment and woeful self-sacrifice, and even after she has gone to bed with him, in his garden lodge overlooking the English Cemetery (clearly one of Léontine's less upbeat settings), he is filled with suffering because she has had other lovers. "I wish," he mutters, "to possess your past."

Presently Le Ménil arrives in an agitated state and forces Thérèse to confess to her transgression. In a hotel-room scene that many readers of the 1890s found excessively shocking, he raises his hand to strike her, then backs shamefacedly out of the picture. But his presence in Florence has meanwhile been discovered by Dechartre, and when Thérèse, in her desperate fear of rejection by her new lover, lies transparently to Dechartre about the nature of her former tie to Le Ménil, his jealousy becomes ungovernable. He begins to brood, one almost might say to dote, on her erotic past, as if it were a cherished relic, like a pair of baby shoes; he hectors her pedantically. "A woman," he says,

cannot be jealous in the same manner as a man, nor feel what makes us suffer. . . . Why? Because there is not in the blood, in the flesh of a woman that absurd and generous fury for ownership, that primitive instinct of which man has made a right. Man is the god who wants his mate to himself. Since time immemorial woman is accustomed to sharing men's love. It is the past, the obscure past, that determines our passions. We are already so old when we are born! Jealousy, for a woman, is only a wound to her own self-love. For a man it is a torture as profound as moral suffering, as continuous as physical suffering. You ask the reason why? Because . . . you are matter and I am the idea; you are the thing and I am the mind; you are the clay and I am the artisan. . . . I know what there is in my jealousy. When I examine it, I find in it hereditary prejudices, savage conceit, sickly susceptibility, a mingling of rudest violence and cruel feebleness, imbecile and wicked revolt against the laws of life and of society. . . . To desire a woman in all the brilliancy of her beauty and her wit, mistress of herself, who knows and who dares; more beautiful in that and more desirable, and whose choice is free, voluntary, deliberate; to desire her, to love her for what she is, and to suffer because she is not childish naïveté [or] pale innocence, which would be [surprising] in her if it were possible to find them there; to ask her at the same time that she be herself and not be herself. . . . —Oh, this is absurd! . . . If you deceived me, my dear, I should not reproach you for it; on the contrary, I should be grateful to you. Nothing is so legitimate, so human, as to deceive pain. What would become of us if women had not for us the pity of untruth? Lie, my beloved; lie for the sake of charity.

In the end, Dechartre cannot reconcile himself to life with Thérèse, and in a fit of despair he abandons her.

It is, after all, an old story. A sensitive and insecure man, perhaps no longer young, falls in love with a painfully desirable woman, who to his amazement returns his affection. But since he cannot believe that she has chosen, out of all the men in the world, someone as defective as himself, he also has no faith in her fidelity. He is diminished, not exalted, by his love, and he comes to despise himself for his enslavement to a craving that he cannot believe is requited. Soon he lives in the daily expectation of betrayal, an expectation confirmed by his knowledge of the woman's sensual past, which subjects him to morbid imaginings. Yet his suffering makes his desire hypertrophy, turning him into a sort of priapic super-male, and so he grows secretly attached to it. He's like an aging river god in some old Italian fresco, to whom the proximity of a lovely nymph restores a heightened virility. And meanwhile, the woman herself, flattered to inspire such unbridled lust, submits to his vengeful cruelty—more than that, she incites and relishes it. But even this is to no avail: her past, which she has already forgotten, precludes any possibility of a future.

Because it's so difficult to sit down and fill even one page with graceful, readable sentences, any writer who can regularly do so is prone to believe he's in control of what he writes: the enormous discipline of the act itself poses as a deeper self-mastery. Perhaps all writers labor under this illusion; certainly France did when he set out to tell the tale of *The Red Lily*. The novel was his revenge on his former self—the blasé Anatole of 1893, no longer so painfully, so humblingly in love, whipping the pathetic, anxiety-gnawed Anatole of five years earlier. Yet in hindsight we can see that the avenger, however inspired, was venturing a little out of his depth; and we may also doubt whether the notion of a research trip to Italy was really so well advised. Setting off for Florence, Anatole may have believed that he was watching his old self bob off into the wake of a stronger new identity, while Léontine almost certainly hoped that the voyage would restore him to his earlier passion. Yet in Florence itself the pair's search for the picturesque only emphasized Anatole's lack of self-evolved dramatic ideas, while Léontine's tireless accumulation of locations for scenes grew so like a shopping spree that it alarmed and overburdened her partner. It was the classic story of the antique-collecting couple who go out cruising the shops and wind up quarreling about how much they can really cart home.

Can the house of art ever be so directly furnished with the memories of life? To Flaubert and to many of those who came after him, the two realms, though corresponding, were incommensurable. France agreed in theory, yet in practice he returned compulsively to his bundles of letters, his "store of erotic reminiscence." Stores, collections, reliquaries, troves: the bookseller's son left few of their metaphorical implications unexplored, yet a germ of frustration lurked amid his taste for musty hoards. People obsessed with collecting often lack one crucial quality, and that is a sense of proportion. They buy sets of porcelain they can't afford to insure; they try to fit huge sofas into tiny living rooms. And it was so, too, with Anatole France: when he attempted to squeeze himself and Léontine, with all their shapeless biographical lumps, into the framework of a fashionable fiction, he ran into unforeseen problems. It became part of his working method to cull phrases almost directly from their love letters and pack them into *The Red Lily*; though the reader may have already noticed a few examples, Jacques Suffel's edition of the *Lettres intimes* indicates that there are many more to be found. We discover that Anatole's written warning "I will never forgive you anything" crops up as Dechartre's outcry "I can't forgive you what I'd forgive another. . . . I can forgive you nothing!"; and that Léontine's "Don't make your letters so very cruel!" becomes Thérèse's "You're hurting me! . . . I wonder if you're naturally cruel." Sometimes the quotations are practically verbatim. In a letter of late August 1889, Anatole writes to Léontine: "I hallucinate, I'm haunted, I can never envision you *alone*"; and this phrase makes a fairy-queen appearance on the very last page of the novel as Dechartre's "I no longer can envision you alone, I see you always with *the other*."

Now, the incorporation of letters into novels is far from uncommon, and sometimes it works pretty well; one thing Anatole had going for him was the rough congruence between Dechartre's character and his own. There was, of course, the danger that the larger organism would reject the grafts as mere irritants, but this doesn't happen in *The Red Lily*—the problem is the reverse. The snatches of dialogue that France adapted from his and Léontine's letters, for all that they were originally written rather than spoken, seem more, not less, real than the rest of the dialogue, some of which is painfully grandiloquent. On this score Marie-Claire Bancquart, who understands Anatole France better than anyone else, has expressed understandable impatience. She gives short shrift to the way *The Red Lily*'s lovers converse, which, as she notes, isn't even the way a normal person would write. "The grace of your thoughts, your elegant courage, your spiritual pride," Dechartre says, chatting up Thérèse—it's enough to put her to sleep. But such stilted language is the least of what irks Bancquart, who comes very close to scoffing at *The Red Lily* in her life of Anatole France (she accords it a little more sympathy in her splendid Pléiade edition of 1994). Generally Bancquart treats France not as a great artist but as a representative figure, what is called "a man of his time," and doubtless her approach is the right one. But in so doing she often shows more interest in France's turgid novels of ideas or historical extravaganzas than in his eminently readable tales of modern life, which win her approval only rarely and under sufferance. What appalls her in *The Red Lily* is the character of Thérèse or, rather, what France decided would be alluring in a worldly heroine. She is especially irritated by those moments in the novel when Thérèse is portrayed as advanced or liberated because she eats ice cream or French fries with workgirls in the streets. Can it be true, Bancquart indignantly asks, that a leisure-class lady of her type might be found attractive not because of some labor or achievement but merely because she dares snack on fast food outdoors? "Thérèse is a creature not a hundred years old. We're astonished to find her so remote from ourselves," writes Bancquart. Yet for all the brilliance of her reasoning, for all her mastery of social detail, it may be that Bancquart treats *The Red Lily* and its heroine too reductively. Thérèse may not be the modern heroine Bancquart wants, but that doesn't mean she's no heroine at all.

The character of Thérèse cannot be considered apart from France's desire to write a society novel, and it must be conceded that this ambition put him in a corner. The consumers of *romans mondains* were mostly middle-class females, and they wanted nothing but the rank and fashion—they'd have turned a very cold shoulder on France's usual cast of artisans, bohemians, impostors, actresses, and demimondaines. Consequently France ended up demanding that his characters be taken at a level of social valuation that he often couldn't quite handle. Almost everybody had to be fancy or famous; almost every home had to be stately. It wasn't merely that he turned

Jews like Léontine and her father into Gentiles, or that he made Montessuy's château a facsimile of Vaux-le-Vicomte, one of the grandest old piles in France; it was that he consistently glamorized his entire story, even trying to portray political disputes at high governmental levels that he knew nothing about. An opera-hater, France insisted on writing the society novel's compulsory opera scene; is it any wonder that it got out of control? Yet faults of transposition are not the only ones in this novel, because the entire plot is seriously overengineered—full of superfluous machinery. The high-society milieu is neither causally nor morally integral to the story of Thérèse and Dechartre, which, provided that the Thérèse have some money of her own, could actually have been set in any corner of the French panorama. The lovers come packaged in a social situation that doesn't profoundly affect them, and we sense that they're structurally detachable. The *grand monde* may be this tale's backdrop and its mass-market hook, but the tale is really one of erotic fascination. And if we decide to take it not as a failed society novel but as a sort of hybrid of genres—say, one part *roman mondain*, one part *roman d'analyse*, one part comedy of manners—we may still be able to enjoy it.

By much the same token, we cannot require Thérèse to be something she is not. Bancquart seems to think she's a mere phantasm of masculine desire, an innocent object of a man's deranged jealousy, and she summarily clears Thérèse of any wrongdoing; but that's not the sense of the story. There Thérèse is both more guilty and more interesting than Bancquart makes her out to be. The novel's earlier chapters portray her as a woman of pluck, even audacity. She likes to go slumming in the "old streets where misery dwells," she believes that "life is a continual betrayal," and she gives herself "quickly, simply" to her first lover, Le Ménil. When Le Ménil congratulates himself on the secrecy of their affair, she reproves his naïveté with the shrewd comment "Not everything is known, but everything is said." And consistently she trumps Le Ménil in conversation.

When he objects to her forthcoming trip to Florence in the company of the "immoral" Choulette, she replies, "Yes, morality, I know—duty! But duty—it takes the devil to discover it. I can assure you that I do not know where duty is. It's like a young lady's turtle at Joinville. We spent all the evening looking for it under the furniture, and when we had found it, we went to bed." Try reading this aloud, and you'll know what in France's prose sent Proust into ecstasy: these lines, surely, are the purest Bergotte. And it's no accident either that France gives them to Thérèse, because she is in many ways the most willful person in the book. Tiring of Le Ménil, she declares, "I have—impulses! . . . What do you wish? You shouldn't have loved me." Later, in bed with Dechartre, Thérèse "trades love against love with unsuspected fury . . . and dares what she would not have found possible to dare." The woman is by no means a Goody Two-shoes; isn't it possible that her cool dropping of Le Ménil presages what she could, if necessary, do to Dechartre, and that his artist's intuition roughly seizes this uncomfortable truth? There's a scene in the book where the charlatan-prince Albertinelli, returning to Florence from a tour of his country estates, mentions to Thérèse and Dechartre that he has earlier seen Thérèse in the railway station talking to an unknown gentleman. "Forgive, Madame, in a rustic, a certain pretension to knowing something about the world," Albertinelli says to Thérèse. "In the man who was talking to you I recognized a Parisian because he had an English air; and while he affected stiffness, he showed perfect ease and particular vivacity." The unknown gentleman is, of course, Le Ménil, who, having hurried down to Tuscany to win back his former mistress, is about to return to Paris; in this scene, as in much of the book, the writing is simply impeccable, with three acute (and still valid) observations—that French aristocrats perennially dress like English gentlemen, that Italians can always see through such sumptuary codes to the actual nationality of the dresser, and that a man naturally approaches a woman he desires with "particular vivacity"—all elegantly telescoped into one brief speech. Thérèse, of course, is unsettled by the Prince; and she starts, too carelessly, to lie. She says, as Dechartre pretends not to listen, "I have not seen [Le Ménil] for a long time. I was much surprised to meet him at Florence at the moment of his departure." Listening to her duplicities, we remember that remark about the turtle at Joinville.

When all is said, to demand of *The Red Lily* that it accurately reflect social reality or echo common speech seems grudgingly unresponsive. It does have characters that France failed to spank into life, and scenes for which he found no happy turn. Yet here the truism that French fiction comes alive largely through the handling of registers of tone finds an incisive illustration: the novel is all ironic pose and conscious verbal choreography. Aware that such stories rely on a repertory of romancer's conventions, Anatole France plays the old Gallic game, winking mischievously at his public as he winds up the clockwork of a tale of doomed desire. If a portion of the dialogue is adapted from his correspondence with Léontine, the bulk of the narrative wordplay is derived from wholly different quarters, notably from contemporary tendencies in verse; certain passages have a delicate tartness—what Proust called "hoarseness" or "dissonance"—that the age came to crave and that passed into the style of many an Edwardian writer in English. Jean-Jacques Brousson, who became the secretary of France's old age and wrote several treacherous memoirs of the not-so-*cher maître*, offers a wicked account of France's advice on how to spin out good prose. The with-it writer, Brousson has France say, should look for occasions to use negative epithets (like "unbetrayed"), he should try to jangle two ill-assorted words together (as in "eyes worn by science and voluptuousness"), and he should never overlook an occasion to cut a paragraph into its component units with a pair of scissors and paste it back together in the most *outré* fashion. It's hard to guess the accuracy of Brousson's sketch of France the prose robot, but such devices do turn up often in *The Red Lily*. Entire scenes are engulfed in a fey comicality that barely nods at the evolving story; the largely nonrealistic plot and dialogue toy with French fiction's standing requirements, of which the most firmly established, as Henry James once pointed out, was the infraction of the seventh commandment. No French novelist of this period ever forgot that the only really interesting kind of play, from the reader's point of view, was byplay; this was as true in 1893 as it had been in 1833, when the Baroness Dudevant, better known as George Sand, ran away to Venice with Alfred de Musset.

With the recollection of these two names, we stumble on a fertile coincidence. Remember that we are now well into the Belle Epoque: *The Red Lily* appears, as we've seen, in the summer of 1894, and a little over two years later, in November 1896, for the first time and after much bickering of interested parties, a substantial portion of the Sand–Musset correspondence is published, in the *Revue de Paris*. The coincidence, of course, is only apparent. As it happens, there were certain material links between these two events—the *Revue*'s editors were not unknown to France—but of far greater moment is the general temper of the times. The fin-de-siècle seductress, so menacing to male self-esteem, has made her debut; scary and sexy at the same time, perhaps a revelation of the true nature of woman, she mesmerizes the public and has become an eminently marketable commodity. In this climate, the acquisition of the Sand–Musset correspondence would have constituted a coup for any literary magazine.

What apparently passed unnoticed, however, and what has continued unnoticed to our day, was the thematic kinship of the tale embodied in that exchange with the one recounted in *The Red Lily*. It is true of course that the first is real and the second fictional, but both stir the same heady brew. Both take place in Italy; both involve a married lady of self-reliant disposition and independent means who falls in love with an unmarried gentleman; both call into question the sexual morality of the lady, not the gent; and both depend on a tiny inadvertency—George's empty teacup, Thérèse's posted letter—to serve as the mainspring of a vicious mental mechanism. More generally, the idea, given currency by Benjamin Constant, that two opposed feelings can run along side by side in the same person is offhandedly enlisted in the Sand–Musset letters and consciously stressed in *The Red Lily*, where the couple's mutual and self-inflicted tortures are portrayed as part and parcel of love. But *The Red Lily* takes matters further than George and Alfred had cared, or dared, to do. Whereas they had giddily forsworn all proprietary rights, Anatole France insinuates that it is only through jealousy that love becomes, properly speaking, passionate; the passion springs from the imagination of betrayal. Male jealousy, a coursing, Darwinian force, is virtually written in the blood: "We are all so old when we are born." This atavistic need of sexual ownership explains why Dechartre perversely rejoices in his own jealous feelings; and it may also explain why he welcomes, with what Proust would have called "hysterical satisfaction," the evidence of Thérèse's lying.

But if there is a rough correspondence between Alfred de Musset and the fictional Jacques Dechartre, their situations are dissimilar in one crucial respect: Musset had every reason to be jealous, whereas Dechartre, by all sensible standards, has no reason at all. Whereas Alfred had been wounded by what George had *done*, Anatole was tormented by what Léontine *was*—an independent woman who could not be acquired. And it is just here that Proust, of whose great novel certain passages by France seem flashing premonitions, throws a backward light on his predecessor. Always attracted to medical metaphors (his father was a physician and an eminent epidemiologist), Proust insists that jealousy is not only a feeling but also an appetite, a strangely extrinsic appetite of the sort that might belong to an invading virus. That is why jealousy "rejoices" at evidence of betrayal: it is as though this emotion had an "independent existence, fiercely egotistical, [and] gluttonous of every thing that would feed its vitality," even to the cost of the one who nurses it. The fervor springs spontaneously from its own loins. Like a parasite within a host, it battens, Proust tells us, on the host's lifeblood; and no more appropriate metaphor could be found for Dechartre's jealousy of Thérèse, or for Anatole's of Léontine. If it is a commonplace of the psychology of love in nineteenth-century France to assert that one cannot know the beloved, that we are all sunken ships to one another, still there is something new in *The Red Lily*, something that foretells the Proustian discovery that we can regain the past only through an act of relinquishment. Jealousy of another's past is really existential jealousy—a sort of rage against the freedom of some-one we love to have emotions we shall never divine.

5

THE UNSEEN LEAF

SOMETIME LATE IN THE spring of 1890, after the success of his revue at the Pouquets', Gaston de Caillavet pressed into Jeanne Pouquet's hand a copy of George Sand's epistolary novel *Mademoiselle la Quintinie.* This book is in some measure an anticlerical tract: giving vent to her exasperation with the French Church hierarchy, Sand weaves a tale in which a devout Catholic girl is courted by a freethinker who succeeds in converting her to his views. The basic dramatic idea, which was derived from the eighteenth-century equation of secularism and sex appeal, must have tickled Gaston's vanity: unbaptized, with no religious convictions, he probably felt that Jeanne's interest would be piqued by the spectacle of a lover marching to a different moral code. He could not have been more mistaken. She began reading the novel, underlined a few sentences, and then left off, confiding to her diary that the thing was "the opposite, almost to a word, of everything I believe and care for in the way of religion. . . . Being deeply fond of [Gaston], I cannot read such a book without sorrow, since it only reveals the abyss between us." The next day she showed her diary to Gaston, who suddenly perceived that religion—or, rather, Jeanne's attachment to the formalistic Catholicism of her girlhood—might soon defeat all his hopes. "You are kind and sweet," he told her, "but it is your destiny to make people suffer."

The Pouquet family was patriotic, paternalistic, and provincial in the manner of those French families who maintain their local allegiances and peculiarities even after moving to Paris. Their large but ill-heated and ill-lighted residence in the rue Miromesnil, not far from the doors of three dauntingly prominent hostesses, Madame de Chevigné, Madame Straus, and the venerable Madame de Beaulaincourt, who occasionally received the ex-Empress Eugénie and Princesse Mathilde, flaunted a grand-bourgeois comfort that somehow lacked the final polish: neither the Pouquets' tastes nor their accomplishments were a patch on those of the Arman de Caillavets. The father was a right-wing Catholic stockbroker who was mad for hunting and the outdoors but had no discernible cultural interests; the mother, as far as one can make out, lived for and through her children, particularly her daughter. Mme Pouquet prided herself on her prophetic powers, and on meeting Gaston she had seen, as in a sudden illumination, her little girl on her way up the aisle. Money played a role in this vision, since Gaston was Léontine's only heir, but Mme Pouquet also rather fancied the boy, in a matronlike way. She was amused by his habit of poking fun at people, of finding them absurd while forgiving them for it: he was like one of those music-hall comics who continually fling asides at the crowd. She kept her eye on Gaston and Jeanne, observing their every gesture and glance, and only a few weeks after registering their mutual infatuation, she approached the young man with a brazenness that today seems bizarre and perhaps was so even then: on behalf of her daughter, she wrote him a veiled declaration of love. "I'm afraid I feel frightfully careless in condoning, and sometimes even arranging, the little meetings of you two," Mme Pouquet confided to Gaston. "If, with my clairvoyance, I were to hold my tongue, I might one day have bitter regrets." Like a procuress out of some old libertine novel, she begged Gaston to say nothing aloud at their next encounter, but to squeeze her hand if he had taken her point; and apparently he complied, for a clandestine betrothal was soon concluded. It was agreed that the wedding would be held after a lapse of two or three years; Jeanne was thrilled by this informal pact; but the bluff, overworked M. Pouquet, who was not clairvoyant, was left in the dark.

Both Mme Pouquet and her daughter knew that the match was far from a shoo-in. There were some technical, operetta-style problems, in particular the prior claim of a certain tedious cousin, but most of all they worried about the difficulties of allying two such very different houses, one conservative and Catholic, the other republican and freethinking. What would M. Pouquet think? And that was why the George Sand novel —or, rather, Gaston's approval of it—was causing Jeanne such grief. Unaware that Gaston was a stranger to the font, Jeanne wanted to induce him to receive his First Communion, which, as she'd gathered from whisperings out at the lawn-tennis courts in Neuilly, he had not been instructed to do. Failing this—failing his conventionalization in all respects—the wisest course was to conceal the marriage project from her father; and it was here that Gaston's friend Marcel had a useful bit part to play.

Lately Marcel, too, had been lavishing attentions on Jeanne, whose beauty, as he would say in later years, put him in mind of a "spring of clear water." On learning in August that she and her mother were about to make a trip to Orléans, where he was serving, he offered to procure them accommodations, redecorated at his own expense, in the town's best hotel. Some-body, presumably Mme Pouquet, made short work of this rash proposal, but, as Jeanne reported to Gaston in a letter,

> Marcel spends the whole day [at our apartment] and no-body takes the least exception to it. I chatted with him at length last Monday. He is decidedly an odd boy . . . who

often scares me with his thoughts about us. If he really believes everything that he tells me, we won't have much to enlighten him about in two years' time. I hope everything he says is mere guesswork, floated in an offhand tone to see what sort of mug I put on. I'm strong enough now not to have anything to fear from this little game . . . but often I wonder, when I see how certain he is about us, if he really doesn't know something. . . . I'm afraid and I go all pale. . . . On Monday somebody mentioned your name, and he turned toward me imperceptibly and stared at me with such a curious expression that I looked away because I felt so uneasy. I'm afraid that you aren't cautious enough with him. Please do me a favor, *put on a big show of indifference toward me*, don't look all indignant when he says things to me that you don't like, etc., etc. I don't much trust your friend Marcel, and I'm always afraid that he'll blurt out something unfortunate in front of other people. He's certain that you're going to marry me, so certain that he said when we parted, "I'm afraid I've overstayed my welcome. Don't tell Gaston, it might upset him and then he'd forbid me to see you."

So if Marcel was carrying a torch for Jeanne, he had also become her decoy or cover: by inviting him to her home, by being seen with him at the tennis courts or in the Parc Monceau, she was using him to divert her father's gaze from her real beau. There had been some question of her enlisting another friend for this role, the engineer's son René Lévi-Alvarès, who, despite the "little black mark" of his unfortunate racial origin, had charmed M. Pouquet, but as long as an "Israelite" had to be enlisted—and many of the Pouquets' newer friends had this peculiarity—Marcel, who was half-Jewish, would do better than anyone else, because he was so often at Gaston's side. And so it was that Marcel found himself pinned in a very uncomfortable position. He knew of Gaston's feelings for Jeanne and guessed that the pair were "semi-betrothed," yet his coltish impulses went to his head, preventing him from grasping his place in her stratagem. By degrees he grew achingly obsessed with her, yet decades later he would recall that he had refused to "permit himself the slightest shred of hope."

Jeanne was tallish, with high cheekbones and blue eyes. She took singing lessons and played the harmonium for her family's country church in Périgord; her mother called her "my little lark." A natural performer, always up for an evening at the Comédie-Française, Jeanne might have trained for the theater if the customs of her class had permitted such ambitions. But her talents were imprisoned in her parents' drawing room, and her beauty, too, was already at its fullest, like an April torrent that will soon dry up: there was every reason to expect that marriage and a succession of pregnancies would blight her looks as surely as they would stifle her artistic aspirations. Less effusive than her mother, physically frail, chronically ill dressed despite her svelte figure, fiercely self-critical, and suspicious of servants—"What a plague is that race of flunkies!" she scrawled in her diary at this period—Jeanne was torn by contradictory forces. Though hooked on attention, she was also morbidly secretive and convinced, like many adolescent girls, of her peers' implacable envy. She felt that to disclose any of her feelings might invite unforeseen aggression, and her days were spiced with the fear that her diary might fall at any moment into treacherous hands.

If, today, you untie the ribbons binding Jeanne's surviving letters or open the faded green copybooks containing her intimate journal, you at once notice her habit of swinging back and forth between two handwritings. One is an angular, over-disciplined, schoolgirl hand, while the other is a rounder, much wilder hand, often produced by lead pencil; and this polarity expresses a split-mindedness of which she is perfectly aware. Her summer diary of 1890 is wholly in the schoolgirl hand: its chief subject is the inadvertent suffering she feels she has been causing Gaston. It is Gaston whom she rhetorically addresses as she struggles to explain that there are really two Jeannes, the one false, the other genuine:

I've changed a lot in the past 7 months. I am still the excessive little person, passionate and somewhat mad, of last year, but is it because I've gone out a bit this year and got to know the world or is it for some other reason? that I've become serious and above all that I've managed to acquire a large measure of self-control. . . . It is to honor the promise I made you, my poor G., that I straightaway begin to set down my thoughts. One day perhaps I'll be able to show them to you, and on that day you will no longer curse my ironic coldness. You have begun to know my character but you still know nothing of my heart, and that ignorance is what causes your cruel suffering! You'll be amazed to see how much the heart of a little girl, even of a laughing, silly little girl, can conceal in the way of tenderness. I have often been reproached with not having a feminine nature, with not being romantic, with not being tender; this is just what dismays my beloved mother . . . [but] since these leaves are intimate confidences I'm going to admit to you that such reproaches are unjust and ill founded on a simple appearance. I feel everything very keenly, even too keenly, and it's to dissimulate this excess in my sentiments that I affect to be what I am not. I am also ashamed of my impressions, so strong are they, and I prefer to be taken for a "fin de siècle" girl than for the ridiculously passionate little person who is now delivering her confession. Nobody in the world suspects it, not even Mamma with whom however I so often talk. With her a sort of stupid timidity prevents me from parting the veil that covers my heart. There are in me two persons so distinct that I never have any trouble shifting them about. The social one you know, she can control herself, she's gay, she laughs, she sings, she is exuberant etc. etc. the other, the real one does not resemble her. I find it unbelievably hard to contain her and make her accept the yoke of the other. For several months she has found it harder than ever to accept domination. Terrible fears come over her before a world so cruel, so wicked, before life, before everything. . . . How I would blush dear Lord, if anyone found these pages and could see just how mad I am! If I allowed myself to be guided by the "real me" I'd rave on like this until tomorrow.

"Mad" is a word that Jeanne often uses to describe herself in her diary and letters. It refers not only to her vestigial childishness (in the sense of "silly") but also to emotions ranging from inadmissible erotic longings to the mere wish to be frank about a painful wound or another person's devious behavior. As a marriageable, upper-class girl of good tone and regular habits, Jeanne doesn't feel she should say what she thinks; when her girl friends or cousins try to thwart her desires, and this seems to happen all the time, she sees no point in "unmasking their game" but fills her diary with invective. There's an air of ill-concealed visibility about her: she's like a woman always worried that her slip might be showing. Her attempts at composure, at a self-control so repressive that it seems a planing down of all feeling to some flat, socially prescribed level, seldom succeed for long, and very early a word appears in her letters that will never entirely desert them—the word "sedative." Over and over Jeanne is on the verge of tears, about to break down, in need of a day's "repose," and over and over we find her doctor or her disconsolate mother proposing to sedate her.

One reason this jumpy young girl craves Marcel's company is to help her keep tabs on Gaston. During the summer, when Gaston's mother or maternal relatives lure him away to various country houses, spas, and beach resorts, the danger arises that he'll fall for somebody else. "If at least I could see Proust today I'd know what you're up to," Jeanne notes in her diary on July 20. "I've got to have plenty of faith in you not to be anxious about your stay by the seaside. If you're going to fall in love with some fresh-faced beauty—if Marie de W. intends taking advantage of my absence to bring up all the light artillery of her coquetry, and if you succumb to this formidable assault . . ."—alarmed by her own thoughts, Jeanne breaks off; but the following day she returns to her diary to unburden herself of the spite she feels toward the many female "vipers" who daily contrive her ruin.

Marcel continued to frequent the Pouquet establishment, and occasionally to bring news of Gaston. But to have this uniformed *cavalier servente* dancing attendance upon her was very cold comfort for Jeanne, who worried that Gaston might give her the brush. "You vex me no end with that little M.!" she complained to her secret fiancé.

> If you want to make me happy you won't tease me any-more about that little cardboard officer. Before I got to know you* he was very much in love with your humble servant but I made him understand that he bored me. You see that I do not find him as perfect as you seem to believe I do.

Lovers can seldom conceal their feelings, and the secrecy of Jeanne and Gaston's romance began to wear thin. One day as Léontine was going over her bills from the Bon Marché, she noticed an invoice for some unfamiliar items. "Just who, may I ask," she demanded of her son, "is this [woman] to whom I have the honor of purveying silk stockings and gloves?" So Léontine, herself well versed in deception, knew; and one may doubt whether M. Pouquet was really so blind as to what was going forward under his nose. It is curious that in her attempt to put her father off the scent of Gaston, who was an unbeliever, an artistic type, and Jewish on his mother's side, Jeanne chose to be seen with Marcel, who was an unbeliever, an artistic type, and Jewish on his mother's side. The great mystery was

---

* Jeanne may be mistaken here. The order in which Jeanne, Gaston, and Marcel got to know one another is not clear.

perhaps more imagined than real, offering both a flirty duenna rôle to the otherwise idle Mme Pouquet and the illusion of invisibility to her self-conscious daughter.

By the summer of 1890, Jeanne and Gaston were fairly drowning in each other: she implored him to review her outfits, to redefine her tastes, to give her some good books to read. When Gaston went away to Capian and Jeanne to her family's château of Essendérias in Périgord, he sent her an engagement ring which winked so noticeably that she returned it in favor of a more modest stone. The marriage project thrilled her but made her nervous. Incessantly fussing, she drank milk to lighten her southern complexion, tinkered with her dresses and hair, wondered if she should pierce her ears. She wanted Gaston to visit her at the family château, but only if accompanied by a male decoy, and she implored him to move heaven and earth to lay hands on a suitable friend. Though her father had taken a shine to René Lévi-Alvarès, she insisted that Proust made a better escort. Gaston replied in guarded tones: Marcel had just written an "impenetrable" letter, and if, as seemed likely, he couldn't or wouldn't leave his regiment, René would take his place and arrive by early October. "My dearest," Jeanne wrote back, ". . . can't you win over that little boobie Proust? Mamma's going to write him—and yourself, too—an official letter; if necessary, you can show it to your mother. Our situation is so extraordinary . . . ! A real novel . . . but not a fin-de-siècle novel—not at all!" And even as she wrote, her mother was plying Gaston with honeyed words. "It is good, fine, and strange, this great tenderness which will soon grow between us," she told him, still greatly impressed with her own sibylline faculties. Yet these faculties failed to impress Léontine, who harbored grave reservations concerning the wisdom of uniting two such immature young people. Gaston had recently broken down and shared his "secret" with her, and Léontine had given him her blessing only on the condition that he was truly in love and proceeded with all due caution.

By late September, Gaston was free to visit Jeanne. But Marcel had never turned up at Capian, so Gaston arrived at the Pouquets' château with René in his place and Jeanne was outraged. "I'm furious against Proust, against his family who won't let him come, and against that commanding officer of his who will give him only a short leave," she lamented. Jeanne spoke of Marcel with ever-increasing harshness, but this may have been for tactical reasons: Gaston was getting somewhat jealous of the brilliant boy with the beautiful manners, and she didn't want his jealousy to get out of hand. To Gaston and to Jeanne, Marcel was unplaceable in the deeper scheme of things: though he didn't seem to desire women very strongly, he was plainly attracted to them emotionally and aesthetically. The young people's ignorance or denial of Marcel's sexuality is apparent in a letter that Jeanne wrote at summer's end, after she and her mother had returned to Paris. Passing through Orléans on their way north, they had rented a landau for a country drive and invited Marcel to join them. "I've seen Proust!" Jeanne wrote to Gaston.

He announced his desire, as soon as he gets out of his regiment, to go to some wild, picturesque, and deserted seashore, where he won't have to worry about any indiscreet friends troubling his reveries. I do think, however, that a discreet girlfriend would only add to the charms of this melancholy solitude, as long as she had real blond hair and could be an agreeable third party between the poetical Marcel P. and Mother Nature. Is this supposition an atrocious calumny? . . . After several more minutes' worth of digressions, he quitted us with exquisite phrases, in which, if I understood them, he prostrated himself at the feet of the mamma and groveled at those of the daughter. He's agreeably besotted.

A few months later, toward the end of 1890, Marcel was discharged from the army and returned to Paris. He started showing up regularly at the weekly *soirées dansantes* that Mme Pouquet held for Jeanne, and at least once he was invited to tea. Arriving several hours early, he was offered a chair in the linen room by Jeanne's former nanny Fifine, now the Pouquets' housekeeper and the only domestic whom Jeanne didn't despise; doubtless the ever-voluble Marcel drew Fifine out, as was his custom with household help, and made careful mental notes as to her speech patterns and social attitudes. He also asked her to purloin a photograph of Jeanne for him, and when Fifine indignantly refused, he proceeded to make a series of surreptitious overtures to Jeanne's family, her friends, even her relatives in Périgord, all of whom proved unable to oblige. Frustrated, he began to circulate photos of himself among Jeanne's friends in hopes of starting an all-around exchange that would eventually shake out a picture, but to no avail.

When spring came and the weather improved, Marcel often joined Jeanne and Gaston and some other friends out at the Neuilly tennis courts, which were situated off the boulevard Bineau; though his asthma didn't allow him to play, he took charge of the refreshments and chatted off court with a bevy of girls. Céleste Albaret, the handsome young woman from the Auvergne who in 1913 or '14 became Marcel's housekeeper, recalled in *Monsieur Proust*, her sometimes hazy memoir of 1973, that Marcel had once told her that he'd been as deeply in love with Jeanne

> as it was humanly possible to be. . . . She had magnificent blond hair. . . . I couldn't sleep because of her. When we went to play tennis in the mornings, I'd leave home with provisions, little cakes and sandwiches of every flavor and color. I didn't know what to do to please her, I bought her flowers, presents—I gave myself such pains! . . . When I knew I was going to see her, I didn't walk—I ran! I liked to watch her blond tresses fly when she played tennis.

Long afterward, Jeanne would recall that

> sometimes a tennis ball fell into [Marcel's] circle of conver-
> sation, making the glasses and the misses jump. Marcel al-
> ways accused the players of having shot it there . . . "for
> no reason," but perhaps there was a reason . . . namely
> Marcel's charm, the tenderness he gave and elicited, which
> often annoyed his male companions.

One assumes in one's thirst for a neatly rounded narrative
that what Jeanne did not bring to Marcel she brought to Gaston, and perhaps, at the outset, she did. Yet signs of a fatal
dissension came early, and one of those signs was especially
telling. Scarcely had Gaston left the Pouquets' house in Périgord in the autumn of 1890 when he got a note from Jeanne
asking why he had begun to refer to Capian by its oenological
denomination of "Caillavet." "I'm going to admit to you under
my breath," she said, "that I don't much care for the name,
and if you want to make me happy when I become your wife,
we'll rectify it." At this Gaston froze. The place wasn't his yet,
much less hers, and here she was telling him what to call it.
"I keenly, *very keenly* desire to know the source of these reflections concerning our family property," he wrote back, "because I'm convinced that someone else is behind them." He
was patronizing her, of course, but he was right: several of
Jeanne's girl friends had shared with her their thoughts concerning the suitability of such a tiny domain, an acreage not
even listed in the directory of Gironde estates, bearing the dubious appellation "Château Caillavet." Gaston might have
pointed out that Capian, or "Château Caillavet," or whatever
the devil one wanted to call it, was merely his father's harmless
avocation, but instead he had rounded on Jeanne; and stung
to the quick, she struck back. "Wicked, wicked," her next letter
railed,

if you were beside me on this big sofa where all alone I sit wretchedly weeping I'd beat you and bite you. You say I'm not sincere, well you'll see if my love isn't sincere. You think I'm cold! Very well then, I'll throw away my little-girl mask, which I was only keeping on a little while longer so as not to shock you, and you'll see what I'm like, so much the worse oh so much the worse for you! I'll come to you and scream out my love like some poor madwoman!

This lovers' spat is unusual in the girl's intense and premature concern about property—the pair were to wed only two and a half years later. It seems that to be an adult, for the sixteen-year-old amateur actress, is to strut in borrowed feathers—to talk knowingly about houses and titles and to command a smirky, superior tone ("I don't much care for the name"). When Gaston bats her demands aside, she reels in humiliation and reaches for her mask of impossible innocence, while nearby, always, we sense the shadow of her mother.

At this time Mme Pouquet was thirty-seven years old, dripping with jewelry, plump, pretty. It does not seem that she had ever loved her husband, though she had probably honored and obeyed him. But now that was changing, and changing fast. Her clandestine maneuvers began to weigh on her conscience, which she tried to salve with long, exalted, self-exculpatory letters to Gaston. Though her husband was no bigot, Mme Pouquet explained, he tended to opt for the tried-and-true; he continued to favor the suit of Jeanne's cousin, who was not only a Catholic but rich into the bargain, and he would resent any betrayal of conservative tradition, having served—this Mme Pouquet disclosed with particular solemnity—in the Pontifical Zouaves during the Franco-Prussian War. It is hard to imagine Gaston reacting to the name of this corps with anything but a smile, but then he probably read all Mme Pouquet's letters with amused indulgence. Her handwriting wasn't as wayward as her daughter's, but some of her capitals, especially the *B*'s, ran to the flamboyant, and she could drift into eyebrow-raising confidences. "I hardly slept a wink last night," she wrote Gaston one morning, "and it's all your fault." Though the good lady was trying sincerely to be helpful, her penchant for secrecy had clouded her vision and produced uncontrollable results. One of these was Mme Pouquet's meddlesome intimacy with her daughter's fiancé; another was the suppression of Jeanne's right to speak freely with her father. Jeanne was sixteen years old, an awkward age; her forfeiture of moral independence only compounded the self-contempt engendered by her devious behavior. As time went by, she felt more and more guilty, and the guilt crept into her letters to Gaston. She had, she told him, a "deplorable character"; she believed that only "the whip, the whip" could correct her vicious impulses. She felt "anguish" or "vague sadness" that often kept her from sleeping at night; and one day a tremor in her hand prevented her from writing. Though she longed for an openhearted chat with her father, he seemed too stiff, too distant, to address. "Papa absolutely paralyzes me," she told Gaston.

Throughout most of 1891, the Pouquet home is the scene of intensely dramatic mother-daughter quarrels. Both are hot-blooded southerners, born actresses, what the age would have called "hysterics." The distraught Mme Pouquet writes to Gaston that

> this mystery with regard to Jeanne's father, which she can no longer bear, has become an obsession, [about which] she won't allow me to console her. . . . And then the religious question terrorizes her and throws her into despair. . . . She blames me at present and puts on that little glacial look of hers, which really hurts. . . . I feel such pain, my dear Gaston. . . . With her I am absolutely in the wrong. . . . I

think I understand, alas! (because that's the way people are)
. . . that she holds me responsible for her current suffering.
. . . She reproaches herself terribly for all these hidden
things.

By October 1891, Jeanne is in the throes of what Mme Pouquet calls a "crisis of spleen" and has shamefacedly confessed
to her mother that she feels she's "behaving as badly toward
Papa as a wife betraying her husband"—a covert accusation.
And indeed Mme Pouquet's letters of this period do show a
slippage into frank disloyalty. Writing to Gaston, she refers
jokingly to her husband as "the terrible Papa"; she instructs
Fifine to pick up Gaston's letters and keep them out of M.
Pouquet's hands; and she talks to Gaston about Jeanne with a
superiority verging on scorn: "There's still a lot of the baby in
her despite her little pretensions to being a grownup . . . indeed, there's a lot of the badly spoiled baby." To what degree
was Mme Pouquet's prophecy of Jeanne's march to the altar
an attempt to live her daughter's life for her? Jeanne, in her
writings, never touched on this topic, but she left an inadvertent clue to her feelings. At some point in the course of her
later life, while rereading a letter from her mother, she ran a
blue pencil so violently under one of those phrases about div-
ination and destiny that she made a rent in the paper.

The Pouquet household was not alone in its distress. As
Marcel redoubled his attentions to Jeanne, Gaston's mind grew
overcast. All this fawning, this sweet talk, this begging for a
portrait photo of her—what sort of young man would permit
himself such liberties with a friend's intended? "He is mad,"
Gaston told Jeanne. "No, merely a little absurd, chimerical,"
she later remembered answering. "And in love," Gaston re-
torted. "Hardly—Marcel is not in love with me." And she
proceeded to explain how Marcel always overdid everything,
how he always applied the most florid language to the mildest,
most innocuous affections, reminding Gaston that he himself

had received such tender letters from Marcel that he had felt ridiculous and had torn them up. Marcel, she said, knew nothing about girls—he had no sisters or female cousins—and he was entirely ignorant of the rules of proper conduct toward young ladies. He was merely expressing his friendship, and there was no reason for Gaston to get hot under the collar. Yet when Marcel, a while later, did manage to secure a photograph of a different girl, a courtesan with whom he'd struck up an acquaintanceship—this was the Laure Hayman who would impart some of her traits to the character Odette de Crécy in *Swann's Way*—Jeanne was hurt and shocked to be supplanted by another person, a conspicuous beauty who happened, infuriatingly, to resemble her. And discovering that Laure had given Marcel a book bound in the silk of one of her stockings, Jeanne protested the "indecency" of the gift and refused briefly to talk to Marcel, with the consequence that Gaston refused briefly to talk to her.

"A light cloud, an imperceptible shadow"—these were the terms Jeanne used to describe such sulks in her memoir *Quelques Lettres de Marcel Proust*; but that was almost forty years after the fact. Time, like a prism, had a way of refracting all Jeanne's perceptions, and if, today, you try to put yourself in her place, or in Marcel's, mulling over their youthful anguish, strolling by their old haunts (such as Léontine's townhouse, until recently the Paris office of BankAmerica/Chicago), or the Temple of Love in the Parc Monceau (now a public toilette), it is hard to get a grasp of what they really felt. Did Marcel actually suffer as much as he claimed? And was Jeanne at all aware of his suffering? Most probably she wasn't—Jeanne lacked her mother's mind-reading powers—but it is unlikely that she would have spent so much time with him if his attentions hadn't flattered her female pride. In her memoir Jeanne belatedly claimed to have perceived, almost to have discovered, his genius, but her actual letters of 1890–91 tell another story, and as late as 1912, on the eve of the publication in *Le Figaro* of a segment of *Swann's Way*, the still-wounded Marcel sent her a letter saying that she would find in this narrative "something of the emotion that I felt [on those days] when I wondered if you would be at the tennis courts. But what's the point of remembering things which you took the absurd and unkind decision to pretend that you'd never noticed." A letter Jeanne wrote to her daughter as late as November 1947 does suggest an abiding ambivalence toward Proust:

> I fume when I remember that in a stupid row with your father I stupidly threw on the fire (in the coke-burning grate in my room . . . remember?) a great many letters. . . . There were in this bundle of letters infinite treatments of the "love" (?) that Marcel claimed to feel for me. His analysis of it would have graced *Time Regained*. He returned to it with a curious stubbornness in almost all his letters. It was precisely these constant allusions that exasperated your father. Admit that being jealous of Marcel, a notorious pansy . . . was the essence of absurdity.

It seems, then, that Jeanne consigned to the flames a suite of love letters in the grand manner by the young Proust. As an elderly woman she regrets her old coolness toward him, and she tries to dodge the accusation of unkindness on the grounds that he was, after all, a homosexual. She implicitly portrays the little Jeanne of the early nineties as a wised-up young lady who knew exactly who and what Marcel was; yet her testimony is belied by her own letters of 1890, especially the one to Gaston in which she suggested that Marcel, who was planning a seaside vacation, would be happier in the company of a pretty girl, preferably an authentic blonde like herself. The truth seems to be that Jeanne's attitude toward Marcel during that distant summer whiled away at the Neuilly tennis courts, that summer of rallies and persiflage, consisted in the most commonplace sentiment known to man, which is the conviction that what you feel for another person that person must also feel for you. Jeanne was unmoved by Marcel, so Marcel had to be unmoved by Jeanne.

AFTER HIS FALLING OUT with Gaston over Jeanne, Marcel distanced himself from the entire Caillavet clan, including Anatole. It was perhaps the first of his many self-distancings, and Jeanne suspected that it had as much to do with his social ambitions as with any strains he had felt with the denizens of 12, avenue Hoche. On this score she may have been right. By now Marcel had begun his penetration of the Faubourg Saint-Germain, a quest inspired less by conventional snobbery than by his belief that high society afforded a privileged post of observation. France is a very centralized society, and this was a very French idea: like a walker in one of Le Nôtre's great parks, he felt that a prospect of the whole layout could be gained only from certain specific and elevated vantage points. This impression was purely subjective, a half-truth of his sensibility, but it had the unintended (if not wholly unwelcome) consequence of separating him from his old friends, whom he merely caught sight of now and again, in the rare encounters afforded by his restless and ever-renewed climb. And so his relations with them became by degrees a matter of mere glimpses. He glimpsed Léontine trying to ensure a positive reception for *The Red Lily*, and he tried to help her out. He glimpsed Jeanne and Gaston now and again at the salon of Madeleine Lemaire, and somewhat later, during a reading at Madame Lemaire's of his prose cycle "Portraits de peintres," he caught sight of Anatole France amid the listeners. He continued to admire France (though progressively less), and it may be that France, who had held a nominal position for over a decade as assistant at the Senate library in the Palais du Luxembourg, played some role in Marcel's application, in May 1895, for a similar post at the Bibliothèque Mazarine (where, some fifty years earlier, Sainte-Beuve had also worked). During the Dreyfus Affair, Marcel, Anatole, and Léontine took the side of the unhappy captain; but Marcel by and large moved in different circles now, and when he tried to get France to write a preface for his first book, he found that he needed to call in all his chits with Léontine, and that the lines that Monsieur France eventually disgorged were even more equivocal than was usual with that master of the ambivalent epithet. Of all the avenue Hoche set, it was always Léontine who most warmly supported Marcel, urging him never to throw out anything he wrote, and after his duel with Jean Lorrain, the critic who had insinuated, viciously and accurately, that Marcel was a homosexual, she sent him a note of rejoicing: "My dearest Marcel . . . I take you to my heart for being so brave and coming back to us safe and sound from your adventure."

Though Marcel soon grew notorious for his contradictory views on the pleasures and indentures of friendship, his relations with Gaston seem a special and melancholy case. With Gaston he was evasive, almost aloof. When it came time for Gaston and Jeanne to marry, the groom invited Marcel to be his best man, but Marcel declined, on the grounds of his feeling for the bride. Though Jeanne herself refused to accept this emotion as genuine or deep, she would later remember that

for two years already it had filled [Marcel's] letters to Gaston with a theme that had a thousand delicate and absurd variations; it set them at odds, then helped to bring them back together, and in the end it served as a pretext for Marcel to quit a milieu that no longer held for him the charm of the unknown. A great curiosity tormented him. . . . Shortly after our marriage, when we invited him to dinner, he answered, "How, Madame, can you invite me to your house! If you have not understood that I cannot come, you will be equally unable to understand the grounds for my refusal." And he continued to refuse for fifteen years.

Today the name Gaston de Caillavet is known only to older French theatrical people—he figures marginally in the big Proust biographies—but within a few years he was to become one of the most famous writers in Paris, far more famous than Proust himself, who found a measure of worldly success only after World War I. Together with his collaborator, Robert de Flers, Gaston was to ply his trade as a popular "digestive" author, a creator of bubbly middlebrow comedies, one of which, *Le Roi* (to which Emmanuel Arène also contributed), ran for several straight seasons. Despite Marcel's delight at Gaston's success—which was certainly too shallow, in his eyes, to inspire any real envy—those stuffy old theaters were infernos for asthma sufferers, so it was only from a distance that he watched Gaston's rise, and only for special occasions, such as his old friend's dramatization of *The Red Lily*, that he dragged himself, full of sentimental memories of the amateur productions in the rue Miromesnil, to the Variété or the Vaudeville, where he apprehensively seated himself in a carefully selected box. When Gaston, in his turn, fought a duel with a detractor—a fiercer contest than Marcel's, which ended with both duelists slightly gored—Marcel sent him a note telling him how much he had admired his bravery. "Along with my parents' sincere compliments for what you have done," he ventured to add, "please convey to your wife the humble respects of her old admirer."

THE WORLD KNEW LITTLE about Jeanne Pouquet until the rediscovery of her private papers. One thing that it did know, however, was that she had served as a "model" for the character Gilberte Swann in *Remembrance of Things Past*. As readers of Proust will recall, Gilberte is the Narrator's first love, for whom he long harbors a frustrated affection; though she soon evolves into someone quite unlike Jeanne, her physical appearance, disdainful manner, and love of playacting owe much to Gaston's fiancée. "Gilberte's braids seemed to me a matchless work of art," Proust has the Narrator write of the exquisite young girl.

> For a strand, however infinitely small, what celestial herbal would I not have chosen as a reliquary. But despairing of being able to obtain a real lock of those plaits, if only I had been able to possess a photograph of them! . . . To acquire one, I made with the friends of Swann and even with photographers base deeds which failed to procure me what I wanted, but bound me forever with very wearisome people.

The daughter of Charles Swann, a wealthy neighbor in the Narrator's village of Combray, Gilberte enters *Remembrance* as part of the legend of Bergotte: it is known that the writer, who admires her precocious understanding, likes to take her on tours of churches and monuments. The adolescent Narrator has no way to meet her; but one enchanted afternoon in late lilac time, while he is out strolling with his father and his grandfather at the edge of Swann's estate, he pauses by a hawthorn hedge to gaze up a flower-bordered alley, and there, at the alley's farther end, in a haze of vernal color, appears a girl with long tresses who is holding a gardening trowel. He gazes steadily at her, praying that she will notice him, but she only glances his way with what seems a look of haughty indifference; and then, to his horror, she thumbs her nose at him. In part because of Gilberte's closeness to the glamorous Bergotte, the boy is irresistibly taken with her, and he regards her as a sort of nymph who will lead him into the land of gratified desire. Yet Gilberte's obscene gesture bars his way into that land, and inwardly he rages against her. "I loved her," he later confesses, "and I was sorry not to have had the time and the presence of mind to insult her, to hurt her, and to force her to keep some memory of me. I thought her so beautiful that I should have liked to retrace my steps and shake my fist at her and shout: 'I think you're hideous, grotesque—how I loathe you!' "

Jeanne Pouquet recognized herself in Gilberte. In a letter of 1945, to her daughter, she mentions that she is rereading Proust in a "new edition illustrated by Van Dongen. . . . I'm finding things there that have taken on a great interest for me with the passage of . . . lost time! If one reads 'tennis-courts off the boulevard Bineau' for 'Champs-Elysées' in the descriptions of Marcel's love for Gilberte, I find, almost word for word, the evocations of his love for me in the letters that I so absurdly destroyed." There is no point in recalling for the reader this long, lyrical part of *Remembrance*, other than to say that it all has to do with unrequited love and comes to hinge on a letter that never arrives. Any attempt to compare a real person with a fictional character is inherently hamfisted, but it may perhaps be said that Jeanne Pouquet is both present in and absent from Gilberte. Though there is a superficial correlation between the real-life Caillavet family and the fictional Saint-Loup family, which Gilberte joins by marrying Robert de Saint-Loup, Gilberte rapidly shades into someone less like Jeanne than like Marcel's friend Marie de Bénardaky. With this tall, attractive Greco-Russian girl he really "bonded," as we might say today, late in his adolescent years; and however peculiar that bond may have been, it more closely prefigured the Narrator's attachment to Gilberte than did his self-thwarted courting of Jeanne. With Marie there was at least some reciprocity; with Jeanne there was none. Yet there *is* a correspondence between Jeanne and Gilberte, and for any aficionado of the Proust story who does not demand a living-color resemblance between "model" and "character," its visibility steadily grows. One has to forgo comparing nose with nose and make out the functional analogy.

The function of Jeanne in life and Gilberte in fiction is to bridge or span, to provide both the first experience and the terminal reconsideration of heartbreak. For this kind of suffering, like everything else in the Proustian field of possibilities, where people and emotions appear, vanish for a while, and reappear transformed, has an earlier and a later phase. In *Re-membrance*, unrequited love begins as a mere pea in the bed of a young boy's happiness, but by the later volumes it will be costing him all his sleep. His whole life will come to resemble his earlier, unanswered letter to Gilberte; yet when he revisits her toward the end of the novel, what he feels is only boredom and disillusionment, a sort of shrinkage of the world. This, too, is a form of sorrow; and when the Duchesse de Guermantes vilifies Gilberte, saying, "Don't you see, she is nothing," she may be voicing Proust's own regret about ever having cared for Jeanne Pouquet. Yet there is also a great difference between Proust's fondness for Jeanne and the Narrator's for Gilberte, and this difference has to do with homosexuality. One of Proust's most urgent early wishes was the desire to be hetero-sexual, and his frustrated abandonment of Jeanne and Gaston obviously embodied a farewell to this quixotic hope. The homo-sexual element does not (and, given the circumstances, could not) figure in the tale of the Narrator's loss and rediscovery of Gilberte; what does is some echo of Marcel's middle-aged crav-ing for Jeanne to reassure him that their youth had a mean-ing—to give him some hope for the past.

In the Gilberte story one's imagination is haunted by the Narrator's unvoiced response to his first vision of her as a girl: *I think you're hideous, grotesque—how I loathe you!* These words, so similar to those in which Anatole France expressed his "hate-ful love" for Léontine, give us an inkling as to the manner in which that lady's salon became fruitful for the literature of the fin de siècle. Now that we have reached the end of another century, we may perhaps be forgiven for not knowing just how to take a world so veiled by half-tones, so picturesquely undulent and dusky—a world whose "period" feel is unmis-takable and whose inhabitants seem a little contrived. The se-ductive hostess, the bent and bearded writer, the witty young playwright, the blond ingénue, the pale, dreamy soldier—their entwined destinies suggest some worm-infested orchard where vines prey on one another in their struggle for light and life. Yet the more we reflect on Léontine's salon, the more it may appear that France's obsession with erotic wounding and Proust's account of a boy's first mute vision of what Elizabeth Bowen once called "sadistic love-tactics" can, and perhaps must, be read as variations on a theme. Love, as a succession of French writers have been telling us all down the century, is a way of remembering; if memory is strongest when it bruises, then Eros must be allowed to sharpen his teeth and leave his nails unpared. Of course, we can read Proust's passage about the boy's amorous loathing of Gilberte as a crossing of the threshold into homosexuality, and we can also read it as a metaphor about the power struggle between the sexes, and people have read it in both these ways; but if we read it in the light of Proust's debt to France, we can see that it has wider implications.

"What do you do, Monsieur France," the younger man once asked the older, "to know so very many things?" "It's very simple, my dear Marcel," France replied. "When I was your age, I wasn't handsome like you; in fact, I wasn't attractive at all. I had no social life, so I stayed at home reading and did nothing else." This malicious remark makes us wonder what the two writers' friendship really yielded in the way of enrichment. The usual way of talking about France's effect on Proust is to run through the many intersections of their lives—their common engagement on behalf of Dreyfus, their mutually flattering prefaces and dedications, France's supposed wish that Marcel marry his daughter, Suzanne—but in the ledger of sympathies none of this adds up. On balance, France was not a major influence on his younger confrère, and in most areas of taste their sensibilities differed. Many of their shared views may be found among other novelists of their day, and even their insistence that love is a mnemonic act is a recurrent theme in the French writing of the period. Both, however, had a strain of preciosity; both protected this strain from any lapse into the poetically obscure; and both found artistic uses for that most universal of experiences, social embarrassment—for slip-ups, pratfalls, impossible-to-forget gaffes, unquiet phrases that return to trouble the mind. To be shown up as an insensitive oaf, to be caught out in a bald-faced lie—for both France and Proust, who were alive to a Parisian theatrical tradition that saw the cliché and the social solecism as a prime source of comedy, such moments were keys to character and spurs to drama. It is, however, in their heightened depiction of the emotion of jealousy, in their aggressive way of scratching it onto the screen of the reader's consciousness, that the two may have most in common. Twice in *Remembrance* Proust enlists an allegory, picked up from an article by France, about a man who believes he has trapped the Princess of China in a bottle, and this image can be read as the dominant (if unspoken) trope in both *The Red Lily* and Proust's great tale of erotic suspicion, "Swann in Love." Suffocatingly possessive, both the Dechartre of *The Red Lily* and Proust's Swann derive masochistic pleasure from being lied to by their mistresses or, rather, from wondering whether they are being lied to. Gnawed by doubts, they are inquisitor lovers who repeatedly force their female prisoners to regurgitate some allegedly self-impeaching testimony. The paradox, of course, is that if the defendant were to confess to her real or imagined sins she would lose all her mystery, all her power of seduction, and so cease to be desirable—mendacity being a catalyst for the erotic imagination. "To hear lies," says Proust's Narrator, "opens the world to us," and elsewhere he tells himself, echoing Dechartre, that an untruth may be touching if prompted by affection: "We lie all our lives, even—especially—perhaps only—to those who love us." Proust, like France, was mesmerized by the glamour of evil, whose scaly sheen had illuminated so much of the best French writing of the century—one thinks of Baudelaire, of Barbey d'Aurevilly —and would never really lose its literary luster. All his life, despite the misgivings, despite the disappointments, Proust felt a sly kinship with France and knew what he'd inherited from him. Wasn't it true, he asked shortly before his death, in an article for the *Revue de Paris*, that in France's best prose the "catlike impression of mixed savagery and sweetness prowls within the cage of an admirable phrase . . ."?

NOT ONCE IN THE first fifteen years following the marriage of Gaston and Jeanne did Marcel visit them at their apartment, in the boulevard de Courcelles. But according to a letter that Jeanne wrote to André Maurois in 1941, when the biographer was at work on a book about Proust, Marcel "saw us *constantly*"—though never at home. His refusal to look in on them, she informed Maurois, "exasperated Gaston, who deemed this abstention an ostentatious charade, considering that Marcel sought out *our* company wherever he could find us, and that he inundated us with letters, cards, notes, cables, and express messages sent over the pneumatic tube." But, once again, this claim is questionable: by 1941, when Proust had come to be widely regarded as the greatest French novelist of his day, Jeanne had a stake in whatever glowing memories of him she could summon up and amplify. Several notes to Jeanne in Marcel's hand have indeed survived, but they merely show him grubbing for "material," questioning her about people, current social forms, clothes, scraps of gossip. Was it true, he would ask her, about the mischievous tricks that the Comtesse de X was playing on the Comte de Y? Why did Madame G. and Madame S. wear such differently styled evening gowns? And was there any possibility that Jeanne might ask the publisher Calmann Lévy to look at something Marcel had written? The queries had little to do with Jeanne herself, and if she replied with a few impatient words, he would go into a sulk and vow not to trouble her again, only to press her a while later with fresh questions about slang or dress or manners.

And so it went, year in and year out, until, quite unexpectedly, late in the autumn of 1906, Jeanne wrote a full-scale letter to Marcel. She told him that she had fallen ill with what she called "neurasthenia," and she asked him (or so we may presume from his reply, since her letter hasn't survived) to recommend a doctor or perhaps even a cure. His reply was freighted with ironies both deliberate and unwitting.

Dear, dear, dear Madame! Since the day you wrote me I've been wanting to write. And already I have so much to tell you that I feel that it won't be possible. . . . I've been at Versailles for four months, but is it really Versailles? I haven't got out of bed, I haven't been able to visit the palace one single time, nor the Trianon, nor anything; I open my eyes in the dark and wonder whether the hermetically sealed and electrically lighted place where I am is really somewhere other than Versailles, of which I haven't seen a single dead leaf fluttering down toward a single sheet of water. Such is my palmy youth, my whole life. Even so in my extremely resigned thoughts your letter, as to one who has lost everything and has nothing left to lose, has brought so very much sadness. You, the radiant apparition of so many of my dreams, you have been ill? and you are discouraged? and sad? That's impossible and once back in Paris I must see you. If there is a *material* cause for your illness you must see a doctor. Whom are you seeing now? This is very important. And if there is no material cause, then *I will cure you*. And if I do not succeed, I shall ask Gaston to entrust you to me, which is hardly very compromising and I shall take you to Berne to consult Dubois and you shall be cured. . . .

Farewell Madame, I hope to be in Paris soon; I have rented an apartment there since the month of October and still cannot get in on account of epic complications, the more epic in that I myself am by way of being part-owner of the house. I don't know when I'll be able to move in and I don't know if you'll want to come to see me there. It's a very ugly apartment, in a dusty place, in the shadow of trees, everything I hate, which I've taken because it's the only one I could find that Mamma knew and having gone through the heart-wrenching business of quitting the rue de Courcelles which was too expensive, I haven't the courage to take an apartment where I'd feel that her eyes had never seen anything, that she hadn't been able to get to know it, to say what she thought of it.

Though Marcel was clearly touched that Jeanne had written, his response had wandered far afield. To her message that she was sick he had replied, in effect, that he was *more* sick: her plea posed a threat to his sense of belonging to an invalid elect. One might say that his letter revealed a valetudinarian attitude that had always played a latent role in his relations with her. He had always been lovesick and wounded, a supplicant, a man on his knees. He had never stood and fought to win her for himself but had stayed—as during those tennis matches in Neuilly—off court. His eternal illness, like that of the hero of his novel, had served as a sort of ringer for his homosexuality, a pretext for his laggardness toward girls. And now that he was beginning to write longer letters to Jeanne, his manner of expression harked back to his earlier suffering and reawakened dormant emotions. Criminal lawyers are familiar with the situation in which the courtroom testimony of the accused unconsciously reenacts his crime, or at least the state of mind that accompanied that crime, and something of that sort was occurring here. Nothing was really over for Marcel; everything that had ever happened between them was happening again. His letter, in consequence, was deeply embarrassing, and of course nothing came of it. Jeanne must have been especially distressed by his knowledge, or intuitive recognition, of the emotional nature of her "neurasthenia" ("if there is no material cause, then *I will cure you*"). Somehow, perhaps through the grapevine, Marcel knew that Gaston had proved chronically unfaithful; what he did not know was that Jeanne had just taken a lover.

PROUST SELDOM SAW Léontine de Caillavet after a regrettable falling out with her in 1896, which can be reconstructed as follows: Colette and her first husband, Willy, turn up at one of Léontine's receptions, Willy makes a pass at Jeanne, and Léontine finds out about it and has words with Colette. Why, of all people, Colette? One cannot exactly say, but it is certainly part of the salonnière mind-set always to see the woman as the instigator of such flaps. Colette takes it all in very bad part and develops a "hysterical" pain in one eye. She turns to Marcel, that walking directory of medical specialists, and he, dismayed by the whole incident, asks Léontine kindly to explain to him how Colette was at fault. Léontine snaps at him, Colette's mortification is multiplied a hundredfold, and Marcel is rewarded for his bumbling goodwill with a strong suspicion that he is *persona non grata* with both parties.

As time goes on, Marcel is (or claims to be) largely confined to his bed, and he asks himself if it is really worth his time and trouble to repair his ties with such bothersome, if admittedly admirable, people. Indifference masquerading as renunciation? Perhaps. Anti-asthma powders have clouded his room, his brain is befogged by sleeping draughts, and his old friends wobble in memory's middle distance as though seen through scrims or in mirrors, always at one or more removes, unreachable, perhaps irrecoverable. And, well, so be it. It is so much more important to get on with one's work!

And then, on January 13, 1910, Marcel unfolds the *Journal des Débats* and discovers that Léontine is dead. "My dearest Gaston," he writes to his old friend,

in a flood of tears all the past, all the beginning of our
great friendship . . . once again fills my heart, and I assure

you that mine is a very fraternal heart, very tenderly bending today over your own which grieves. . . . I have heard
how exquisite your adorable wife was for [Léontine] in her
last illness. Her sweet tenderness will give you in your suffering something that I have never had, for I have always
wept alone.

And to Jeanne Marcel sends a note of admiring recognition of
her kindness to Léontine and Gaston, adding, "I can hardly
write, but even if I were able to, I could never tell you how
much I love you."

Marcel arranged to have a large wreath—camellias, arum
lilies, lilacs, roses, and violets—placed on Madame Arman de
Caillavet's bier during the funeral service that was to take place
the following day at the church of Saint-Philippe-du-Roule; it
is not known if he was actually present. He lamented to Jeanne
that he was being daily assailed by terrible asthmatic fits, and
although she informed him through a friend that she was eager
to pay him a visit, he regretted that he couldn't encourage her
to come: it would be too embarrassing for both of them, since
he carried on conversations lately by writing on little scraps of
paper. But he was at work, he wrote her, on a new novel—
this was *Swann's Way*—"that I would have been so curious to
show to your mother-in-law. I think again of her wonderful
intelligence." He remembered Léontine fondly, sadly; and
then, at the end of the month, as his health improved and he
began to get out and about a little, he caught sight late one
evening of Gaston's collaborator, Robert de Flers, and his wife
at the Restaurant Larue, and as he sat down beside them, Robert told him how Léontine had died. The story, as Marcel
wrote to Robert the following day, seemed "a nightmare, most
painful in all that I learned that was horrid, inadmissible, about
a person who for years, and without any personal stake or
reward, showed me so much devotion and kindness. I recall
certain words, certain times, and comparing them to what you

have told me, I cannot believe [your story]. It's not possible! And it's true!"

What had happened was this. Madame de Caillavet, in the period between the publication of *The Red Lily* and her death, at age sixty-three, had grown ever more imperious. Proust's friend Marie Scheikévitch, a painter and writer who had come to know her in 1905, would remember her as a generous but caustic lady who "paid no heed to the passing years" and "despised sentimentality." Léontine tried her hand at fiction, with indifferent success; she continued to advance the careers of others; and as befitted one who in her private life had championed both the arts in their modern form and the frank expression of female sexuality, she spoke with appalling candor, shrank from no verbal combat, and showed only contempt for anyone else's lapses of wit or intelligence. She had, Marie thought, a "streak of cruelty." Her views often collided with Anatole's, who had never quite mastered his halting tongue ("When I talk, you hear me crossing things out"), but they liked as of old to visit antique dealers and antiquarian bookshops, together ferreting out the rare and refined. Her husband, Albert, continued to plan all the menus and choose all the wines, secretly relishing his role as house buffoon.

Though photographs reveal that Léontine had become quite stout by the early years of this century, her interest in clothes had only grown. She seemed unaware that she no longer looked youthful, that an expensive overelaboration of dress now stood in for her former daintiness. With her dyed hair, overweening hats, and busily patterned dresses, she had come to appear slightly ridiculous, a rouged-and-powdered caricature of a mannequin in the *Gazette du Bon Ton*. Her enemies thought her the acme of bad taste; but the real problem was the contrast she struck with her nominal consort. At this time Anatole France often cocked a concupiscent eye at the admiring young females in his entourage; he was sixty-five, and Mme Scheikévitch, among others, found him attractively repellent. In the spring of 1909 he sailed to South America for a lecture tour —a vain attempt to bring Rabelais to the pampas—and presently Léontine began to receive anonymous letters hinting that he was not traveling altogether alone. She was also shown a shocking newspaper article about the appearance of "M. and Mme France" at an official function. Yet even before these revelations, Léontine had been gnawed by premonitory despair. As soon as her lover had arrived in the antipodes, she had written him that she no longer dared, as before, "to speak with you heart-to-heart. For I've come to know too well, and so suddenly, the bitterness of displeasing, and it has made me so timid, so fearful, and I shrink back so as not to incur any blame. . . . There is in you a god, and sometimes, too, a child spoiled rotten, willful and occasionally wicked."

She was heartsick; too heartsick to soldier on. Anatole, returning late that summer, tried to conciliate her, and they went down to Capian for the grape harvest, but she began to run a fever from a respiratory infection and had to be brought back to Paris. "Too old, too old," she murmured to Jeanne, who tended her devotedly. "I should die—I haven't the courage to face what life has in store for me—but do stop crying." About this time Marie Scheikévitch, who later described the incident to Proust, received a letter from Léontine asking her how to kill oneself with a revolver. (Marie herself had already tried to perform this experiment, on account of amorous problems of her own.) But no revolver proved necessary, for in the meantime Léontine had gassed and very nearly asphyxiated herself, further weakening her pulmonary tissues. She lived on only a few more weeks, nursed by a despairing France.

Many years earlier, while working on his preface to Constant's *Adolphe*, Anatole had discovered in himself a violent antipathy to the character of Ellénore. He had been struck by the injustice of her complaint against the novel's muddled protagonist. At that time, all his fellow feeling, and probably all of Léontine's, too, had gone to Adolphe rather than to his "vengeful fury" of a mistress. For France, Ellénore's death, apparently of a respiratory infection, was really a vindictive suicide, an attempt to shackle her lover with eternal remorse. In this, of course, France differed from Balzac. Balzac, while writing *Muse of the Department*, had read Ellénore's death as a metaphorical demise, a stylization of the agony that rejected lovers pass through. It was part of the baggage of romantic neoclassicism, a purely literary strategy that connected Constant to Racine and the tragic sense of closure. People didn't actually die of a broken heart, of that Balzac was sure; the notion was the romancer's equivalent of one of those articles of religious faith that no sensible person takes at face value. And Proust, as his correspondence reveals, was (like most of us) just as much an infidel as Balzac on this score. In January 1910, when Proust learns from Robert de Flers about the circumstances of Léontine's death, his first impulse is to disbelieve. Nevertheless, he is doubt-ridden, anguished; and after a day of despondency, he writes Robert the letter containing his startled admission: "It's not possible! And it's true!" But that is not all Proust says, because, unguardedly, he deepens his confession. "The great consolation of lives like mine," he confides, "and certainly part of the reason why one adopts such a life, is that one prefers not to be tortured by the spectacle and the knowledge of such things." The note of remorse is unmistakable here. Marcel has made a bonfire of his friendships, and now, however briefly, he is gagging on the fumes.

Over the years, Léontine, aided by Anatole, had amassed a large, if distinctly minor, collection of pictures and statuettes. Her house was populated by dancing Tanagra figurines, Meissen milkmaids glancing over their shoulders, baby fisherfolk, baby peddlers, baby musicians, mothers and children in fond attitudes, a faithful widow weeping over an urn, a surprised nymph. These now stood as a monument and a tribute to the couple's thirty-odd years together; but Madame Arman de

Caillavet herself was gone, having been laid to rest in a crypt in the Cimetière Montmartre.

MARCEL PROUST'S FRIENDSHIP WITH Jeanne Pouquet cannot really be understood without some reference to the architecture of *Remembrance*, a design at once intricate and astonishingly symmetrical. Wishing at all costs to avoid the effect of plane geometry, Proust the architect craved a deeply sculptural, ever-shifting structure, a sort of revolving stage set in which the work of building would become part of the building itself. The characters also were to be shown in the round, all being seen at two or more widely separated points of their lives, as in a tale by Balzac or Hardy; and toward the end of the novel a new generation would be introduced to suggest a sort of closing of the circle. By 1908, Marcel began to feel that this generation would have to be represented by a very young girl, whom he referred to as "the girl with rosy cheeks," and as we track the gathering weight of this new preoccupation, we begin to suspect that if Jeanne and Gaston had not had a daughter, Marcel would have had to invent her.

In December 1908, Marcel wrote Georges de Lauris a letter (much quoted by Proustologues) stating that the only females who attracted him anymore were very young ones. He debated marrying the so-called girl of Cabourg, a real person whose identity has remained a mystery, but then decided against it. At roughly the same period, he also started asking around after a pretty creature he had seen in society, a certain Oriane de Goyon, and tried, as usual, to secure her photograph. When, at length, he came face-to-face with her, she bored him, yet all the while the young-girl theme skipped in and out of his notebooks, in and out of his prose sketches and letters. Proust seems to have felt (and no doubt a psychohistorian could make a meal of this) that he could recapture his lost youth, and also expiate his guilt toward his dead mother for being an "invert," if he found such a girl for himself. He was primed for his first meeting with Jeanne's daughter, Simone—the "model" for Gilberte's daughter, Mademoiselle de Saint-Loup.

One evening in April 1908, Marcel arrived unexpectedly a little before midnight at the Caillavets' apartment and insisted that their fourteen-year-old daughter, who was sleeping, be awakened. Her governess acquiesced, and when Simone appeared, groggy and resentful, she instantly charmed him with her fetching looks and her way of warming slowly to his presence. The girl, with her long, curving nose, looked a good deal more like Léontine than like Jeanne. A few days later, Marcel wrote Jeanne to tell her how much he had liked Simone: her teenager's parlance was delicious, he said, and her comeliness made him feel, as he never did, tongue-tied. He added helplessly that Jeanne herself had looked lovely with her neck bare and her hair up in a chignon.

Years later, Simone de Caillavet, who was to become a writer and salonnière and the second wife of André Maurois, would make light of the significance of her childhood meeting with the great writer. She would proclaim herself "a mere finial" atop the edifice of his work, and actually the image is appropriate, for the encounter was psychologically weightless, a matter of Marcel's ongoing research, of his concern for narrative structure. Yet his disinterested enjoyment of Simone left touching traces in his letters, where his voice now sounds so lonely that it comes close to utter desolation: though he has always admired this fascinating family, he is still very much the outsider. At the time of Léontine's death, we find him writing to Simone to tell her how affectionately her grandmother always spoke of her; a little later, he asks her for a picture of herself. "When I was in love with your Mamma, I did prodigious things to get hold of her photograph. But it was no use. Every New Year's Day I still get greeting cards from certain people in Périgord whom I got to know solely in order to possess that photograph." Some days further along, as the Seine threatens to flood its embankments, Marcel writes Simone that she must read *The Mill on the Floss*; there are other fleeting exchanges; and then, about June 4, 1912, comes the inevitable letter to Jeanne in which Marcel, scrupulously following his life script, declares his feeling for Simone:

> Here I am in love with your daughter. . . . I am trying to think of the name of the flower whose petals are like her cheeks when she smiles. I should so like to see her smile again. It is true that if I should see her she might thumb her nose at me: a symbol besides of the attitude of her parents to me and notably of her father, to whom I wrote the tenderest things without his ever responding.

But the "love" this time is a literary event, quite unlike his former baffled passion for Jeanne; and the metaphor of the thumbed nose, once a sign of Gilberte's dominion, is now reassigned to Gaston, as if to acknowledge Marcel's long migration from sexual confusion to a greater degree of self-knowledge.

IN MID-JANUARY 1915, WHILE waiting to be called up for his army physical in a cold and blacked-out Paris, Marcel read in *Le Figaro* that Gaston had died, at the age of forty-five, in the Pouquet château in Périgord. The renowned playwright had been ill for many months with uremia, but Marcel, despite his constant inquiries, had not been kept informed of Gaston's suffering and descent into morphine-induced oblivion, and he was devastated by the news. The death of Gaston, a man of such sweet good humor, and one of the few heterosexual male friends of Marcel's adolescence who had unreservedly accepted him, seemed to sweep away a vast province of his past, and as he tried to collect himself, he sat down and wrote Jeanne a bitterly heartbroken letter:

These tears that are choking me—what I should need is to shed them by your side. I adored Gaston, my tenderness for him was infinite, my heart is broken with suffering, I cannot stop weeping. I had no inkling of his condition, I was thunderstruck. And it's an equal suffering to think of your own, to imagine it, to feel it, how unbearable it is; and to think of your daughter's suffering—her papa loved her so much and was so proud of her. Every time I met him he would say: "Come and see for yourself what a marvel of intelligence she is."

No I can't believe that I shall never see Gaston again, just think that I knew and *adored* him even before he knew you!* that the only cloud that ever came between us resulted from the fact that we were both madly in love with you and that I'd wanted to have the consolation of owning some photographs of you which put him in a terrible and very natural temper the poor dear man. . . .

Ah Madame if we could only cry together. If I could only tell you the things he always said about you, things full of tenderness, of adoration, but I wouldn't even be able to speak.

When Jeanne returned from Périgord to Paris, Marcel was the first person to share his sympathy with her. Though too ill for several weeks to call on her, he contacted her almost daily by pneumatic or through his housekeeper Céleste, who would go downstairs and phone from a nearby café. He made and broke innumerable rendezvous, fussing, wavering, revising his plans, and when at length Jeanne sent him a note, he wrote back confessing that Gaston's death had horrified him.

I cannot get used to the idea that his life, which he would have enjoyed so much, has been taken from him in the fullness of youth. I can still see your engagement, your

_____
* Again, the chronology of their early friendship is uncertain.

274

wedding, and the thought that you are a widow—you who are still for me that young girl of yesterday—is heartrending. I do not know if I can see you, it would be a very great balm for me. Next week I must be examined by the induction review board; in my present state of health that's an exhaustion for which I must prepare myself with lots of rest, and afterwards (supposing that I am not drafted, and who knows?), I shall certainly be ill. But then again if I can one day summon up a little strength, and especially if my daily attacks finish early enough, I'll have somebody notify you at once by telephone. It's such a bitter thing for me to mourn Gaston all alone that it would soothe me to do so together with you.

I've thought so much about that daughter of whom he was so proud, your dear Mademoiselle Simone, that I don't even know any more if I actually wrote her, so many times have I written her in thought. If I haven't done so (but I have, I have, the letter has probably stayed in the jumble of papers next to my bed) tell her that she can pile up as many letters as she wishes from among those she has received without amassing as much constant thought for herself as there is in my heart.

When Jeanne wrote back, explaining the circumstances of Gaston's death and doubtless pointing out that it had come as a release from his agony, Marcel told her that this fresh information had only added to his sorrow

by making me realize how dreadful it all was. . . . I had made arrangements to see you when something just now happened that will deucedly complicate things. The charming and perfect housekeeper who for several months now is at once my valet and sick-nurse—I don't say cook, except on her own behalf, since I eat nothing—came into my room wailing with sorrow! The poor young woman had just heard of her mother's death. She left at once for the Lozère and has been replaced by her sister-in-law, whom I don't know, and what is more serious, who doesn't know the apartment, can hardly find my room if I ring, and wouldn't know how to make my bed if I got up. Yet I still hope to be able to come. As for the other possibility (your coming here), that's much more difficult. My room is almost always full of a thick vapor, which would be as intolerable for your breathing as it is necessary for mine. If my housekeeper had been here, and if one day the atmosphere had been breathable, I would already have sent her to you (because I don't have a phone any more and so can't ring you). With this new maid it's harder. And yet, maybe, if a day or two from now it's unnecessary to fumigate. . . . But what time would suit you? How about six o'clock? But then at what time should I notify you (either by sending you my driver, or by having someone telephone you—which would perhaps be more difficult—from a nearby [café] with a telephone)? Do you promise me not to look at the mess in my room nor at my personal disorder? I admit that I'd greatly prefer to come to see you. But as long as my housekeeper hasn't returned this will be very difficult, and when she has come back, even if I take all the medicines in the world some days may go by before a day comes along when I'm well enough to get out of bed. At any rate, it seems to me that it wouldn't be impossible at my place in two or three days, or in a little while longer (perhaps a week, I don't know, not having dared to talk to her about myself in the midst of her suffering, whenever she comes back, but I think that the burial ought to be tomorrow, and I don't know what she could do down there once it's over). If she returns rather soon, I'll send you a note one day to announce my visit, if it is materially possible for me for before dinner, and if my attack is over too late then for after dinner. Don't bother yourself much with replying, I'll try to arrange it so that it doesn't impose on you too much. But I know how very much the things that I desire the most, and believe myself certainly able to do, become unrealizable to execute [sic]. I can't tell you how much I think of you two; my anxious way of missing the departed one is not selfish and does not prevent me from thinking mostly of his dear wife, of his dear little girl from whose side he has been so barbarously removed.

Though Jeanne persisted in her attempts to confirm a rendezvous with Marcel, new objections and obstacles continually arose: the notion of his paying a visit to her seemed to dissolve amid the fast-closing vapors of his sick chamber. The project, she began to feel, was chimerical; and then one day, like a bolt from the blue, a tightly stuffed envelope was hand-delivered to 12, avenue Hoche by a chauffeur who said something about a certain monsieur who was too sick to come around in person. As Jeanne would recall in *Quelques Lettres de Marcel Proust*, Marcel's letter was a sort of bill of indictment that began with the words "Madame, I know now what I always should have known, which is that you have never felt the slightest friendship for me." It went on, if we are to believe her, for sixteen pages, and consisted of one long, bitter reproach for her unwavering indifference to him, which, at last, he had admitted to himself. "A thousand recollections," she later remembered, "precise, luminous, and incontestable, now rose from his past to confirm this sad revelation. . . . And with a prodigious effort of his memory he recalled all the events of [our] life that seemed to strengthen his conviction. He distorted them with morbid ingenuity, gave them a painful meaning in order to confirm his ravings." As it happens, no such sixteen-page letter has come down to us, and we can only suppose that Jeanne destroyed it. But there exists another letter in Marcel's hand, of roughly one page, which says somewhat the same thing, and which briefly mentions an earlier missive, perhaps the one containing his long accusation. In this one-page letter, Marcel describes to Jeanne the events that have brought on the sudden revelation of her supposed indifference to him. He writes that having felt well enough the previous evening to go out, he had requested someone to telephone her, but

no one answered. Taking my chances, I came around, but [there was no] time to alert [you]—it was too late; it was twenty to eleven (or quarter to eleven) when I arrived in front of the portal with the three arches. Your lights were off, everywhere, on all floors. I let the motor idle for an hour to see if a curtain would be pushed aside, but since nothing happened, I didn't dare ring, thinking that perhaps you'd gone to sleep. . . . I hadn't stood in front of 12, avenue Hoche since one evening when I'd seen Gaston home, very late. That evening I'd been moved to see this house, which brought back so many memories. But what was any of that beside the feeling that overwhelmed me yesterday evening? What I experience now is not touching memories but an inconsolable grief. Well, I don't know when I'll be able to get up again, and doubtless by then you'll have gone. And perhaps it's better that way. For me, *the dead live*. For me, this is true for love, and also for friendship. I cannot explain why in a letter. When all my *Swann* has come out, if you should ever read it, you'll understand me. I wrote you the other day. I hope you got my letter; I don't know what happens to those charged with delivering my letters once they've left my room, since I'm bedridden. I think tenderly of you, your daughter, and Gaston.

The setting of this non-meeting is strangely evocative. The silent house, with its three tall, darkened windows; the attractive widow, restlessly sleeping; the taxi purring at the curb, with an old admirer waiting inside—we have here (or would have, if something weren't very wrong with the picture) all the makings of some spectacular crime or riveting courtroom testimony. And Jeanne in her memoir seems conscious of this. Subpoenaed by history, she fervently disputed Marcel's side of the story (and offered, as Henry James might have pointed out, a suspect superfluity of evidence). According to her summary of Marcel's sixteen-page letter, which, she claimed, told a story substantially different from the brief one quoted above, Marcel had actually come *after* midnight; he *had* rung her doorbell; he had also honked under her window for ten minutes; yet still—and on this point she regretfully corroborated his testimony—she had not opened her door. But the conclusion he had drawn from her silence, which was that she'd never re-turned an iota of his affection, seemed to her a willful non sequitur. In reality, she'd been fast asleep, she hadn't heard any of his ringing or honking, and even if she had heard it, she wouldn't have opened her window at that hour—what woman would have, in a city at war? Even so, to her distress, Marcel had used what she called "the taxi scene" to sum up the whole history of their friendship. There was his galling phrase, "For me, *the dead live*," which insinuated that she did not genuinely mourn Gaston; there was his surly suggestion that she wouldn't trouble herself to read *Swann*; and there was also the fact that Marcel, like the incorrigibly unpunctual night owl that he was, had arrived much later than he'd claimed. It was all so incred-ibly unfair! Yet Jeanne's outpouring negligently disclosed some-thing else, something crucial: this was that Marcel, earlier that same day, over the phone, had asked her maid if she would be in. And since the woman would presumably have reported this call to her mistress, it would have made perfect sense for Marcel to assume that Jeanne would wait up for him, or at least ac-knowledge his arrival. After all, she knew his habits; she'd known them for years.

What are we to make of this squabble? Well, it's very hard to say whose face had more egg on it, and obviously no one cares anymore. What's interesting is the fact that Jeanne simply couldn't let go of the incident, that over a decade later she was still turning it over in her mind, still feeling that it was the key to something in her life. And for this the best explanation is that she had a guilty conscience. Among other things, Marcel had been absolutely right about her feelings toward Gaston, for in fact she had *not* mourned her husband—she hadn't even gone to his funeral. (The one who missed him most was Mme Pouquet, who would never again mention him without tears in her eyes.) It's also very likely that Jeanne had indeed been aware of Marcel at her window; ten minutes of honking had surely wakened *somebody*, if only a servant who would have alerted the mistress of the house to the commotion outside. Yet the real reasons for Jeanne's chagrin may be deeper still, and though we shall never be certain what they were, certain facts leap to our attention. She had spent twenty years with Gaston; he had ceased early to love her; another man had loved her all those years, or at least, he had loved her in his memory; and now, suddenly, that man was back, a writer with a growing reputation who still prized her and worried about her and remembered . . . well, everything. We cannot know, of course, whether such thoughts actually ran through Jeanne's mind on receiving Marcel's angry letter. But we do know that she contacted him at once with a proposal that *she* visit *him*.

There was the usual dithering—Marcel's health was on the fritz again—but one evening after dinner Céleste telephoned Jeanne to tell her that the invalid was feeling better. That very night he was going to carry out an hour and a half of anti-asthma fumigations, after which he would be able to receive her. If she wished, she might come at eleven-thirty and stay for a period of forty-five minutes; he regretted the brevity of the proposed meeting, but he feared that by a quarter past midnight he would again be subject to horrible fits of breathlessness. Doubtless the planned interview showed an exquisite sense of plot structure—it was a Proustian revisitation worthy of *Time Regained*—but Marcel was also making the classic Proustian mistake, which is to fail to know when to relinquish a precious person to the netherworld of memory. If the meeting probably served Jeanne as a sort of halfhearted apology for whatever suffering he had borne for her sake, it became for Marcel a contemplation of irrevocable loss. There was, simply, an enormous difference between their perceptions of the value of unconsummated experience. For the middle-aged matron, with a history of family life and an established lover, such non-consummation was an emptiness, a blank; for the lonely bachelor writer it was the void at the heart of existence.

Arriving at the appointed hour at 102, boulevard Haussmann, Jeanne in her black veils was shown into a room entirely lined with cork, in which stood a large pianola; reclining on his bed was Marcel, who immediately began to weep, crying, "Gaston! My dear Gaston is dead!" For a while he continued to sob, and she tried to comfort him; after his grief had subsided somewhat, he lifted a large cardboard box onto his bed and removed the lid. Then, to her amazement, he placed on his bedcovers two photographs from their early days together. There was a picture of Gaston posing in his artilleryman's uniform, and one of Marcel himself, in the posture of a serenading Pierrot, strumming a tennis racket in place of a guitar. He was kneeling at the feet of three girls by the courts off the boulevard Bineau, and he looked so silly that the flesh-and-blood Marcel burst out laughing at him before dissolving again in tears.

THE IDEA THAT ALL writing germinates directly from other writing—that sense of a happy filiation so noticeable in the work of Anatole France—fills much of the French prose of the last century, in which the continuous retailoring of hand-me-down characters and predicaments can sometimes remind one of the folkways of preliterate societies. Such recycling requires considerable inventive power. Since style is the transformation of the world into a new substance, a uniform idiom in which no leftover lumps of rhetoric or shards of journalistic note-taking are permissible, elaborate tactics of citation evolve. The heirlooms are rotated, or inverted, or viewed from an unsuspected angle; the quoting itself is slyly oblique. We may find a fictional woman openly doing her darnedest not to be like an earlier fictional woman, or a deceased writer from recent history popping up as a literary character, or a couple from an old tale reappearing in a new one with their genders reversed. The lingo previously reserved for talking about things inside pictures is suddenly applied to the real world, and words thought appropriate only to the real world are applied to what's inside pictures. Sometimes it seems, as it did to Proust himself, that all the writing of the century is scrolling itself along inside one cosmic brain.

Many of Proust's fictional characters are piggybacked on historical personalities. The Narrator's grandmother is partly a derivative of George Sand—not, of course, the Sand of Musset and Pagello, but the warm "supersensuous" grandmother (to enlist Henry James's inspired adjective) of the 1870s. The Narrator's mother quotes from Madame de Sévigné's letters so often that she sometimes seems a chip off that older block. And traces of Sainte-Beuve appear, mostly to cartoonish effect, in the accents of Madame de Villeparisis, Madame de Cambremer, Monsieur de Norpois, and others. Sainte-Beuve is a dominant figure in Proust's world, an obnoxious grandpa who moves into the younger man's mental house spouting infuriating opinions and demanding attention and life support—he won't die or shut up or clear out. And as the world has known since 1954, when Bernard de Fallois published an edition of Proust's manuscripts of 1908–10 under the title *Contre Sainte-Beuve*, the first volume of Proust's great novel began as a critical attack on Sainte-Beuve—or, rather, it grew out of a number of prose fragments flanking that attack in the writer's leatherette-bound notebooks of this period. If *Contre Sainte-Beuve* is an excellent place to study Proust's intuitive search for a literary program, the transformation of personal experience into fiction does not seem, however, to be one of its subjects. The collection packs sixteen pieces, among them an essay on homosexuality, another on "Rooms," and another on "Sleep," which tries, ingeniously, to retrofit Chateaubriand's descriptive machinery for modern purposes. Already present are the family housekeeper Françoise, the first voyage to Balbec, and the Baron de Charlus—all, of course, under different names—and also a bevy of girls from "the world of finance," young things looking much like Jeanne Pouquet, "who seem with a glance to put a distance between you and them, a distance which their beauty renders painful." The book is a gift assortment of bravura sketches, yet in its central and least conventionally "creative" section, where Proust lashes out at Sainte-Beuve's critical method, the question of life-into-art is addressed; and it is settled on lines that will permit Proust to carry out the diciest of all his fictional operations—the assignment of the female gender to characters loosely "based" on male acquaintances.

Proust's approach is frankly combative here: he's convinced that Sainte-Beuve's method is based on a single idea: namely, that a man's role in society is what best explains his writings. But this, Proust complains, is a shallow idea, which fails to recognize what every sensitive reader knows: "that a book is the product of another self than the one we reveal" in everyday life. Sainte-Beuve shows an enormous interest in women, in the creative role of the hostess, in salon conversation as an archetypal Gallic form of expression; but what a writer creates in solitude, for his own spiritual satisfaction, has nothing whatever to do with the prime virtue of the salon, which is wit in one form or another. Sainte-Beuve is so taken with the salon as a sort of performance genre that his classic *Chateaubriand et son groupe littéraire sous l'Empire* resembles "an enfilade of salons in which the author invites various people to be interviewed about the personalities they have known." Priding himself on his critical freedom, Sainte-Beuve is in reality so unfree that he squirms in misery in Madame Récamier's drawing room in the Abbaye-aux-Bois, terrified that he'll give in to his impulses and hurl a brickbat at Chateaubriand. He positively grovels at the feet of the two celebrities; yet once they have passed on to the next world, he instantly makes up for lost time and erases his previous judgments word by word. He begins, in what Proust sees as the most unforgivable vulgarism of his critical manner, to apostrophize the shade of Chateaubriand, addressing him as "you" and calling him ugly names, like the famous "ingrate."

Proust's points are clever and amusingly illustrated, but you can't help feeling that he's more ambivalent about this over-bearing ancestor than he's willing to let on, and by-and-by his uncertainty is explained: Sainte-Beuve has grown so real in Proust's mind that Proust is beginning to be captivated by him, to see him as a potential fictional character. After all, the two writers have some points in common: what is Sainte-Beuve's exaltation of the salon but a sort of historical premonition of Proust's own salonomania, his own compulsive running around in the Faubourg Saint-Germain? "Whom Proust loveth, he chasteneth," we might say, with apologies to Saint Paul; and soon, in his discussion of Sainte-Beuve's failure to appreciate Baudelaire's genius, we realize that Proust has unwittingly *become* Sainte-Beuve. Not that he endorses Sainte-Beuve's opinion of the poet—far from it; but it's so much more natural for Proust to criticize people than to analyze books, so much more fun for him to retail an anecdote than to explicate a text, that his attack on Sainte-Beuve rapidly degenerates into an account of the critic's betrayal of Baudelaire's candidacy to the Académie Française; and so, out of just the sort of dirt that Sainte-Beuve liked to dish, he ends up making his own mud pies. Proust never consciously perceives that Sainte-Beuve's essays can be profitably read only as vivifications and not as verdicts, but that is the secret direction of his thought. And the ironies keep on piling up: as Antoine Compagnon has noted, the descriptive "impropriety" that Proust detests in Sainte-Beuve's style is remarkably close to his own evolving poetics. What sets Proust's teeth on edge is the so-called unevenness of Sainte-Beuve's epithets, the pairing of adjectives that belong to wholly dissimilar orders of experience; an example, drawn from *Volupté*, is the phrase "poor gray Jansenist roof," in which the word "Jansenist" is wrenched for effect out of a realm of discourse that has nothing whatever to do with roofs. One recalls that such flashy "transposed" adjectives were just what put Proust off Anatole France's more labored manner—Norpois's carping at Bergotte in *Swann's Way* is merely an expression of

Proust's own disenchantment—yet the trick of juxtaposing the observed and the phantasmal comes to fill the whole of *Remembrance*, a novel in which people with no likeness to anyone in creation are constantly dispatched to real places like the Buttes-Chaumont, and in which winged monsters out of Symbolist paintings take their seats in railway coaches and motorcars.

Many readers have been struck by how often episodes in Proust's life and work appear to reprise, however partially or distortedly, events in the literary history of the last century. The dispute and reconciliation, in Venice in the spring of 1900, of the author and his mother, which is recounted in *Contre Sainte-Beuve* (and, in fictional form, in *Remembrance*), and which seems to have liberated so much of Proust's creative energy, took place in the Hotel Danieli, where (in its previous incarnation as the Albergo Reale) Sand and Musset had quarreled some sixty-six years earlier. Victor Hugo's quasi-imprisonment of his mistress, Juliette Drouet, in an apartment in the rue de Paradis in 1834 foreshadows the Narrator's similar treatment of Albertine in *The Captive* (a similarity of which Proust, who was fond of Hugo's poem "Les Tristesses d'Olympio," cannot have been unaware). Many of the traits of Albertine, the football- and automobile-loving chippie who succeeds Gilberte as the Narrator's significant other, were derived from Alfred Agostinelli, the chauffeur whom Proust first engaged in 1907 and whom he later employed as his secretary, lodging him in his own apartment at 102, boulevard Haussmann; more eerily, much in the character and fate of Agostinelli, including his death, is foretold in Proust's early sketches of the Albertine story.

Though Proust may have hoped that his often-aired protests against the biographical interpretation of fiction would cause himself to be spared such manhandling, the sexual transpositions in his writing were cruelly remarked in his lifetime. About a year before his death, his friend Jacques-Emile Blanche addressed him in *Propos de peintre*: "It sometimes seems to me that even in your finest pages you lend to one sex the traits of the other, that in certain of your effigies there is a partial substitution of the attributes of gender—enough that one might read 'he' instead of 'she.' " The jab apparently took Proust by surprise, for he responded to Blanche in a private letter whose air of virtuous fatigue could not conceal its author's lack of an emotional shield against this species of innuendo. And after Proust's death, in 1922, the criticism of the sexual transpositions in *Remembrance* steadily multiplied. The most effective of his critics were themselves homosexuals, and the often-missed irony of this situation was that the very offense he had warned against in his letters and in his portrayal of Bergotte— that of reading a man's works biographically—was now being revived by putative fellow spirits and directed at him. The more restrained of his critics merely asserted that he'd never experienced what he wrote about. Natalie Clifford Barney, a familiar of Anatole France and a self-proclaimed exponent of sapphic love, recalled seven years after his death that just before the publication of *Cities of the Plain* she had told him of her concerns about the accuracy of his portrayal of lesbian life. It was impossible, Barney said, to employ lesbianism to stand in for male homosexuality in a work of fiction, as Proust had done, because their manifestations were too unalike; but she didn't go so far as to assert that his novel could be understood only in the light of his "inversion." It was left to Gide and Cocteau to suggest that one's grasp of *Remembrance* was likely to be weak unless one made a constant mental adjustment to Proust's feints and duplicities, his ambivalence about being homosexual.

As is well known, Marcel Proust publicly denied his sexual orientation and gave no overtly homosexual traits to his fictional alter ego. Yet when Gide visited him toward the end of his life, he found a Proust who vaunted his "uranism" and claimed never to have loved a single woman "except spiritually," never to have known any sexual relations outside of those he had enjoyed with males. Gide's account is in his *Journal*

1889–1939; if we were to credit it, it would put a very odd complexion on Proust's twenty-five-year-long correspondence with Jeanne Pouquet, since as late as 1915 we find him fingering the wound she dealt him in his youth and complaining of the salt she rubs into it. One has to be skeptical of Gide's reminiscence, not because he was especially untruthful but because he would have been deeply gratified by any perceived remorse on Proust's part for his lifelong denigration of homosexuality. This, after all, is a Gide who arrives with his *Corydon*—his defense of sexual diversity—in hand, a Gide who has been at pains in his work to stress the protean, multifaceted nature of love; having heard from Proust what he craved to hear, Gide writes that Proust "blamed himself for the 'irresolution' that had led him . . . to transpose to a 'budding grove' of girls everything gracious, tender, and charming that his homosexual memories offered him, leaving nothing for Sodom but the grotesque and the abject." What Gide gives us, then, is a shamming Marcel, a Marcel who has all along been faking his portrayals of young women; and this picture (which would, to say the least, have astonished Jeanne Pouquet) is not rendered any the less troubling by Cocteau's notorious quips about Gide's never having read Proust attentively in the first place.

The first volume of Cocteau's diary, *Le Passé défini*, was composed about 1950 (but not published until 1983, about three decades after Gide's journal). With the entrance of the quintessential bad ol' boy of French letters, writing when he was about forty years longer of tooth than he'd been as serviceable chum to Marcel in the heyday of the Ballets Russes, the squabble over sexual transposition acquires that aura of court intrigue, of footings to be gained and idols to be broken, that hangs over every great publishing business—in this case, that of Gallimard. The elderly Cocteau wants his constituency to rest assured that he has creamed off all the niftiest people for himself, especially Proust, but what we get is really posthumous revenge—Cocteau's status fight with a ghost. He wrestles the ghost to the floor by rereading Proust's weakest volume, *Cities of the Plain*, then exults over the master's bad taste in feminine apparel, incomprehension of the art of painting, unfunny jokes, unwitting snobbery, and obvious or old-hat judgments on high society. ("But [Proust] never got his foot in anywhere," Cocteau recalls the great hostess Laure de Chevigné telling him.) Even the confirmed Proustomane must bow to most of Cocteau's observations, but when, browsing on into *The Captive*, Cocteau finds Proust regaining his verve, he decides he has had enough of *Remembrance* and slams the book shut; he weeps crocodile tears over his failure in the twenties to realize how sick Marcel was, how woefully his sickness was infecting his talent, etc., etc. Cocteau's cavils crop up haphazardly, but rearranged in logical order they add up to a fierce indictment of Proust's transpositions.

The weird cheek of Marcel, to attribute his own sexual behavior to others, while he always has a woman clinging to his [hero's] side. Besides, the young girls of this period did not smoke cigarettes in trains, they did not have that boyish freedom in their ways. . . . It is weird that Gilberte can still be "playing" in the Champs-Elysées when she already has all the allure, all the vocabulary, all the trickery of a woman. And Gilberte at home with the Swanns is not a little girl, a girl who would still go to the Champs-Elysées. . . . One really wonders whether Marcel . . . ever engaged in anything beyond vague fumblings. . . . What happens is that he transposes his fumblings with boys into normal sex and it doesn't hold up. . . . One can't imagine Proust in a young man's clothes. One pictures him always as a little gentleman in a waistcoat, with a hat and cane, just as he describes himself waiting for Elstir when Elstir is chatting with the budding young girls. If those young girls had really existed they'd have found him awfully silly, they'd have burst out laughing at his "pretty waistcoat" and his "prettiest cane." . . . And then that Paris of Proust where young men don't need to work, since there are girl milkmen, girl butchers, girl cabmen, girl messenger boys, girl telegraphists—the simpleminded insistence on of this fraud *spells boredom*. . . . One feels that he's much more at ease in the domain of Charlus, which he knows like the back of his hand, than in that of Albertine, which he invents out of whole cloth and which has to do with love which he knows nothing about. Like friendship, love escapes him. . . . Poor, poor Marcel. Poor invalid with his madman's gaze. He knew nothing of love. He knew nothing but the maniacal tortures of his lies and his jealousy.

It is possible, as the American novelist Louis Auchincloss once argued in an essay for *The New York Times Book Review*, that Proust might have handed Gallimard a better book if someone had waylaid him into writing a story closer to his own. An unrequited homosexual passion for a chauffeur might have made more sense than the Albertine story, which is—let's just say it— -basically incomprehensible; and if the hero's homosexuality had been rendered explicit, his floppy-dog passivity with Gilberte would also have had a plausible explanation. (It's already hard, Lord knows, to see the Gilberte story as anything but a touching tale of a boy's uncertainty about his sexual orientation.) Auchincloss's assumption is that Proust simply needed a little more courage; a leaner, meaner Proust would have told it like it was and closed the "gap between the two Marcels." Auchincloss has a point here—he's probably closer to the way Proust is actually read by young people nowadays than those academic expositors who fuss over his sacrosanct *texte*—and given the persistence of this Marcel-who-lacked-courage construct, it was probably inevitable that the whole debate would spill back into the biographical domain.

Which lately it has, in a topsy-turvy way. What we now know about Proust's interest in Jeanne Pouquet suggests that his experience of love was broader than we might previously have thought; but what if his long obsession with her was actually feigned? What if it was really *Gaston* that he cared for, all along? Ghislain de Diesbach's ambitious *Proust*, which appeared in 1991, replays Marcel's adoration of Jeanne as just such a real-life transposition. Diesbach, an often charming stylist, is one of the preeminent French biographers of our time, and his brief retelling of Marcel's involvement with Jeanne offers a young Proust who quite consciously pretends to be heterosexual—who is, in fact, the next thing to an outright liar. In his triangle with Jeanne and Gaston, Diesbach tells us,

> Proust for the first time plays a rôle he likes and will never cease to perfect, that of the helpless adorer of his best friend's woman, a role that enables him to flaunt all the resources of his sensibility. . . . For Proust, to make himself the woman's accomplice is a way of living by proxy an inadmissible love, and in proclaiming from the rooftops that he is smitten with the beloved, a means of deflecting suspicion.

Diesbach's syntax may bother some people, but we have no trouble following him here, nor when he goes on to say that "Proust soon persuades himself that he is in love with Jeanne Pouquet but makes Gaston de Caillavet the first confidant of this passion, which renders its sincerity suspect. If he were genuinely, carnally enamored, he would have the tact to choose another confidant. . . . Would he be so much in love with Jeanne Pouquet if she were available and there were no Gaston de Caillavet?" All this makes such excellent sense, and would apply so perfectly to any number of cases, that it takes us a moment to realize that Diesbach has subtly displaced Jeanne's duplicity onto Marcel. Diesbach implies that it is Marcel who contrives the masquerade, putting Jeanne up for a blind to hide his desire for Gaston, whereas the relevant documents clearly show that it is really Jeanne who schemes to make use of Marcel in order to hide her betrothal to Gaston. And though Marcel declares his love to Jeanne many times over, he never does so to Gaston. Diesbach, who is often drawn to stereotypical thinking, yields to a facile pseudo-shrewdness here. He's practicing the sort of deflation that might work wonders with the local heavy breather but leaves a giant like Proust untouched. In part, it's a problem of language. Because there's nothing in our common speech to describe what Marcel feels for Jeanne, Diesbach assumes that Marcel feels nothing, or at least nothing "genuine" and "carnal." In essence, we're stuck with Gide's and Cocteau's shamming Proust again (though they, unlike Diesbach, knew virtually nothing of Jeanne). What it all boils down to is Diesbach's failure to register the young Marcel's growing pains, but this isn't surprising, because his perceptions are consistently wide of the mark. When Diesbach tells us, for example, that Jeanne is "levelheaded" and has "a sense of reality," he misses the significance of her conspiracy with her mother to conceal her engagement from her father. Teenagers often hide a decision from a parent because they themselves are secretly uncomfortable with it (a fact that may help explain why Jeanne played along so pliantly with her mother's demand for secrecy).

Despite the lack of evidence, though, might it not be that Marcel actually *was* in love with Gaston and that he simply never admitted it? A legitimate doubt lingers on. Yet here we nosy parkers are in luck, because Proust himself volunteers an answer to this question in a letter to Jeanne, written in 1922, just before his death. In this letter he speaks of his fondness for Gaston as having "the effect of an unsought vaccination. It immunized me against the too-keen suffering of my love for [you]." Proust knew his way around medical metaphors, and he chose this one with care: a vaccination usually involves an injection with a tiny, perhaps weakened, quantity of the same organisms that cause the infection to be prevented. His cryptic admission argues a misdirection of sexual energy in his earlier, eighteen-year-old self, a need consciously to refocus that energy on his own sex. "When one is young," the mature Proust jotted in a notebook, "one is unaware of one's homosexuality, just as one is unaware of one's vocation as a poet. . . . It is only when the revolution of thought concerning the ego has come full circle—when a man's intelligence, weary of himself, looks in from the outside, as if he were somebody else—that the words: 'I am . . . homosexual,' come together in his thoughts."

Marcel never shared with his mother, nor indeed with any of his family, his growing awareness that he was "of the violet persuasion." With them he wore a mask until his death. Let us grant, for the purposes of argument, that Proust fastened on Jeanne in order to please his mother, or rather, in order to please the part of himself that was anxious not to displease her. (Marcel's mother's name, for what it is worth, was also Jeanne.) Let's go further and grant that the real cause of his amorous desperation was not his hopeless love for Jeanne but the fact of his being homosexual. Marcel hadn't been brought up in a way that would have made it easy for him to accept this truth about himself; he was just as scared of it as any other teenage boy might have been in those days (or in our own). It may not be unfair to say that Marcel was in love, above all else, with the idea that he was really heterosexual. But even if we assume that this was the case, and there is nothing that obliges us to do so, does any of it imply that his feelings for Jeanne were other than as he described them? French literary history is full of examples of the so-called triangulation of desire, in which some third presence or force—some parental figure or romantic obstacle or compelling form of snobbery—inflates the attractiveness of the love object; but this third force is no more unreal than anything else in the dreamworld of passion. "Everything, in love," as André Maurois put it in a venturesome essay on Proust's sexuality, "is the work of the imagination."

There is no form of cryptography that can decode Marcel's attachment to Jeanne. Most of us are more open than Diesbach to the notion that sexuality is not a two-track system but a raggedly shaped field of experience, and that our words don't only describe that experience but also generate and embody it. What we write in an intimate letter doesn't exactly offer a report on our feelings; it summons them up, alters, denatures, or dispels them, forces us to invent new expressions and to question the adequacy of old ones. This "Constantian" property of speech (which is far from alien to *Remembrance*, where many Constant-flavored phrases are used to portray the Narrator's attempts to break up with Albertine) is just what should put us off the attempt to translate Proust's words into some "clearer" language of our own. The letter written from Versailles in 1906, with its image of the unseen leaf fluttering down toward the unseen sheet of water, cannot be reformulated; its phrases are freighted with a self-deception too opaque and beautiful and, perhaps, too deeply saddening, for us to effectively paraphrase. We don't know, any of us, how to give admissible evidence about our romantic or erotic history; all we know is that we don't quite tell the truth. And so it is that Marcel's great love for Jeanne, which often seems no more than a waking dream perpetually on the point of being washed out by the coldest indifference, has its own sort of poetry, its own sort of drama, which resists psychological reduction.

Marcel Proust died in 1922; Jeanne Pouquet lived on for many decades, until 1961. She remarried and, together with her husband, settled down permanently, and rather happily, in the old family domain of Essendérias. For some years she was joined by her daughter, Simone, who transformed the place into a sort of latter-day Nohant. Among those who would stay at Essendérias and enjoy Simone's hospitality were François Mauriac, René Clair, Jean Dutourd, and Jacques Suffel. The presiding spirit was Simone's husband, André Maurois, who for a while attempted to run a model hog farm on the estate.

From time to time, hearing or reading of goings-on in the wide world, Jeanne, now pudgy and gray, would remember Marcel. And, inevitably, she became aware that the only interest she would ever hold for posterity was the fact that he had once been her friend. In July 1942, when André and Simone Maurois were living as much-fêted refugees in the United States, Jeanne wrote them a letter noting that "a copy of *Swann's Way* belonging to Brun (at Grasset), with a dedication and stuffed full of letters, has just fetched 213,000 [francs]! . . . I fume when I remember that my copy was stolen. The amorous dedication went on for 3 pages." There was no use crying over spilled milk, but in April 1948 Jeanne's thoughts once again turned to Marcel, this time more hopefully. "I have read," she wrote to Simone (who was then, one gathers, in Paris),

> . . . that my little book on Proust is much sought after and
> nowhere to be found. I've learned that some bibliophiles
> have offered sums for it that seem to me outlandish.
> —Couldn't I profit by the momentary curiosity about Mar-
> cel to make myself a little money with a few copies—either
> by selling them to a bookseller or by putting them up for
> auction? To increase their value and interest, I could copy
> onto the first page the recently rediscovered verses that he
> addressed to me when I played in your father's revue. . . .

EPILOGUE

IT IS NATURAL IN looking over the love affairs of the past, especially those with claims to a sort of artistry, to judge them in the light of our own experience. The bygone lovers may appear tiny, doll-like, when seen through the telescope of time; we may feel we understand them better than they did themselves, and wish they could have known what we know today. It's natural to judge them in the light of the expectations and failures of the contemporary American marriage, the wit and wisdom of the American divorce, which we like to think give us all the insight into gender relations that anyone might conceivably require. But the French people of the last century were formed in a world very different from our own, and those who have appeared in this book were far from representative of their society. France was then a country of desperately industrious people, mostly poor Catholic peasants, but only four of our characters—Chateaubriand, George Sand, Sainte-Beuve, and Anatole France—actually had to work for a living, and neither Madame de Staël, Benjamin Constant, Madame de Caillavet, nor the freethinking Anatole France were Catholics. (Marcel Proust sometimes considered himself a "cultural" Catholic.) Nowadays we want to analyze erotic entanglements in terms of a balance of power, but our ideas about what makes a person "strong" or "weak"—shopworn ideas that go back to Nietz-sche, Ibsen, and Strindberg—are always biased in the direction of one moral system or another. People can be strong in many different ways, and the social pressures exerted on a couple bear in from so many different directions that it is generally impossible to say which side, if any, they favor. And so we discover, as we look back at the great shipwrecks in the history of love, that we not only cannot reach back into the past to prevent them but also cannot salvage very much from them. At the mercy of the elements, the crippled vessels founder and go down, leaving nothing but the memory of their passing.

It is sometimes believed, however, that if one shapes events into a story, this shaping will somehow bind or heal them, make sense out of occurrences that are essentially wounded and without hope of meaning. The characters in this book created their own stories, acted out their own metaphors, and if we avoid forcing our own obsessions upon them and instead draw out of their tangled accounts those images and myths that acquire emotional weight over the long haul, we can see that there are perhaps four or five curative themes that hold their tales together. There is Benjamin Constant's Delphic proclamation of the inherent imbalance of all sexual relations, and our consequent curiosity as to whether the oracle will or will not be confirmed. There is the so-called need to have lived, to have experienced love deeply—what George Sand calls "demonic suffering"—which invariably collides with the equally pressing need to discover what she terms "the normal conditions of happiness." There is the problem of veracity, and of how in seeking it one may come to terms with the necessary, but also unrelenting, beauty of the past. There is the strange truth that Etienne Delécluze touched on when he observed to Jean-Jacques Ampère that one thing is always missing in a lover's description of his love, and that it is always, unfortunately, the most important thing. And not least, there is the terrible difficulty of seeing into another person's soul and of baring one's own.

The old technology for this act of reciprocal exposure was the love letter penned in ink, and what did it in (or, at least, gave it the *coup de grâce*) was the telephone. After about 1900, references to the telephone begin to appear frequently in the correspondence of the Caillavet family and of Marcel Proust; it had obviously become the dominant mode of communication, and if the asthmatic recluse had consented to have a phone in his home, there would probably be no letters from Marcel Proust to Jeanne Pouquet for us to scratch our heads over. Proust was captivated by the new inventions of his day—the box camera, the motorcar, the airplane, and a primitive form of wired broadcasting called the *théâtrophone*—but the telephone has pride of place in his work. It rings briskly during one of the most moving scenes in *Remembrance*, in which the Narrator, who is away from Paris, receives a call from his ailing grandmother which turns into an aural presentiment of her death. He realizes that he's talking to someone on her way into the afterlife, and the implicit comparison between the disembodied telephonic world and the netherworld of Greek mythology—between the Narrator's voice moaning, "Granny, Granny!" and that of Orpheus calling his dead wife—lends this episode a mournful spirituality. Exploiting the resemblance between telephonic conversation and the sort of hallucination or hypnagogic dream in which the subject hears the incorporeal voice of a dead person, Proust uses the isolation of the grandmother's voice to convey her isolation as a doomed being.

Many artists of the Belle Epoque made constant metaphorical use of the new inventions of their age, in part because most of these devices seemed to have a metaphorical motive—they were technology's tropes, so to speak. Anyone able to read an advertisement knew that harnessing internal combustion had confirmed the "mobility" of the common man, that the incandescent bulb had "brought light" into countless towns and villages; anyone, in a Europe full of rapping tables and blowing curtains, could see that the telephone had created an artificial replica of the séance, with its "voices from the other side." These innovations were exhilarating and inspiring, but every improvement has its insidious side effects, and the telephone, which ended up sabotaging an entire style of courtship, was no exception. Stylistically, a liaison in the grand manner could not be pursued over the phone; one has only to try imagining Benjamin Constant pleading with Madame Récamier not to hang up, or Madame de Staël being told to "please hold the line," to realize that the idea is unthinkable.

Alexander Graham Bell patented his invention in 1876, and in 1887—the year that Léontine de Caillavet and Anatole France began their long association—the first Paris directory appeared; by the turn of the century, 30,000 telephones had been installed in France. This didn't mean that the French wrote fewer letters—literacy was increasing, and the volume of mail handled by the postal service increased along with it—but the telephone seems to have wreaked havoc on the old-fashioned amorous correspondence, which barely resurfaced after 1918. One can only speculate as to why and how this happened, but it's worth noting that the love correspondence had always been governed by an implicit rule, which was now being regularly infringed.

In order for a couple to record their adventure in a sheaf of letters, they have to keep up a rally, a steady back-and-forth; if they don't—if they begin to intersperse their writing with long telephone conversations—too much of their tale will escape their correspondence for anyone but themselves to follow the plot. It is this short-circuiting, this drainage of narrative current into another medium, that accounts for the seemingly obscure allusions and in-jokes that fill so many twentieth-century published correspondences, whose readership is generally confined to people willing to slog through a mass of footnotes. Yet those of us who admire the classic love letter shouldn't blame everything on the telephone. In a way, the phone was only acting as sensibility's henchman, because at the moment when it hustled the Romantic love letter into oblivion, the genre itself was going out of date. With its ornateness, self-importance, and muzzily stale eroticism, it was headed for the scrap heap of history.

By now the grand liaison is a thing of the past, and nobody, with the possible exception of undergraduates in English or Comp. Lit., bothers to conduct a full-dress intimate correspondence anymore. Since we have not only the telephone but also its avatars, the fax and E-mail, we've given up exploring our emotions in long, inky letters. This situation is not without its drawbacks, however, and one of them may be that the phone does not allow us to dig very deeply into our feelings, especially if we're on the male end of the equation. The letter has always been regarded as a feminine medium, but telephone chatting may be even more lopsided, as cartoonists and comedians have understood. Men, who retain so much of the prehistoric hunter-warrior in their nature, aren't given to spontaneous self-revelation, to spilling their guts out to an unseen squaw: their sexual status requires masks and silences, feints, protective colorations. Even so, women may be no happier with the telephone than men, especially when they are talking *to* men. Such hallmarks of telephonic communication as the unequal preparedness of the caller and the callee, the chopping of speech into expletives and grunts, the taboo against silence (which normally indicates that the line has been cut), the absence of body-language cues, the temptation to mutual (or even self-) interruption, and the use of the hang-up to mark displeasure all combine to create an atmosphere of incipient dispute. Love affairs are fiduciary relationships, and the telephone often works to undermine trust. Men and women tend to remember different things or to remember the same things differently, and the absence of a shared frame of reference can easily lead to a

299

dialogue of the deaf, with its characteristic squabbles over what somebody "actually meant." Whereas a shoebox of love letters is an archive which either party can cite (where would mankind be without the sobering phrases "As I told you in my letter" and "May I remind you of what you said in your letter"?), telephone talkers are stuck with their memories, which bend the truth as inevitably as water refracts light.

The wanton, tricksy ways of memory seem always to bring one around to Proust, with whom it seemed fitting to end this book. By early middle age the great novelist felt that his powers of recall had been terminally damaged by narcotic sleeping draughts, but he had the memory of an elephant when it came to tying together the loose metaphorical strands of nineteenth-century French literature, and in *Remembrance* the recognition that love is a way of remembering and memory a way of loving reaches its absolute plenitude. Proust's novel is the key to the gigantic century that preceded it. What was it, after all, that prevented Benjamin Constant from leaving Madame de Staël, that caused Madame Récamier to pry out of any new friend his or her personal history, that caused Chateaubriand to distort his entire biography and George Sand to doctor her letters, if not the grip of memory? What was it that made Anatole France despair of ever being able truly to possess Léontine de Caillavet if not his morbid fear of the pull of *her* memory? Throughout much of the writing that precedes Proust there is this great yearning to piece together a vivid sense of anteriority, but only in his immense novel about memory do the sentences frustrate the memory of themselves, the proliferating clauses and subclauses waylaying all perception of mileage or a measured trajectory, so that in the unwinding of a river or a hawthorn hedge or a hazy afternoon one cannot finally remember where it was that one started or how it was that one got where one is, and one goes astray in a timeless, living past. Rich in harmony at any given moment, Proust's water-treading prose rarely drives toward resolution, and it probably has to be understood in chamber-music terms, in terms derived from Fauré or Debussy. This, of course, is the way we want love to be—we want it to develop but also to stand still. The moment when the boy in Combray stops and stares at little Gilberte is fraught with infinite consequences, like some marvelous, exotic chord, but it will never have any decisive outcome. It is a revelation, very nearly the final one in this tradition, of the musicality of love.

SOURCES AND NOTES

THIS BOOK IS THE product of my interest in relatively recent revelations about old events: chiefly Georges Lubin's disclosure in 1972 of George Sand's doctored letters, Jacques Suffel's 1982 edition of the never-before-published correspondence of Léontine de Caillavet and Anatole France, and Michelle Maurois's reconstruction of the youth of her "stepgrandmother," Jeanne Pouquet, in *L'Encre dans le sang*, which appeared in 1982. It is a work of cultural criticism, not of erudition; and if I have retold a number of episodes central to French literary history, this is only with the aim of providing a context for my own, admittedly subjective, viewpoint and not of making a contribution to scholarship. I have depended not only on primary sources but also on a number of reliable and estimable biographical studies, all of which are listed below; but this is not the place for an exhaustive bibliography of the literary liaisons of the last century, which would fill many volumes and contain material on scores of major figures not discussed here. Solid bibliographies of the main characters in this book may be found in scholarly publications and in the Pléiade editions of their works.

The brief notes to be found here are offered with the sole purpose of crediting recent writers to whom I am indebted for information or interpretive ideas, yet whose precedence may *not* be apparent from my text. In addition, I have noted a few conjectural or possibly controversial opinions of my own.

I believe that a work of this scope must inevitably contain some errors. Since I have not approached my topic with any overriding preconceptions, however, the reader may rest assured that such mistakes are haphazard rather than systemic.

CHAPTER 1. A HOSTILE SENSIBILITY

For the details of Benjamin Constant's life I have often referred to Dennis Wood's exquisitely researched and psychologically sensitive *Benjamin Constant: A Biography* (London and New York, 1994). I have frequently used the notes to Benjamin Constant, *Oeuvres*, edited by Alfred Roulin (Paris, 1957).

10 His mother had died: For a discussion (closely related to Penelope Leach's theories of child-rearing) of the impact on Constant of his mother's death, see Wood, pp. 16 *passim*.

11 The gaming obsession: See Wood, pp. 63–65.

45 The obsessive self-encryption: See Benjamin Constant, *The Affair of Colonel Juste de Constant and Related Documents (1787–1796)*, edited by C. P. Courtney (Cambridge, 1990).

CHAPTER 2. THE TOUCH AND ACCENT OF THE ENCHANTER

This chapter focuses almost exclusively on one question: Why did Chateaubriand willfully neglect to discuss the first year or two of his friendship with Madame Récamier in the *Memoires d'outre-tombe*, then fail to offer an adequate account of their long liaison? The suggestion that Madame Récamier "*l'aimait en secret*," and that he exploited this affection for a period of some months (we don't know exactly how many), was first made by Maurice Levaillant in *Chateaubriand, Madame Récamier, et les Mémoires d'outre-tombe* (Paris, 1936). See also Henri Guillemin, *L'Homme des Mémoires d'outretombe* (Paris, 1965), which is by far the most convincing of Guillemin's ambushes of great French writers. Françoise Wagener, in her *Madame Récamier* (Paris, 1986), sustains Levaillant's point; her book is valuable, but I have made almost no use of it since I do not find her view of Juliette Récamier psychologically convincing. She offers the complete extant Récamier–Chateaubriand correspondence on pp. 513–18.

63 The setting seems to imply . . . and a modern authority: See Anita Brookner, *Jacques-Louis David* (London, 1979), p. 144.

90 In the 1930s: Levaillant, pp. 19–22; Wagener, pp. 294–95.

101 "Consider, my friend": Delécluze's and Ampère's letters were first published in *Deux Romans d'amour chez Mme Récamier*, edited by

R. Julliard (Paris, 1954). All the present translations are from *Two Lovers in Rome*, trans. Louis Deternes (New York, 1958).

CHAPTER 3. PROMISING LITERARY MATERIAL

Here I was interested in Henry James's presentiment of George Sand's lack of veracity (to be found in Henry James, *Literary Criticism* [New York, 1984]) and its partial confirmation by Georges Lubin in his preface to George Sand, *Correspondance*, II (Paris, 1972), which gives all necessary references to the letters in question. Useful on Sand (though not on the subject of her doctored letters) is Curtis Cate, *George Sand: A Biography* (New York, 1975).

161 Henry James's alertness: See James, vol. II, pp. 736 *passim*.

CHAPTER 4. THAT LITTLE DROP OF ACID

Central to this chapter is Anatole France and Madame de Caillavet, *Lettres intimes, 1888–1889*, edited by Jacques Suffel (Paris, 1984). France's essays on Constant and Chateaubriand are in Anatole France, *Le Génie latin* (Paris, 1917). Also consulted were: Jeanne Pouquet, *Le Salon de Madame Arman de Caillavet* (Paris, 1926); Michelle Maurois, *L'Encre dans le sang* (Paris, 1981); George D. Painter, *Marcel Proust: A Biography* (London, vol. 1, 1959, vol. 2, 1965). For *The Red Lily* and France's other fictional works, I used Anatole France, *Oeuvres*, edited by Marie-Claire Bancquart, 4 vols. (Paris, 1994). Bancquart's *"Notice"* and *"Notes"* to *Le Lys rouge*, in *Oeuvres*, vol. 2, pp. 1192–1268, is exceptionally enlightening, and I have plucked numerous details of France's early life from Bancquart's magisterial *Anatole France: Un sceptique passionné* (Paris, 1984). Much of my information on Proust's debt to France is derived from Jean-Yves Tadié, "Proust et France," in *Littérature et Nation*, March 1993 (no. 11, 2d series).

174 A few years later, Balzac got excited: See Chapter 6 ("Constant's *Adolphe* Read by Balzac and Nerval (1972)," in *Imagination and Language: Collected Essays on Constant, Baudelaire, Nerval and Flaubert*, by Alison Fairlie, edited by Malcolm Bowie (Cambridge, 1981), pp. 80–95.

178 Thousands of pages have been devoted: My sense of this triangle has been shaped by the deliciously legalistic, but now obscure, *Sainte-Beuve et Madame Victor Hugo*, by Edmond Benoît-Lévy (Paris, 1926).

187 In time, Michelle Maurois inherited: As per my conversations with Robert Naquet. See also: Michelle Maurois, *Le Carillon de Fénelon* (Paris, 1970), pp. 7 *passim*.

191 When Anatole was thirteen: This and the following paragraph are based on Bancquart's *Anatole France: Un sceptique passioné*, pp. 71–110. The quotations from France's correspondence and the Goncourt *Journal* I also owe to her.

195 "For four years I have read . . .": This translation is from Marcel Proust, *Selected Letters, 1880–1903*, edited by Philip Kolb; translated by Ralph Manheim (New York, 1983).

196 What Proust had no way of knowing: The notion that Léontine de Caillavet coached Anatole France as a salon star is admittedly speculative, but only mildly so. This is the general sense of Jeanne Pouquet's portrayal of France. See also Bancquart, p. 153.

225 "I am harsh and obstinate": All translations from *The Red Lily* are drawn from Winifred Stephens's version (London, 1908).

CHAPTER 5. THE UNSEEN LEAF

For the material on Jeanne Pouquet, Gaston de Caillavet, and Marcel Proust I am indebted to Michelle Maurois's charming chronicle of the Caillavet family, contained in: *L'Encre dans le sang* (Paris, 1982), *Les Cendres brûlantes* (Paris, 1986), and *Déchirez cette lettre* (Paris, 1990). I have also drawn numerous quotations from Jeanne Pouquet's youthful diary and from both her and her mother's letters to Gaston de Caillavet; all of these are in the unpublished archives of the Caillavet family, now in the possession of Robert Naquet. My brief presentation of Proust's position at the tail end of nineteenth-century French literature is derived from Antoine Compagnon's *Proust entre deux siècles* (Paris, 1989), and I relied constantly on his indispensable notes to and commentary on *Sodome et Gomorrhe*, in vol. 3 of the 1994 Pléiade edition of *A la recherche du temps perdu* (4 vols.: general editor, Jean-Yves Tadié). Also frequently used were: *Correspondance de Marcel Proust*, edited by Philip Kolb (Paris, 1971– [17 vols. to date]), and Marcel Proust, *Contre Sainte-Beuve*, edited and with a preface by Bernard de Fallois (Paris, 1954); Jeanne Pouquet, *Quelques Lettres de Marcel Proust* (Paris, 1928); George D. Painter, *Marcel Proust*; Ghislain de Diesbach, *Proust* (Paris, 1991). I owe to Antoine Compagnon's notes in *Recherche*, vol. 3, pp. 1491 *passim*, my acquaintance with Jean Cocteau's criticism of Proust in *Le Passé défini: journal* (Paris, 1983), vol. I (1951–52), pp. 268–78, 281, 282, 284, 286, 288–90.

258 "I loved her," he later confesses: This Proust quotation is from Marcel Proust, *Remembrance of Things Past*, translated by C. K. Scott Moncrieff (New York, 1934), p. 109.

266 This incident can be reconstructed: It has been argued, by Michelle Maurois among others, that there never was any dissension between Madame de Caillavet and Proust. But see *Correspondance de Marcel Proust*, vol. 12, p. 337: "Lettre 167, à Louis de Robert." Also Painter, vol. 1, p. 210.

268 Léontine tried her hand at fiction: Her novella "Histoire d'une demoiselle de modes" was serialized in the *Revue de Paris* in May–June 1908, under the pseudonym "Philippe Lautrey." I have tried in vain to discover her reason for adapting this pen name, but a certain Louis Lautrey, twenty years her junior, published a book titled *Poèmes d'Israël* in 1910. Bancquart writes (and one can't help but agree) that Madame de Caillavet's novel was "*d'une écriture et d'une observation plutôt plates.*"

271 In December 1908: On the "Young Girl" theme, see Antoine Compagnon's commentary on Proust's *Recherche*, vol. 3, pp. 1570, 1209, 1212. It is here that I learned of Oriane de Goyon.

281 Such recycling: See Antoine Compagnon, *La Seconde Main* (Paris, 1979).

284 And the ironies keep on piling up: See Compagnon, *Proust entre deux siècles*, pp. 213–15.

285 Victor Hugo's quasi-imprisonment: I am not aware that anyone has drawn this rather obvious comparison, though surely someone must have. Hugo's great poem, of which Proust was so fond, is in *Les Rayons et les ombres* [XXXIV], (Paris, 1840). See also *Recherche*, vol. 3, pp. 437, 440, and 1593.

INDEX

Todorov, Tzveran: view of *Adolphe*, 51, 52
Trevor, Harriet, 11

Updike, John, 179

van Tuyll van Serooskerken, Belle, *see* Charrière, Isabelle de (Belle)
Verhoeff, Han: view of *Adolphe*, 52–53
Verlaine, Paul, 192
Vigny, Alfred de, 116
Volupté (Sainte-Beuve), 174

von Cramm, Minna, 21
von Hardenberg, Charlotte, 44, 56–57

Wagener, Françoise, 90
Wellington, Duke of, 90
Wilde, Oscar, 122

Zélide, *see* Charrière, Isabelle de (Belle)
Zola, Emile, 192, 205
Zuylen, Belle de, *see* Charrière, Isabelle de (Belle)